Fundamentals of Managerial Economics

Julian GOUGH
and
Stephen HILL

MACMILLAN

First published 1979
Reprinted 1985, 1986

Published by
Higher and Further Education Division
MACMILLAN PUBLISHERS LTD
Houndmills, Basingstoke, Hampshire RG21 2XS
and London
Companies and representatives
throughout the world

Printed in Hong Kong

British Library Cataloguing in Publication Data
Gough, Julian
Fundamentals of managerial economics.
1. Finance   2. Management
I. Title   II. Hill, Stephen
658.1'5   HG4026
ISBN 0–333–26666–8 Pbk

Contents

Preface

The aim of this book can be stated simply: to provide a clear, rigorous and comprehensive text on Managerial Economics. While this objective is simple to define, its attainment is by no means easy. The evidence of this is clear; namely, the plethora of books in the subject area which have singularly failed to achieve this objective. They tend to fall rather unhappily into two camps: the first a watered-down exposition of the theory of the firm with minor concessions to actual decision-making; the second an *ad hoc* mixture of material on decision-making with little unifying theme, founded rather shakily on economic theory.

We believe this book to be distinctive and very different from existing texts with comparable titles. It is essentially the joint view of two individuals, rather than a summary of the work of others. We hope that the result demonstrates the enthusiasm we have for a relatively new and expanding area of economics. Because it is our own work we take full responsibility for any errors or omissions.

There is however another reason why we wrote this book. This stems from our belief that much of microeconomic theory has become so arid and divorced from reality that the very subject-matter of economics is dangerously near being considered irrelevant to the world in which we live. Our aim was, therefore, to keep a firm base in economic theory, but systematically to bring in the complications of real firms – e.g. incomplete information, uncertainty and the time horizon of the firm, managerial objectives, etc. We feel there is a grave danger of economics being dismissed because it has become stylised and rigid, with the attendant risk that readers are forced to turn to other disciplines for the discussion of essentially theoretical issues. It is for this reason that we have attempted to preserve the theoretical basis of the subject-matter and not to be tempted to package the text with descriptive examples and case studies with dubious interpretations and little general significance.

It is our hope that this book will be read by a wide variety of people – students of economics and business, those studying management sciences, businessmen and managers, and other decision-takers where economic factors are of some moment. Our intention is that the book is able to be understood by the interested reader with little (and possibly no) previous knowledge of economics. Obviously some sections of the text will be optional, depending on the background of the reader. Chapter 6, on market structure, can be omitted by those with a firm knowledge of the traditional theory of the firm; for others who do not possess this background the chapter is essential reading to understand the rest of the text. Similarly, Chapter 2, on marginal analysis with sections on introductory mathematics, can be omitted by those already versed in the area, but to others it allows them to proceed with the book without having to resort to consulting other texts on mathematics.

While the book presumes little previous knowledge, it quickly proceeds to an advanced level. In many of the chapters substantially new material is introduced, and elsewhere existing knowledge is presented in a new way. It is hoped that the reader, on completing the book, will feel that a clear definable area of economics has been traced out, and that the analysis is highly relevant to business decision-taking.

We have suggested questions for discussion and further reading at the end of most chapters. Also, where appropriate, we have included worked examples and further problems for the student to follow up. We hope this will help the student where the text is employed as a course book.

Finally, we would like the acknowledge the cheerful typing of a difficult manuscript by Mrs Sadia Matthews and Mrs Margaret Aven.

J. G.

S. H.

Acknowledgements

The authors and publishers wish to thank the following, who have kindly given permission for the use of copyright material:

The Advertising Association, for a table from *The Case for Advertising*, edited by David Dunbar.

The Controller of Her Majesty's Stationery Office, for a table from *Price of a Dental Preparation - By Cost Components*. N.B.P.I. Report 113, Cmnd 4066.

Extel Statistical Services Ltd, for a table published in *The Guardian*, 3 September 1975.

McGraw-Hill Book Company, for two figures from *Corporate Strategy* (1965), by H. I. Ansoff.

Prentice-Hall Inc., for an extract from *Economic Theory and Operations Analysis*, by William J. Baumol, 3rd ed., © 1972.

1
Business Decisions

In a modern economy there are a variety of different enterprises, varying in size from the single entrepreneur to the multinational corporation, in activities, methods of finance, forms of organisation, etc. However, all these enterprises have one basic aim – to utilise resources to best achieve the firm's objectives. The word 'firm' is used in a general sense to encompass the decision-making unit engaged in the transformation of inputs into outputs.

Within the firm, management has a number of roles: policy formulation, planning, the implementation of decisions, administration, operating control, communication, delegation, etc. Of these activities, the one we shall concentrate upon is *business decision-making*.

Decision is the act of conscious choice and involves the identification and evaluation of alternative means of accomplishing objectives. Choice of objective is obviously critical; we shall spend considerable time identifying and comparing the possible aims of firms. However, whatever the objective of the enterprise this can be best accomplished by using resources efficiently. For example, consider an altruistic health organisation with a given budget. This firm's objective will be to provide the maximum health service within the constraint upon funds.

This illustrates another aspect of business decisions. The decision problem is generally to best satisfy some objective, subject to one or more constraints. To do this we use the concept of *optimisation*. This will be considered later when we reduce decision problems to their constituent parts.

The sort of decision problems we shall consider include price and output decisions, optimum choice of inputs, the determination of advertising budgets, stock levels, investment, etc. Each decision involves a trade-off between costs and benefits. All these decision problems are *allocation* problems within the firm.

The process of decision-making can be broken down into four main elements. The first is the recognition of the need for decision. A decision is necessary when there is a difference between desired and expected outcomes. Obviously this involves identifying what we would like to happen and what is likely to happen. The objective may be to maximise profit or growth, or minimise cost or effort. Objectives may sometimes be multiple or inconsistent.

The second stage is to generate alternatives and define the *decision environment*. Normally the alternatives considered will be only a small subset of the complete range of alternatives. Empirical research into actual business organisation suggests that the search for alternatives is often terminated once a satisfactory rather than optimum solution has been found. This may be justified if the costs of search are high, but a more general reason is the desire to minimise effort rather than maximise performance.

The decision environment encompasses all the characteristics of a situation that may be relevant to the decision problem. The decision environment itself may be subdivided into those variables external to the firm, such as general economic and social conditions which together define the broad environment within which firms operate, and the narrower environment of the firm itself. Consider, for example, the investment decision. Among the variables to be taken into account are:

1. The growth of national income.
2. The market rate of interest.
3. The projected rate of inflation.
4. The physical requirements of the firm, i.e. labour, raw materials, etc.
5. The availability of funds to the firm.
6. Government regional incentives for investment.

The first three of these variables help form the broad decision environment, while the last three are part of the narrower environment of the firm itself.

Often the most useful means of defining the decision environment is in the use of *economic models*. An economic model is a simplified representation of reality which attempts to pick out the essential economic relationships, often in equational form. Models normally specify the relationship between essential elements and contain some indicator of performance (objective function) which is then optimised subject to the necessary constraints.

The third stage is the estimation of future variables necessary for the evalua-tion of alternatives. All decisions concern future behaviour and events and there-fore are characterised by uncertainty. Information about the future is both imperfect and expensive to obtain. Techniques for taking account of uncertainty are discussed later, but can never eliminate completely the uncertainty surround-ing future outcomes. An essential part of these techniques is the estimation of the future costs and revenues associated with different actions. The traditional business estimation procedures include both intuition and guess-work.[1] In attempting to raise management to a more scientific level we would normally use statistical methods of estimation. However, business decisions must often be taken quickly. A compromise must then be found between the speed and accuracy of a particular estimation procedure.

Constraints in particular may be difficult to quantify. Physical constraints present no particular difficulty, but institutional, social or legal constraints may be more problematical. The common procedure is to optimise subject to quanti-fiable constraints to achieve a solution and adjust this solution to satisfy un-quantifiable constraints.

The final element in decision problems is the actual choice among alternatives. Logic is applied to achieve the best possible solution, normally by the use of some mathematical or statistical models. The optimisation approach is more a method of thinking than any particular technique. This methodological approach consists of systematically evaluating alternatives until an optimal solution is found.

Further reading

W. J. Baumol, 'What Can Economic Theory Contribute to Managerial Economics?', *American Economic Review*, 51 (May 1961) pp. 142-6.

Bryan Carsberg, *Economics of Business Decisions* (Harmondsworth: Penguin Books, 1975) chap. 3.

2
Marginal Analysis and Decisions

Introduction

In many decision problems it is often our concern whether the benefit of a particular action is greater than the cost. The economist's traditional technique involves the use of marginal analysis. We may call this the neoclassical approach to decision-making, widely used in microeconomic analysis. As the technique is developed its limitations will become apparent. These limitations provide us with the reason why the technique is not widely used in practice. However because marginal analysis is widespread in microeconomics, and because there are specific circumstances where it will be useful (e.g. see Chap. 14), it is worth spending some time developing these techniques. Before we can do this, attention must be paid to the economist's methods of expressing relationships. This will stand us in good stead for other chapters in the book, where functional form is important.

The most useful way of expressing relationships is often the equation. To illustrate a functional relationship we use algebraic notation, e.g. $TR = f(Q)$,[1] to show total revenue as an unspecific function of output. Then the value of the dependent variable, total revenue, is determined by the independent variable, output. Tables and graphs, theoretically at least, are equivalent ways of expressing relationships, although it is often difficult to express tables and graphs in a specific equation form. This is a particular problem in cost and demand analysis, where we seek to fit an equation to empirical relationships in order to extrapolate to find what cost/demand would be at future output/price levels.

To see that the three forms are equivalent, consider a simple example. Suppose a perfectly competitive firm faced a market price of £2 for its product. Then we could write the total revenue function in the form $TR = £2Q$. Equivalently the corresponding table or graph could be constructed (Fig. 2.1).

Totals, averages and marginals

A marginal relationship is defined as the change in the dependent variable associated with a unitary change in one of the independent variables. For ex-

$$TR = £2Q$$

Tabular form		
Q	*TR*	
1	2	
2	4	
3	6	
4	8	
5	10	

Graphical form

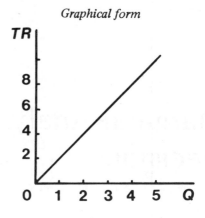

Figure 2.1

ample, marginal revenue is the change in total revenue associated with a unit change in output.

It is helpful to write

$$MR = \frac{\Delta TR}{\Delta Q}$$

where Δ refers to a small change. This notation will help us to see the relationship between marginals and the calculus, introduced later.

Totals, averages and marginals bear a relationship to each other that can be examined in algebraic and graphical forms. Suppose we have the following simple tabular relationship between output and total cost:

Q	*£TC*	*£AC*	*£MC*
0	6	–	–
1	10	10	4
2	16	8	6
3	24	8	8
4	36	9	12
5	50	10	14

The average cost (column 3) is simply total cost divided by output. Marginal cost is the change in total cost associated with a unit change in output. If output changes from 2 to 3 units, total cost changes from £16 to £24, therefore the marginal cost of the third unit is £8. Both average and marginal cost are derived from total cost.

These points can be plotted (Fig. 2.2):

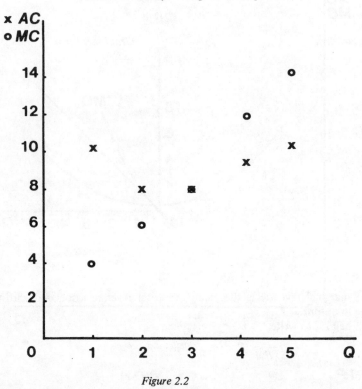

Figure 2.2

The economist usually draws this as a graph by fitting curves approximately to these points. To do this is to assume output is continuous rather than discrete, because marginal cost is not defined between units. From Fig. 2.3 some general rules can be formulated which hold for all relationships.

1. When the marginal is less than the average, the average must be falling. Conversely when the average is decreasing, the marginal must be less than the average.

2. When the marginal is greater than the average, the average must be rising, and conversely.

From 1 and 2 it follows logically that when the average is at its lowest; the marginal equals the average. Consequently the marginal cost curve always intersects the average cost curve at its lowest point.

Geometrically the marginal and average curves bear an exact relationship to the total curve. Suppose we have a total product curve as follows, where total product is determined by the quantity of factor (L) employed (Fig. 2.4). Average product at any point is equal to the slope of a line from the origin to the total curve at that point. Thus at X average product equals OB/OA (total product divided by the quantity of factor).

Marginal product at any point on the total product curve is equal to the slope of the total product curve at that point, for example at point Z marginal product equals the slope of the line CD.

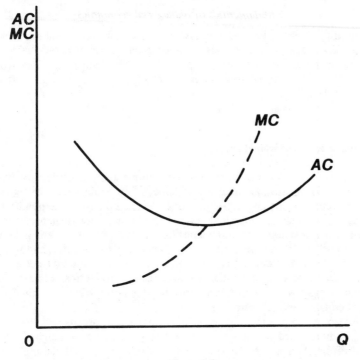

Figure 2.3

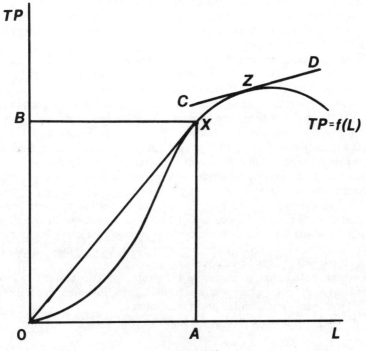

Figure 2.4

At point X a line from the origin is also tangential to the total product curve. Thus at X average product equals marginal product. Immediately before X the slope of the total product curve is greater than the slope of a line from the origin; therefore marginal product is greater than average product and average product is rising.

The application of marginal analysis

Marginal analysis is helpful in the microeconomic analysis of decisions because of two rules for profit maximisation, which can best be illustrated by example.

To maximise profit any activity must be carried on up to the point where its marginal cost equals its marginal revenue (i.e. where marginal profit is zero). Given normal cost and demand conditions, if marginal revenue is greater than marginal cost profit can be increased by expanding the activity, and if marginal cost is greater than marginal revenue profit can be increased by decreasing the activity. This rule can be applied to advertising, production, etc., so that, for example, factors will be purchased up to the point where marginal revenue product equals marginal factor cost.

The second marginalist rule for the maximisation of profits says that activities should be performed to the levels where they yield the same marginal return per unit of effort. This is the efficient allocation rule and says that a multi-product firm, for example, should allocate a factor between two production activities so that the marginal profit per unit of input is equalised in each activity. If this were not the case total profit could be increased by reallocating the input among the outputs (allocating more input to the activity with greatest marginal profit and less to the other activity).

For a number of reasons decisions must sometimes be made on the basis of average rather than marginal data. Almost all accounting data are in terms of averages and totals.[2] Also marginal data by their nature are often hypothetical. For example marginal revenue data would be provided by changing sales by one unit, but the decision to change sales must be made before marginal revenue can be found. Finally less data are needed to find averages. For example if total cost is £10 and output is 5 units average cost can be calculated, but to find marginal cost we would need to know total cost at different output levels.

However, under certain conditions averages can be used to estimate marginals. If average cost increases as output expands we know that marginal cost must be greater than average cost, so average cost can be revised upwards to estimate marginal cost. Moreover the degree of adjustment necessary will be indicated by the rate at which the average is changing. If average cost falls as output expands the converse must hold. Only if we know that average cost is constant at different output levels will marginal cost equal average cost.

We have stated that to maximise the profit from an activity it should be carried out to the point where marginal profit is zero. However, this is a necessary but not sufficient condition for profit maximisation.

Consider the following total profit function (Fig. 2.5):

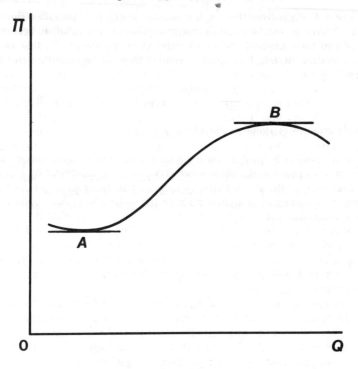

Figure 2.5

We can see that marginal profit (the slope of the total profit function) is zero at points A and B. It is also obvious that A is a minimum and B a maximum. The condition that marginal profit equals zero only indicates a turning-point for the function and is referred to as the first-order condition. To ensure a maximum we must consider the second-order condition, which can be developed intuitively from Fig. 2.5. As output changes from just less than A to just more than A, the marginal profit changes from negative to positive, and at B from positive to negative. At this stage this is all we can say about second-order conditions. When we proceed to examine calculus the second-order condition can be developed more rigorously.

The concept of a derivative

We know that a marginal value is the change in value of the independent variable associated with a unit change in the dependent variable.

Consider $\qquad y = f(x)$

then[3] marginal $y = \dfrac{\Delta y}{\Delta x}$

A derivative is a precise value of the general marginal relationship $\Delta y/\Delta x$. To find a derivative we need to find the value $\Delta y/\Delta x$ for very small changes in x. We use dy/dx for the derivative of y with respect to x.[4] We are now generalising the marginal relationships to refer to very small changes in the independent variable, i.e. assuming x to be continuous rather than discrete. This is an assumption that need not cause distress for large magnitudes, as long as we note that the derivative may not be defined in particular circumstances, i.e. where x is small and discrete.

We have already said that marginal refers to the slope of a line tangential to the total curve at a particular point. Strictly speaking, however, marginal cost for example, refers to the slope of a line from a particular point on the total cost curve at say output Z, to another point on the total cost curve at output $Z + 1$ units. The derivative on the other hand refers to the slope of the tangent at that point because the change in output associated with the derivative tends to zero. The derivative dTC/dQ shows precisely how cost and output are related at specific output levels (Fig. 2.6).

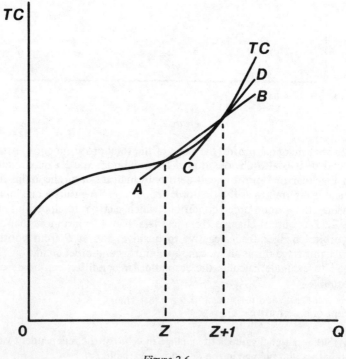

Figure 2.6

The marginal cost of the $Z + 1$th unit is equal to the slope of the line AB, while dTC/dQ at this point equals the slope of the line CD. The derivative of total cost with respect to output is greater than marginal cost at this point because marginal cost is increasing.

Rules for differentiating functions

We shall consider certain rules for finding the derivative of particular forms of functions. These can then be applied in all circumstances where the function used fits that particular form. This will also give us the opportunity to discuss how particular functional forms can be expressed.

1. Constant functions[5]
A constant function can be expressed in the form $y = c$, where c is a constant. The derivative of a constant is zero, i.e. if $y = c$, $dy/dx = 0$.

2. Power functions
A power or exponential function can be written in the form $y = ax^b$, where a and b are constants referred to as the coefficient and exponent respectively. The derivative is then equal to the exponent b times the coefficient a multiplied by the variable x raised to the power $b - 1$.

i.e. $$y = ax^b$$
$$\frac{dy}{dx} = bax^{b-1},$$

for example if $$y = 4x^2$$
$$\frac{dy}{dx} = 2 \cdot 4 \cdot x^{2-1}$$
$$= 8x$$

3. Sums and differences
Let $u = g(x)$ and $v = h(x)$ be two unspecified functions of x. The derivative of a sum is equal to the sum of the derivatives,[6]

i.e. if $$y = u + v$$
$$\frac{dy}{dx} = \frac{du}{dx} + \frac{dv}{dx}.$$

For example if
$$u = 3x^3 \text{ and } v = -x, \text{ and } y = u + v, \text{ then}$$
$$y = 3x^3 - x$$
and $$\frac{dy}{dx} = 9x^2 - 1.$$

4. The product of two functions
The derivative of a product is equal to the sum of the first term times the derivative of the second plus the second term times the derivative of the first.

Thus if $y = uv$, where u and v are again unspecified functions of x (a terminology retained throughout this chapter), then $dy/dx = u \cdot dv/dx + v \cdot du/dx$,

for example if
$$y = x^3 (1 - x)$$

$$\frac{dy}{dx} = x^3 (-1) + (1 - x)3x^2$$

$$= 3x^2 - 4x^3.$$

5. Quotients

The derivative of a quotient such as $y = u/v$ can be found by writing it in the form $y = uv^{-1}$ and using the product rule. Alternatively, it is often easier (although it may not appear so at first sight) to use the rule that the derivative of a quotient is equal to the denominator multiplied by the derivative of the numerator minus the numerator times the derivative of the denominator, all divided by the square of the denominator.

If
$$y = \frac{u}{v}$$

then
$$\frac{dy}{dx} = \frac{v \cdot \dfrac{du}{dx} - u \cdot \dfrac{dv}{dx}}{v^2},$$

for example if
$$y = \frac{x^2 - 1}{x}$$

$$\frac{dy}{dx} = \frac{x(2x) - (x^2 - 1)1}{x^2}$$

$$= \frac{x^2 + 1}{x^2}.$$

6. Function of a function

If $y = f(u)$, where $u = g(x)$ then

$$\frac{dy}{dx} = \frac{dy}{du} \cdot \frac{du}{dx},$$

for example if
$$y = 2u^2 + u$$

and
$$u = x^3 - 1$$

then
$$\frac{dy}{du} = 4u + 1$$

and
$$\frac{du}{dx} = 3x^2$$

then $\quad \dfrac{dy}{dx} = (4u + 1)3x^2$

$\qquad\qquad = (4(x^3 - 1) + 1)3x^2$

$\qquad\qquad = 12x^5 - 9x^2.$

Maximisation and minimisation – the application of derivatives

We have seen that for a function to be at a maximum or minimum its slope must equal zero. The derivative gives the value of the slope of a particular point, and therefore when the derivative is zero we can find the corresponding value of the variable for a maximum or minimum.

To illustrate, consider a simple example. Suppose we had the profit function $y = 12x - 2x^2 - 10$, where x is output and y refers to profit.

Then we could easily plug in different values of x to get the following table or graph (Fig. 2.7):

x	y
1	0
2	6
3	8
4	6
5	0

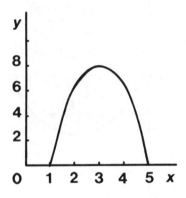

Figure 2.7

From this we can see that profit is maximised when $x = 3$.

Alternatively we could maximise profit by finding the derivative and setting equal to zero (so that marginal profit is zero).

If $\qquad y = 12x - 2x^2 - 10$

$\qquad\quad \dfrac{dy}{dx} = 12 - 4x.$

If $\qquad \dfrac{dy}{dx} = 0, 12 - 4x = 0,$

i.e. $x = 3$.

However, the derivative equalling zero only indicates a turning-point for the function, which may be a maximum or a minimum. In order to distinguish between them we need the concept of a second-order derivative, which enables us to formalise the second-order condition referred to earlier in marginal analysis.

Consider the function

$$y = a - bx + cx^2 - dx^3.$$

Graphically, Fig. 2.8 shows:

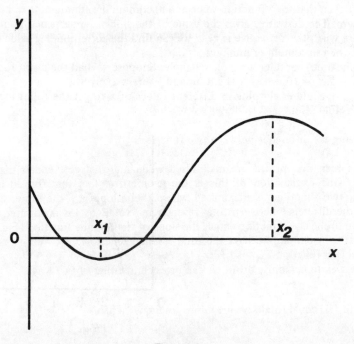

Figure 2.8

The first derivative will be zero at both x_1 and x_2. Now the second derivative is just the derivative of the derivative. Formally:

(1) When the first derivative is zero a turning-point is indicated and;
(2) If the second derivative is negative at this point the turning-point is a maximum, and if the second derivative is positive at this point the turning-point indicates a minimum.

Thus at x_1 the second derivative is positive, and at x_2 it is negative.

We had $y = 12x - 2x^2 - 10$ as a profit function and found $dy/dx = 12 - 4x$, so that when the first derivative is zero x equals 3.

Now for the second derivative we write d^2y/dx^2 and $d^2y/dx^2 = -4$ (merely differentiating the first derivative with respect to x).

Consequently, from rule 2, x equals 3 indicates a maximum for this function. Consider the average cost function;

$$A = x^2 - 4x + 10$$

and suppose our objective was to find that level of output (x) to minimise average cost.[7]

Now $\dfrac{dA}{dx} = 2x - 4$

if $\dfrac{dA}{dx} = 0, x = 2$, so $x = 2$ indicates a turning-point for average cost.

We find $\dfrac{d^2A}{dx^2} = 2.$

Therefore average cost is minimised when $x = 2$.

Maximising the difference between two functions

We have seen that profits are maximised when marginal cost equals marginal revenue. One explanation of this is the geometrical fact that the difference between two functions is maximised where their slopes are the same, so that profit (the difference between total revenue and total cost) is maximised when the slope of the cost function equals the slope of the revenue function (Fig. 2.9). Suppose, for example, we have the total revenue function[8] $TR = 6x - x^2$, and the total cost function $TC = 10 + 2x - x^2 + \frac{1}{3}x^3$ $(x = \text{output})$.

If we seek to maximise profit we can proceed in either of two ways.

Method 1
Let profit (Π) equal total revenue minus total cost. Then

$$\Pi = 6x - x^2 - (10 + 2x - x^2 + \tfrac{1}{3}x^3).$$
$$\Pi = 4x - \tfrac{1}{3}x^3 - 10.$$

To maximise this function we find x such that $d\Pi/dx = 0$, and check this is a maximum via the second-order condition.

$$\frac{d\Pi}{dx} = 4 - x^2.$$

If $d\Pi/dx = 0$, $x = 2$ (ignoring negative values of x which have no economic meaning).[9]

Now $\dfrac{d^2\Pi}{dx^2} = -2x < 0$ if $x > 0.$

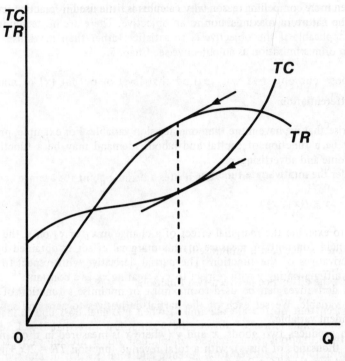

Figure 2.9

Method 2

We know that profits are maximised when marginal cost equals marginal revenue.

Now $\qquad MR = \dfrac{dTC}{dx} = 6 - 2x$

and $\qquad MC = \dfrac{dTC}{dx} = 2 - 2x + x^2.$

If $MR = MC$, $6 - 2x \qquad = 2 - 2x + x^2$

$$4 - x^2 = 0.$$

Ignoring negative x, $x = 2$ maximum profit.

The reader should now be aware of the power of these tools of calculus. However a word of caution is necessary. It was mentioned earlier that these techniques are rarely used in practice. The most obvious reason is that to maximise profit in this manner requires the total revenue and total cost functions to be made explicit. An incorrectly specified function would mean an inappropriate solution. Revenue and cost functions are notoriously difficult to estimate (for confirmation see Chaps 7 and 9).

An even more compelling reason why calculus is little used in practice revolves around the nature of maximisation as an objective. There are no techniques of calculus applicable if the objective is to satisfice rather than maximise. For a discussion of maximisation as an objective see Chap. 5.

Partial differentiation

It may arise that we have more than one decision variable. For example, production may be a function of capital and labour, demand may be a function of price, income and advertising, etc.

Consider the multivariate function

$$y = f(x_1, x_2).$$

In order to examine the marginal effect of a change in x_1 or x_2 on y, the other must be held constant. A measure of this marginal effect is obtained by the partial derivatives of the function. The partial derivative with respect to x_1 is found by differentiating y with respect to x_1, treating x_2 as a constant.[10]

Partial derivatives can be used to maximise or minimise a function of more than one variable. We set each of the partial derivatives to zero and solve for the dependent variable.

A firm produces two goods, x and y (where x is measured in thousands of cars, y in thousands of buses), with a total revenue function $TR = 2(x + y)$ and a total cost function $TC = 2x^2 + y^2 - xy + 2$. Suppose the firm seeks to produce x and y to maximise profits. Then we form the total profit function:

$$\Pi = 2x + 2y - 2x^2 - y^2 + xy - 2,$$

find the partial derivatives with respect to x and y, set these equal to zero and solve the resulting simultaneous equations.

To find the partial derivative with respect to x we differentiate Π, keeping y constant:

$$\frac{\partial \Pi}{\partial x} = 2 - 4x + y$$

$$\frac{\partial \Pi}{\partial y} = 2 - 2y + x.$$

To maximise profit we set each of these to zero, to get the following simultaneous equations:

$$2 - 4x + y = 0$$
$$2 - 2y + x = 0.$$

To solve these, multiply the first equation by 2 and then add to the second equation:

$$\begin{array}{ll} & 4 - 8x + 2y = 0 \\ + \\ & \underline{2 - 2y + x\ = 0} \\ & 6 - 7x\qquad = 0 \\ \therefore\ x\qquad\ \ = 6/7. \end{array}$$

Substituting back into the first equation

$$2 - 24/7 + y = 0$$
$$y = 10/7.$$

The profit-maximising outputs are therefore $x = 6/7 \times 1000 = 857$ cars, and $y = 10/7 \times 1000 = 1428$ buses. Any other output combination will result in smaller profits.

Constrained optimisation

In determining the output levels of x and y we have assumed the firm has perfect freedom of choice. In reality the firm would operate under constraints such as its contractual obligations. Where the constraints take the form of inequalities, such as that the firm must employ at least 25 men, but could employ more, calculus is unable to assist in finding a solution.[11] However, where constraints take equality form, such as that the firm must employ 25 men, no more and no less, calculus can help. Where there is just one equality constraint, substitution can be used. The constraint is solved for one of the decision variables, and then substituted into the objective function to convert into an unconstrained optimisation problem which can then be solved in the normal manner.

Reconsider our two-product firm, with the total profit function

$$\Pi = 2x + 2y - 2x^2 - y^2 + xy - 2,$$

where x refers to thousands of cars and y to thousands of buses. Suppose the firm had contracted to provide 3000 vehicles and no other outlets exist. Then the firm would maximise profit subject to the constraint that $x + y = 3$.

The constraint can be rewritten as $x = 3 - y$ and this substituted into the profit function, then

$$\Pi = 2(3 - y) + 2y - 2(3 - y)^2 - y^2 + (3 - y)y - 2$$

Simplifying, $\Pi = 15y - 4y^2 - 14$.

This can be maximised in the normal way by finding the derivative with respect to y, setting equal to zero and then solving

$$\frac{d\Pi}{dy} = 15 - 8y.$$

If $\quad \frac{d\Pi}{dy} = 0, 15 - 8y = 0, y = 15/8.$

Substituting back into the constraint, if $y = 15/8$ then $x = 9/8$, i.e. to maximise profit subject to providing 3000 vehicles, 1125 cars and 1875 buses will be produced.[12]

However, substitution is only satisfactory when the constraint is of simple form. When there is more than one constraint, or if the constraint is of complex form, the technique is inadequate. In these circumstances we can, however, use the Lagrangean multiplier technique.

With this technique an artifical variable is created for each constraint. Using these artificial variables the constraints are incorporated into the objective function, leaving the value of the function unchanged. This becomes the Lagrangean function, which is then solved by setting the partial derivatives equal to zero and solving the resulting simultaneous equations.

With our constrained motor manufacturer we first put the constraint into implicit form; that is, rearrange it to equal zero.

We write $\quad x + y - 3 = 0.$

The artificial variable λ is multiplied by the constraint and then added to the objective function (profit function) (L).

i.e. $\quad L = f(x, y) + \lambda g(x, y)$

$\quad L = 2x + 2y - 2x^2 - y^2 + xy - 2 + \lambda(x + y - 3).$

Now as long as $x + y - 3 = 0$ the profit function is unchanged, and maximising the Lagrangean is equivalent to maximising total profit.

The partial derivatives with respect to x, y and λ are found, set to zero, and the resulting simultaneous equations solved.

$$\frac{\partial L}{\partial x} = 2 - 4x + y + \lambda$$

$$\frac{\partial L}{\partial y} = 2 - 2y + x + \lambda$$

$$\frac{\partial L}{\partial \lambda} = x + y - 3.$$

Setting equal to zero

$$2 - 4x + y + \lambda = 0$$
$$2 - 2y + x + \lambda = 0$$
$$x + y - 3 = 0$$

From the third equation $x = 3 - y$, which can then be substituted into the first two equations to get:

$$2 - 12 + 4y + y + \lambda = 0$$
$$2 - 2y + 3 - y + \lambda = 0,$$

i.e. $$-10 + 5y + \lambda = 0$$
$$5 - 3y + \lambda = 0.$$

Subtracting

$$-15 + 8y = 0$$
$$y = 15/8.$$

Substituting into the constraint, $x = 9/8$, which of course is the same result obtained by the substitution method.

Further reading

W. J. Baumol, *Economic Theory and Operations Analysis*, 3rd ed. (London: Prentice-Hall International, 1972) chaps 3 and 4.

J. Parry Lewis, *An Introduction to Mathematics for Students of Economics*, 2nd ed. (London: Macmillan, 1972) secs III and IV.

Jean D. Weber, *Mathematical Analysis: Business and Economic Applications*, 3rd ed. (New York: Harper & Row, 1976) secs I to III.

Questions (see Answers to Numerical Questions, p. 248)

1 Determine the marginal products of capital (*MPK*) and labour (*MPL*) in the following production functions:
(i) $Q = 5L - L^2 + LK + 4K - 3K^2$;
(ii) $Q = 10L + L^2 + 3L^3 + 2LK - L^2K + 4K^2 - 2K^3$.

2 A monopolist has a demand function $P = \alpha - \beta Q$ and an average cost function.

$$AC - \frac{a}{Q} = b + cQ$$

with all coefficients > 0 and $\alpha > \beta$.
Find Q (output), which gives
(i)   maximum revenue;
(ii) minimum average cost;
(iii) maximum profits.

3 Maximise $Z = x_1 x_2 + 2x_1$ subject to the constraint

$$4x_1 + 2x_2 - 60 = 0,$$

using the method of Lagrangean multipliers.

3
Uncertainty

The nature of uncertainty

The essence of any decision is that it is made in an environment of incomplete information. The decision-maker cannot know all that is relevant to a particular decision. This lack of relevant information is due principally to three causes.

First, decisions involve the future, which is 'imaginable but not knowable'.[1] Predictions must be made that may well turn out to be incorrect.

Second, the past presents a record of the outcomes of earlier decisions which were themselves made in an environment of incomplete information. Consequently historical data may be a record of earlier mistakes.

Finally, decision implies a choice among alternatives. At any given moment the decision-maker is faced with an infinite number of alternative actions, some of which he cannot be aware of. Therefore information even about the present is incomplete.

In recent years techniques of decision-making have been developed which attempt to provide a systematic framework for analysing decisions under uncertainty. These will be outlined in the following pages, but it is necessary to remember that decision-making is essentially subjective, and no technique exists which can be mechanically applied to all decision problems, i.e. uncertainty can never be completely eliminated. The 'art' of management cannot be replaced by the 'science' of decision theory. Where decision theory can help is in providing the systematic framework for 'better' decisions.

Economists traditionally make a distinction between risk and uncertainty. Risk is a decision environment where we know the likelihood of future outcomes. Large losses are avoidable in risky situations because of the possibility of insurance against unfavourable outcomes. Because the likelihood of future outcomes is known, insurance companies can profit by charging a premium for risk small enough to make the avoidance of risk worth while to the decision-maker and yet sufficient when summed to cover the cost of those unfavourable outcomes that do occur, and leave a surplus as profit for the insurance company.

Uncertainty is a decision environment where the likelihood of each future outcome is not known. One of the techniques of decision theory is to try to remove uncertainty from the decision environment by estimating the likelihood of future outcomes.

Probability and expected value

A variable is random if it changes in no predictable sequence; for example, the sales of bread at a bakery tomorrow. Values of a random variable are the numerical values corresponding to each possible outcome. In assessing the likelihood of each possible level of future sales, one of the most simple methods is the relative frequencies approach. Suppose we have kept a record of bread sales over the past 100 days. Table 3.1 shows the distribution of outcomes.[2]

Table 3.1

Sales level	Frequency	Relative frequency
20	30	0.3
25	50	0.5
30	20	0.2
	100	1.0

Probability is a measure of likelihood. By convention the probability of an event x (which we call $p(x)$) is 0 if the event will not occur and 1 if the event must occur. Consequently we have incomplete information if the probability of the event occurring is greater than zero and less than one.

If we expect bread sales to follow the same pattern in the future, we can estimate the probability of sales being a particular amount (x) by the relative frequency approach.

i.e.
$$\text{let } P(x) = \frac{\text{the number of times } x \text{ occurs}}{\text{total number of outcomes}}$$

Following this procedure we can find the *probability distribution* shown in the third column of Table 3.1, e.g.

$$P(x = 25) = \frac{50}{100} = 0.5.$$

The value of the random variable (sales) is not known until after the event occurs. However, using the past record in Table 3.1 we can find *expected* sales $(E(S))$ by multiplying the values of the random variable by the individual probability of each. Therefore from Table 3.1:

$$
\begin{aligned}
\text{Expected sales } (E(S)) &= 20 \times P(x = 20) + 25 \times P(x = 25) + 30 \times \\
&\quad P(x = 30) \\
&= 20 \times 0.3 + 25 \times 0.5 + 30 \times 0.2 \\
&= 24.5
\end{aligned}
$$

Thus expected sales is the weighted average of possible sales using as the weight for each possible sales level the probability of its occurrence. Obviously we cannot infer that the baker will sell 24.5 loaves tomorrow, merely that over a sufficient period of time we expect him to sell an average of 24.5 loaves.

The random variable and expected value concepts are useful to decision-making under conditions of risk. However, these are only useful if the probabilities have been correctly assessed. If conditions change, the respective probabilities must be re-estimated. For example, our baker may find that bread sales vary with the day of the week. The probabilities could then be adjusted to take account of this.

Elementary decision theory

The baker must decide how many loaves of bread to stock tomorrow. If he stocks too many he will be left with stock of no value. If he does not order enough he will forgo the opportunity for profit.

Assume our baker buys loaves for 15 p. each, and sells them at 25 p. There are two crucial elements to the decision problem. The first is the baker's decision of how many to stock, which we call an 'act'. The second is the number actually sold, an 'event'.

We can find the profit or *pay-off* the baker will receive for each combination of act and event. If he stocks 20 and sells 20 he will make a profit of 20(25) − 20(15) = 200 p. However, if he stocks 30 and only sells 25 his profit will be 25(25) − 30(15) = 175 p. We can thus find the conditional profit table (sometimes called a pay-off matrix) for the outcome corresponding to each combination of act and event (Table 3.2).

Table 3.2

Conditional profit table

Act (Stock)

		20	25	30
Event	20	200	125	50
(Potential Sales)	25	200	250	175
	30	200	250	300

If the baker stocks 20 loaves he will always make a profit of 200 p. If he stocks 25 loaves some days he will make a profit of 125 p., but on others his profit will be 250 p. Obviously the best choice depends on the number of times he received 250 p. relative to the number of times he receives 125 p., compared with the certainty of receiving 200 p.

The decision thus depends on the probabilities of each level of sales. These are given in Table 3.1. Using these probabilities, we can find the expected profit from each stock option. To do this we weight each possible value of conditional profit by the probability of that profit.

Therefore the expected profit from stock 20 loaves is:

P (sales 20) $\times$ profit from this given that stock is 20+
P (desired sales 25) $\times$ profit given stock 20 + P (desired sales 30) $\times$ profit given stock 20

$$= 0.3\ (200) + 0.5\ (200) + 0.2\ (200)$$
$$= 200\ p.$$

Similarly,

E (profit from stocking 25) $= 0.3 \times 125' + 0.5 \times 250 + 0.2 \times 250 = 212.5$ p.

and E (profit from stocking 30) $= 3 \times 50 + 0.5 \times 165 + 0.2 \times 300 = 162.5$ p.

Given the decision criteria of maximising expected profit, the baker will stock 25 loaves and make an expected profit of 212.5 p. per day.

We have not introduced certainty into the baker's problem. Rather we have used past experience to determine the best stock option. There is no guarantee of a profit of 212.5 p. tomorrow. However, if he stocks 25 loaves he will average profits of 212.5 p. each day, which is higher than average profits if he stocks any other number of loaves.

The expected values of perfect information

Suppose our baker could remove all uncertainty about tomorrow by obtaining extra information. With perfect information the baker would know exactly how many loaves would be sold tomorrow, and therefore stock exactly the number of loaves customers would buy.

Table 3.3

Conditional profit with perfect information

Bread sales	Profit under certainty	P (sales level)	Expected profit
20	200	0.3	60
25	250	0.5	125
30	300	0.2	60
			245

Table 3.3 shows the conditional profit values that would apply if the baker had perfect information. He could avoid all losses on obsolete stock as well as the opportunity losses of forgone profits that would occur if he did not stock enough.

With perfect information the baker could expect an average profit of 245 p. per day. By eliminating uncertainty the baker could increase average profit from 212.5 p. to 245 p. Consequently it would be worth 32.5 p. to the baker to have perfect information. If someone with perfect predictive powers were to offer to sell this information it would be profitable for the baker to pay up to 32.5 p. for it.

Determining the value of additional information is a serious problem for managers. Here the *expected value of perfect information* (*EVPI*) is 32.5 p. However, perfect prediction is somewhat rare. In most decision-making situations managers must try to assess the value of information which would enable them to make better rather than perfect decisions.

Minimising losses

The problem of how many loaves to stock has been solved by maximising the baker's expected profit. Alternatively we could calculate the amount by which maximum possible profit (245 p.) will be reduced by various stocking options and then choose the action that will minimise these reductions or losses.

Table 3.4

Conditional loss table

		Stock (Act)			
		20	25	30	Probability
Sales	20	0	75	150	0.3
(Event)	25	50	0	75	0.5
	30	100	50	0	0.2

Table 3.4 shows conditional losses for our baker, with each value in the table corresponding to different combinations of act and events. To find this table we must take account of two kinds of losses.

The first is called 'obsolescence loss' caused by stocking too many loaves and is equal to the cost of unsold bread. The second kind of possible loss is 'opportunity loss', the profit forgone by not stocking enough bread when demand is high. When the number stocked on any day is the same as desired sales, neither of these losses are incurred. Therefore, we get a diagonal row of zeros. However if 25 are ordered and only 20 sold we reduce maximum possible profit (given sales are 20) by 5 times 15 p. (5 loaves unsold costing 15 p. each) equals 75 p. If 20 are ordered and 25 could be sold, there is an opportunity loss of 5 × 10 = 50 p., which represents the profit that could have been made.

We now reassign probabilities to the different levels of sales and calculate the opportunity cost of each stock option (expected loss)

E (loss of stocking 20) = 0 × 0.3 + 50 × 0.5 + 100 × 0.2 = 45 p.
E (loss of stocking 25) = 75 × 0.3 + 0 × 0.5 + 50 × 0.2 = 32.5 p.
E (loss of stocking 30) = 150 × 0.3 + 75 × 0.5 + 0 × 0.2 = 82.5 p.

To minimise expected loss our baker would stock 25 loaves with an expected profit (maximum possible profit − minimum expected loss) of 245 − 32.5 =

212.5 p. per day, which is of course the same result we achieved from maximising expected profit. This illustrates the symmetry of the two approaches. Maximising expected profit is exactly equivalent to minimising expected losses.

We can see that the expected loss of the best decision (32.5 p.) is the *expected value of perfect information* (the loss that could be avoided by removing uncertainty).

Salvage values

So far we have assumed that unsold bread is worthless at the end of the day. This may not be realistic. If the product has some salvage value this must be taken into account in calculating our conditional profit (loss) tables. If the product has salvage value then the cost of ordering too many is reduced. Suppose our baker can sell any unsold stock to a local farm, for pig food, and receive 5 p. per loaf. The cost of not selling a loaf is then reduced from 15 p. to 10 p.[3] Any time stock exceeds sales, profit is increased or loss reduced. The conditional profit table can then be recalculated.

If we stock 25, and sales are 20, we can dispose of surplus bread for 5 p. each, and so conditional profit is now $20(25) + 5(5) - 25(15) = 150$ p. The effect is to increase profit by 5 p. for every loaf unsold. Similarly we can find conditional profit when 30 are stocked and less than 30 sold.

Table 3.5

Conditional profit with salvage

		Stock		
		20	25	30
Sales	20	200	150	100
	25	200	250	200
	30	200	250	300

We can then use the conditional profit table together with the estimates of probability for each sales level to find the new expected profit of each action.

E (profit from stocking 20) = 200 (0.3) + 200 (0.5) + 200 (0.2) = 200 p.
E (profit from stocking 25) = 150 (0.3) + 250 (0.5) + 250 (0.2) = 220 p.
E (profit from stocking 30) = 100 (0.3) + 200 (0.5) + 300 (0.2) = 190 p.

We can see that the expected profit from stocking 25 or 30 loaves has increased, due to the lower cost of ordering too many. Ordering 25 is still the optimal policy, with a new expected profit of 220 p. This has increased 7.5 p. from when bread had no salvage value. In fact we could have calculated this more simply. By ordering 25 loaves, given the probability distribution, our baker would have 5 loaves too many 30 per cent of the time. These five loaves have a salvage value of 25 p. and so the expected increase in profit with salvage values = 25 × 0.3 = 7.5 p. Obviously if bread had a salvage value of 15 p. per loaf there would be no cost attached to ordering too many and the baker would stock 30 loaves all the time. In fact, the reader can verify that if bread had a salvage value of 13 p. stocking 30 loaves would be the optimal policy. At any salvage value less than this stocking 25 remains optimal.[4]

Utility and decisions

So far we have assumed *expected profit* (sometimes called *expected monetary value* or *EMV*) as a decision criteria, so that if the expected profit of action *A* is greater than that of action *B, A* would be chosen.

Unfortunately there are some situations where the use of expected profit is inadequate. Suppose we run a factory worth £100,000 and there is one chance in a thousand of it being burned down in a year. Then the expected loss from fire is £100,000 × 0.001 (= £100).

If an insurance company offered fire insurance for £110 the use of expected loss would lead us to disregard the insurance, as the expected loss of insuring is greater than the expected loss of not insuring. But if we felt that the loss of £100,000 was greater than we could stand, we would disregard expected loss and purchase insurance.

To emphasise the point, suppose someone offered you, for just £1, a lottery ticket with a 50/50 chance of winning £10. You would then probably think in

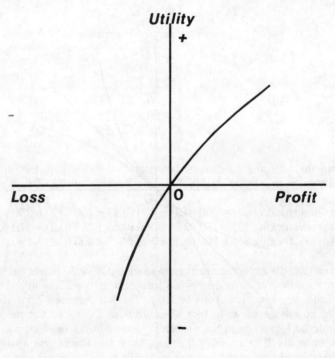

Figure 3.1

terms of expected profit and make the bet as the expected return (£10 × 0.5 = £5) is greater than the cost. Even if you lost, the loss of £1 would not affect you significantly.

Suppose then someone else offered you the same chance of winning £10,000 for a cost of £1000. Then the expected value of the gamble is still greater than the cost, but you would have to think very carefully about it, because to you the loss of £1000 would be a disaster. The point is that the loss of £1000 would be so painful as to be unacceptable as an outcome. £1000 may be too much to lose, despite the chance of winning £10,000. At this stage we are not thinking of expected profit but the utility we would get from different outcomes.

Utility refers to the pleasure or displeasure associated with different outcomes. Theoretically we can plot utility against profit or loss to get the curve (Fig. 3.1). This shows that the displeasure of losing large amounts is much greater than the pleasure of winning the same amount.

The shape of the utility curve is due to psychological factors such as expectations about the future, the decision-makers' conception of his present financial position, the nature of the decision being made, etc. The utility curve is entirely subjective, and therefore likely to vary between individuals or for the same individual at different times.

Consider three individuals, *x, y* and *z*, with the following utility curves (Fig. 3.2):

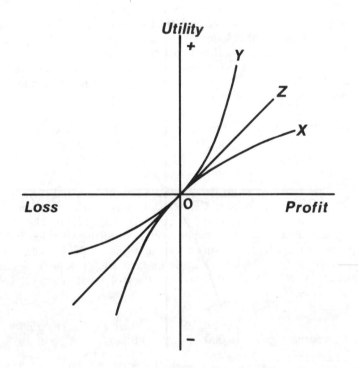

Figure 3.2

Then the utility curves tell us about the attitudes of the three. X is cautious because a positive profit increases utility only slightly, while a loss rapidly decreases his utility. X will avoid situations where a high loss may occur, and is called 'risk-averse'.

Individual Y is different because a profit will increase his utility much more than a loss of the same amount would decrease it. Y would take large risks, feeling that a large loss could not make things much worse than they are, while a high profit would be very rewarding.

Individual Z is indifferent to risk. His utility increases or decreases strictly in proportion to the profit or loss that he makes. We can infer that he is quite wealthy, because losses do not affect him much (however, there will be a point where his utility function turns down quickly, corresponding to the prospect of losing all his wealth). Because Z's utility curve is linear around the origin, Z can use expected profit as his decision criteria for decisions not involving large amounts of money, while X and Y must use utility as a criteria.

Z will act when expected profit is greater than zero, while X will require a high expected profit, whereas Y may act if the expected profit is negative. Consequently we can see that using expected profit as a decision criteria (in particular accepting any action with a positive expected profit) is equivalent to assuming a linear utility function.

The deficiencies of the expected-profit approach are further illustrated by reference to the famous St Petersburg Paradox.

Consider a fair coin (one with a half chance of landing on either heads or tails when tossed) which is tossed until the first head appears and a gambler who wins $£2^n$ when the first head appears on the nth toss. We ask the question: how much should the gambler be willing to pay to take part in the game?

We can calculate the expected return from the game. This is simply the sum of the probability of each outcome times the return from that outcome. Therefore, expected return equals:

$$P \text{ (head on first toss)} \times 2^1 + P \text{ (head on second toss)} \times 2^2 +, \text{etc.}$$
$$= \tfrac{1}{2} \times 2 + \tfrac{1}{2}^2 \times 2^2 + \tfrac{1}{2}^3 \times 2^3 + \ldots$$
$$= 1 + 1 + 1 + \ldots$$

Therefore the expected return is an infinite sum of ones and theoretically the value of the gamble is infinite. Consequently theory tells us someone with a linear utility curve will be prepared to pay a very high price to take part. This is obviously unlikely (for example, the probability of getting £4 or less is 0.75).

Suppose we consider an investment costing £4000. If this is successful we will make a profit of £16,000, but if not we lose our £4000. Assume we know that the probability of success is 0.2, and therefore of failure equals 0.8. We can construct a pay-off matrix:

	Invest	*Don't invest*	*Probability*
Successful	16,000	0	0.2
Unsuccessful	−4000	0	0.8

Then the expected profit from investing equals:

16,000 (0.2) + (−4000) (0.8) = £0,

while the expected profit of not investing is also £0.

Therefore, based on the expected profit criteria, we would be indifferent between investing or not.

Now assume risk-aversion, and a utility function such as the following (Fig. 3.3):

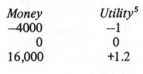

Money	Utility[5]
−4000	−1
0	0
16,000	+1.2

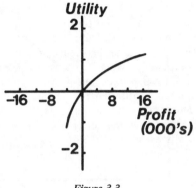

Figure 3.3

Then the expected utility of investing can be calculated:

$$E(U_{\text{Invest}}) = U(16,000) \times \text{prob.}(16,000) + U(−4000) \times \text{prob.}(−4000)$$
$$= 1.2 \times 0.2 + −1 \times 0.8$$
$$= −0.56.$$

While $E(U_{\text{Not Invest}}) = 0$.

Consequently with the given utility function we would not invest, as the expected utility of not investing is higher than that of investing. Obviously in order to formulate decision problems in this utility form we need some sort of assessment of utility functions.

An alternative approach is to consider alternative projects in terms of both their expected return (μ) and the variance of this return (σ^2). Theoretically we can find indifference curves[6] between expected return and variance (Fig. 3.4.). The shape of the curve (Fig. 3.4) then indicates the attitude of the investor towards risk. The indifference curve of the risk-averse investor would have a steep positive slope, showing that as variance increases expected return must increase steeply if the investor is to remain indifferent. This approach emphasises that the dispersion of returns must be taken into account, but estimating indifference curves is even more difficult than estimating utility functions.

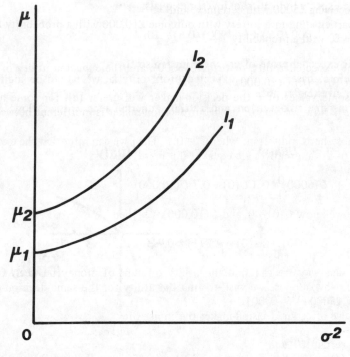

Figure 3.4

Estimating utility functions

This is very difficult at a practical level. However, it seems clear that even a sub-jective assessment of a utility function is preferable to ignoring the problem. There is a procedure which at least theoretically can find the utility of different sums of money, outlined below, but this is really only a more sophisticated form of subjective assessment, enabling the decision-maker's conception of his decision environment to create a utility function that is at least consistent.

A major problem in the modern business environment is that the decision-maker (manager) may make decisions involving actions with money he does not own. Consequently he must try to take account of the preferences and attitudes of those who do own the financial resources of the firm.

One thing that seems reasonable to assume is that the utility function of the decision-maker is everywhere positively sloped because he will always prefer more wealth to less.

Thus the first step in finding utility functions is to assign utilities to any two sums of money arbitrarily, but so that the utility of greater wealth is higher than that of less wealth. For example, set the utility of an outcome of £0 equal to zero and a utility of £10,000 equal to one. Then suppose we wish to find the utility associated with intermediate sums of money, for example £5000.

We offer our decision-maker the choice between:

(a) receiving £5000 with certainty, and
(b) participating in a lottery with outcome £10,000 with a probability P, and outcome £0 with a probability $1 - P$.

Then the expected utility of (a) is $U(5000)$, and the expected utility of (b) is $(1 - P) U(0) + (P) U(10,000)$
For some values of P the decision-maker will prefer (a), for some he will prefer (b). Now we vary P until our decision-maker is indifferent between (a) and (b).
Suppose he is indifferent when $P = 0.7$. Then we can infer that the expected utilities of the alternatives are equal at this point, i.e.

$$U(5000) = 0.3\ U(0) + 0.7\ U(10,000)$$

Since we know $U(0) = 0$, and $U(10,000) = 1$, then

$$U(5000) = 0.3(0) + 0.7\ (1) = 0.7.$$

In a similar way we can find the utility of sums of money between £0 and £10,000. Now suppose we wish to find the utility for the same decision-maker of losing £5000 ($U(-5000)$).
Then we offer the decision-maker the choice of:

(a) a certain £0, and
(b) a lottery with a probability P of losing £5000, and a probability $1 - P$ of winning £10,000.

We again find P so that he is indifferent between (a) and (b), for example when $P = 0.3$.

We then infer $U(a) = U(b)$,
i.e. $\quad U(0) = 0.3\ U(-5000) + 0.7\ U(10,000)$
$\quad\quad\quad = 0.3\ U(-5000) + 0.7\ (1)$
$\therefore \quad\quad U(-5000) = -2.3$

Normally, to avoid problems with negative utilities, we assign a utility of 0 to the worst possible outcome and a utility of 1 to the best possible outcome, and then find the utilities of values in between.[7] We can then make decisions to maximise utilities.
Suppose we are considering the decision whether or not to produce a new good. The investment will cost £100 and the pay-off matrix for possible outcomes is given as (£s):

Sales	Produce	Don't produce	Probability
Good	500	0	0.2
Average	200	0	0.3
Bad	−100	0	0.5

Then we assign a utility of 0 to the worst possible outcome (losing £100) and 1 to the best possible outcome (gaining £500).

Assume that we know that the investor is indifferent between (*a*) and (*b*), and between (*c*) and (*d*) where

    (*a*) is a certain £0
    (*b*) is a probability 0.5 of gaining £500, and a probability 0.5 of losing £100,
    (*c*) is a certain £200,
and(*d*) is a probability 0.8 of gaining £500, and a probability 0.2 of losing £100.

The first step is to assign utilities to the outcomes £0 and £200. We know that $U(500) = 1$, and $U(-100) = 0$. Then because the investor is indifferent between (*a*) and (*b*).

$$U(0) = 0.5 \ U(500) + 0.5 \ U(-100)$$
$$= 0.5 \ (1) + 0.5 \ (0)$$
$$= 0.5$$

and because he is indfferent between (*c*) and (*d*)

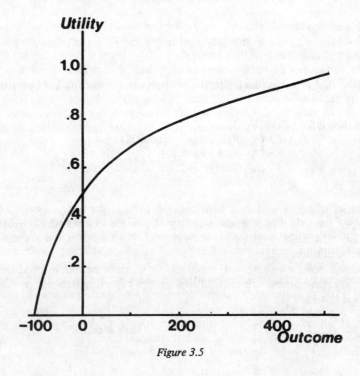

Figure 3.5

$$U(200) = 0.8 \ U(500) + 0.2 \ U(-100)$$
$$= 0.8.$$

From this information we can find the decision-makers utility function (Fig. 3.5).

We then proceed to find the expected utility of the decisions to produce or not to produce.

$$E(U(\text{produce})) = 0.2 \ U(500) + 0.3 \ U(200) + 0.5 \ U(-100)$$
$$= 0.2 \times 1 + 0.3 \times 0.8 + 0.5 \times 0$$
$$= 0.44$$
$$E(U(\text{not produce})) = 0.2 \ U(0) + 0.3 \ U(0) + 0.5 \ U(0)$$
$$= 0.5$$

Therefore to maximise utility the investor would choose not to produce. If the investor had been indifferent between:

(*a*) a certain £0,

and (*b*) a 0.4 probability of winning £500, and a 0.6 probability of losing £100, then

$$U(0) = 0.4 \ U(500) + 0.6 \ U(0)$$
$$= 0.4$$

Then the expected utility of not producing would have been less than that of producing.

Another problem with this method of analysis is that it requires the decision-maker to produce definite answers to hypothetical questions. There is no suggestion that the decision-maker should be given the actual choice between a lottery and its certainty equivalent, because this would obviously be more expensive than the decision is worth. However, by formulating the problem in this way the decision-maker can see the impact of preferences on the decision, which is preferable to making decisions in an environment ignorant of the influence of attitudes.

Decision-tree analysis

Decision trees are diagrammatic representations of decision problems that enable alternatives to be considered sequentially. Both conditional outcomes and probabilities are represented, so expected value (or utilities) can be computed.

In drawing up decision trees, squares are conventionally used to refer to decisions and circles to refer to outcomes. Suppose we are deciding whether to invest £100 in shares or in a bank deposit. If we invest in shares and the market rises we get £130 back, whereas if it falls we get only £80 back. In a deposit account we get £110 back whether the market rises or falls. Assume we know there is a 0.7 probability of the market rising, and a 0.3 probability of it falling.

The choice can be represented in decision-tree form (Fig. 3.6):

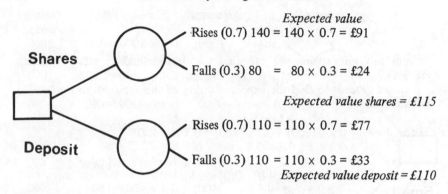

Figure 3.6

Therefore if we choose the alternative with the highest expected value, we invest in shares.

The real value of decision-tree analysis comes with the more complicated problems involving more alternatives and longer time periods.

Suppose we plan to market a new good, with an expected market of five years. We can decide whether to build a large plant costing £2000 or a small one costing £1000. Our estimates of the market future are such that we have the following probability distribution of possible outcomes:

Market demand	Probability
High	0.4
Average	0.4
Low	0.2

The various outcomes are given in the following pay-off matrix, and refer to the annual operating profit in each of the five years.

	Large plant	Small plant
High demand	1000	400
Average	500	400
Low	−200	400

Then the decision tree for the problem can be constructed (Fig. 3.7).

Therefore, to maximise expected value we would choose to build the small plant.

In solving this problem we have made a number of assumptions. We have allowed only three levels of demand and two sizes of plant. In reality there are many possible sizes of both. It may even be possible to build the small plant and then expand if demand turns out to be high. We have assumed the future to be one five-year period. Ideally we would estimate returns in each of the five years corresponding to different states of demand (for example, we could find demand high at first and then decreasing, etc). Profits in the fifth year have been con-

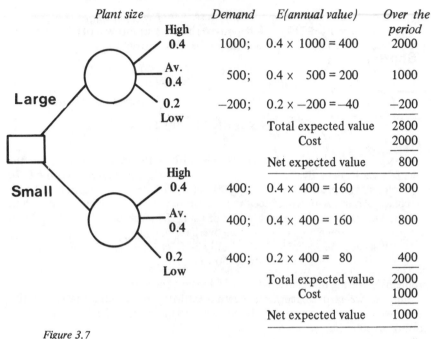

Plant size		Demand	E(annual value)	Over the period
	High 0.4	1000;	0.4 × 1000 = 400	2000
Large	Av. 0.4	500;	0.4 × 500 = 200	1000
	0.2 Low	−200;	0.2 × −200 = −40	−200
			Total expected value	2800
			Cost	2000
			Net expected value	800
	High 0.4	400;	0.4 × 400 = 160	800
Small	Av. 0.4	400;	0.4 × 400 = 160	800
	0.2 Low	400;	0.2 × 400 = 80	400
			Total expected value	2000
			Cost	1000
			Net expected value	1000

Figure 3.7

sidered equal in value to those of the first. In reality we must calculate the present value of profits by discounting. Finally we have assumed a linear utility function and expected profits as the decision criteria. In any event a risk-averter would in this case choose the small plant, with an assured profit of £400 each year.

The point is that each of these assumptions could be revised at the expense of complicating the decision tree. The decision-tree approach can successfully accommodate all these problems – for example, by considering more states of the market.

The decision-tree approach has a number of advantages. The decision process is constructed so that the problem is approached in an orderly sequential manner. Constructing a decision tree forces attention on alternative actions even if they do not appear initially advantageous. Finally, the decision-tree approach can be used with a computer because of its logical process, so that many different sets of assumptions and outcomes can be simulated.

Posterior probability analysis[8]

This is a process by which more information can be used to revise estimates of the probability of outcomes. We use sample results to update prior probabilities with better estimates, which can then be used in the normal way to maximise expected profit or minimise opportunity loss.

Suppose we must decide whether to overhaul a machine or not. The machine has a failure rate given by the following probability distribution:

Failure rate	Probability
0.01	0.6
0.02	0.2
0.05	0.2

i.e. there is a 0.6 probability that 1 per cent of the items produced by the machine will be defective.

We consider a production run of 2000 items, with defectives costing £50 each to replace. An overhaul would set the failure rate to 0.01, but would cost £1000.

First we calculate the expected cost of using the machine as it is (accept) and compare this to the expected cost if we overhaul the machine (reject).

If we accept the machine as it is, and the failure rate is 0.01, we would get 2000 × 0.01 defectives, each costing £50 to replace.

$$\therefore E \text{ (cost accept/failure rate} = 0.01) = 0.01 \times 2000 \times £50 = £1000.$$

Similarly

$$E \text{ (cost accepting/failure rate} = 0.02) = 0.02 \times 2000 \times 50 = £2000$$
$$\text{and} \quad E \text{ (cost accepting/failure rate} = 0.05) = 0.05 \times 2000 \times 50 = £5000$$

However, if we overhaul the machine, the failure rate will become 0.01 and for each initial failure rate the expected cost of overhauling will equal the cost of the overhaul plus the cost of defects after the overhaul, i.e.

$$E \text{ (cost of rejecting)} = £1000 + 0.01 \times 2000 \times 50$$
$$= £2000$$

We can now construct the pay-off matrix or conditional-cost table:

	Failure rate	Accept	Reject	Probability
	0.01	1000	2000	0.6
EVENT	0.02	2000	2000	0.2
	0.05	5000	2000	0.2

Consequently we can find the expected cost of each decision:

$$E \text{ (cost accept)} = 1000 \times 0.6 + 2000 \times 0.2 + 5000 \times 0.2 = 2000$$
$$E \text{ (cost reject)} = 2000 \times 0.6 + 2000 \times 0.2 + 2000 \times 0.2 = 2000$$

Therefore, minimising expected cost we will be indifferent between each decision. If we are at all averse to risk we will overhaul and pay the certain £200, while if we enjoy a gamble we will take a chance and hope that defectives cost less than £2000.

Now suppose we had the further information that a sample production run of ten produced just one defective. Then we can use this information to update the probabilities for a given failure rate. To do this we must find the probability that for each failure rate we would get just one defective in a sample of ten. The probability of one defective in a sample of ten for a given failure rate can be found from the binomial distribution.

THE BINOMIAL DISTRIBUTION

Suppose an event can either occur or not occur – that is, there are just two possible outcomes: success or failure.

. Let the probability of success equal P. Then the probability of failure equals $1 - P$.

If a binomial experiment is conducted n times then the probability that success occurs x out of the n times is given by the formula:

$$P(X = x) = n_{Cx}\, p^x\, (1 - p)^{n-x},$$

where n_{Cx} refers to the number of ways x items can be combined out of n,

$$\text{and } n_{Cx} = \frac{n!}{x!\,(n-x)!}$$

with $n! = n(n-1)\,(n-2)\ldots 1$.

Consequently the probability of one defective in a sample of ten, given the failure rate is 0.01, is $(n = 10, x = 1, P = 0.01)$

$$P(X = 1) = {}^{10}C_1\, (0.01)\, (0.99)^9$$
$$= 0.0914.$$

We call this the likelihood of getting one defective in a sample of ten, given the failure rate is 0.01.

Similarly we can find the likelihoods of failure rates of 0.02 and 0.05. Likelihood failure rate is $0.02 = {}^{10}C_1\, (0.02)^1\, (0.98)^9 = 0.1667$ and the likelihood failure rate is $0.05 =$

$${}^{10}C_1\, (0.05)^1\, (0.95)^9$$
$$= 0.3151$$

We can see that with one defective in a sample of ten, the higher failure rates are more likely.

These likelihoods can be used with the prior probabilities to find the posterior probability of each failure rate.

To do this we use *Bayes Theorem*, i.e.

$$\text{Posterior probability of } A = \frac{\text{prior probability of } A \times \text{likelihood } A}{\text{the sum of posterior probabilities} \times \text{likelihoods}}$$

In our machine example,

Failure rate	Prior probability (P)	Likelihood	P × L	Posterior probability
0.01	0.6	0.0914	0.055	0.364
0.02	0.2	0.1667	0.033	0.219
0.05	0.2	0.3151	0.063	0.417
			$\Sigma PL = 0.151$	1.000

The posterior probability of a failure rate of 0.01.

$$= \frac{\text{Prior probability fr} = 0.01 \times \text{likelihood fr} = 0.01}{P(\text{fr} = 0.01) \times L(\text{fr} = 0.01) + P(\text{fr} = 0.02) \times L(\text{fr} = 0.02) + P(\text{fr} = 0.05) \times L(\text{fr} = 0.05)}$$

$$= \frac{0.055}{0.151} = 0.364.$$

We now have new estimates for the probability of each failure rate, incorporating the sample results, which we can use to find the expected opportunity loss of each decision.

If the failure rate is 0.01 the best decision is to accept the machinery, so one can set the opportunity loss of accepting it, given the failure rate is 0.01, as zero. If, however, we overhaul the machine when the failure rate is 0.01 we incur an opportunity loss, by not making the best decision, of £1000 (2000 − 1000).

When the failure rate is 0.02 the cost of using the machine as it is, is equal to the cost of rejecting the machine. Consequently the opportunity cost of either decision is zero.

When the failure rate is 0.05, if we accept it will cost us £5000 whereas if we reject it will cost £2000. Therefore the best decision is to reject, which we assign on opportunity cost of £0, and £3000 as the opportunity cost of accepting. We can then find the conditional opportunity loss table:

Failure rate	Opp. loss accept	Opp. loss reject	Posterior probability
0.01	0	1000	0.364
0.02	0	0	0.219
0.05	3000	0	0.417

The expected opportunity loss of each decision can be found

E (opportunity loss accept) = $0 \times 0.364 + 0 \times 0.219 + 3000 \times 0.417$
$= £1251$
E (opportunity loss reject) = $1000 \times 0.364 + 0 \times 0.219 + 0 \times 0.417$
$= £364$

Therefore, given the posterior probabilities, the best decision (which minimises opportunity loss) is to reject. Given the sample results, a higher failure rate became more likely and therefore it became less costly to reject the machine.

We can see that the expected opportunity loss of the best decision is £364, which is the expected value of perfect information, as this is the expected opportunity loss which we could avoid if we know the failure rate.

Conclusions

In the preceding pages we have considered how decisions can be made despite incomplete information. The decision theory developed can utilise estimates of the likelihood of outcomes to find expected profit or opportunity loss. The analysis can take account of attitudes to risk and incorporate more information, by revising probabilities.

The major criticism that can be made of the decision-theory approach is that it can achieve decisions only under conditions of risk rather than uncertainty (where the probability distribution of outcomes is known) and as such is of little help in realistic decision situations. However, correct decision-making in uncertainty requires some estimate to be made of the likelihood of future outcomes. One major advantage of this approach is that it focuses attention on these likelihood estimates, which is likely to be superior than any *ad hoc* approach. Decision theory can indicate the sort of likelihood that would make decisions profitable. Suppose we are considering producing a new good and can choose either a large plant or a small one. If the small plant is built a small profit can be made in all situations, but if the large plant is built its success depends on winning a Government contract, whose likelihood is not known. Calculations have been made and the following pay-off matrix constructed.

	ACT	
	Small plant	*Large plant*
Awarded Government contract	200	600
Not awarded Government contract	200	−100

Let the probability of receiving the contract be P, and therefore the probability of not receiving the contract be $1 - P$. Then we can find P so that the expected profit from each outcome is the same.

i.e. E (profit small plant) = E (profit large plant)
$200(P) + 200(1 - P) = 600P - 100 + 100P$

i.e. E (profit small plant) $= E$ (profit large plant)
        $200(P) + 200(1 - P) = 600P + (-100)(1 - P)$
        $200P + 200 - 200P = 600P - 100 + 100P$
        $200 = 700P - 100$
        $P = \frac{3}{7}, = 0.43$

This tells us that when the probability of receiving the contract is 0.43 both actions yield the same expected profit. If the probability of receiving the contract is greater than 0.43 the large plant will have a greater expected profit, and if the probability is less than 0.43 the small plant will yield a greater expected profit. The problem is then not one of calculating the probability of the contract, but subjectively assessing whether P is larger or smaller than 0.43, a much easier task.

Appendix   Decision theory: an example in the use of opportunity loss

Opportunity loss = profit from best decision given the event, minus the profit from the actual decision.

We are considering stocking bread in order to meet demand tomorrow. Each loaf will cost 10 p. and sell for 20 p. Loaves left unsold at the end of the day must be thrown away. We know that the probability distribution of potential sales is as follows:

Sales	Probability
0	0.2
50	0.2
100	0.2
150	0.2
200	0.2

We must decide which of these amounts to stock to minimise *expected opportunity losses*.

There are two types of potential losses. The first is an actual loss caused by stocking too much bread and having to waste it. The second is the profit we forgo by not stocking bread we could have sold.

On the basis of the cost and revenue figures we can find the conditional profit table. This is shown in the following table:

		Stock (Act)					
		0	50	100	150	200	Prob.
	0	0	−5	−10	−15	−20	0.2
	50	0	5	0	−5	−10	0.2
Sales	100	0	5	10	5	0	0.2
(Event)	150	0	5	10	15	10	0.2
	200	0	5	10	15	20	0.2

From this we can find the expected profit ($E(\pi)$) of each action.

$E(\pi)$ stocking 0 = £0
$E(\pi)$ stocking 50 = $-$ 5(0.2) + 5(0.2) + 5(0.2) + 5(0.2) + 5(0.2) = £3
$E(\pi)$ stocking 100 = −10(0.2) + 0(0.2) + 10(0.2) + 10(0.2) + 10(0.2) = £4
$E(\pi)$ stocking 150 = −15(0.2) + −5(0.2) + 5(0.2) + 15(0.2) + 15(0.2) = £3
$E(\pi)$ stocking 200 = −20(0.2) + −10(0.2) + 0(0.2) + 10(0.2) + 20(0.2) = £0

Therefore, to maximise expected profit stock 100 loaves
However, from the information we can also find the conditional *opportunity loss* table.
If the amount stocked equals the amount sold, no opportunity for profit is forgone and no unnecessary costs incurred. Therefore opportunity loss is zero. However, if the amount stocked is greater than the amount sold, we incur extra costs (equal to 10 p./loaf unsold) equivalent to the opportunity loss.
If the amount stocked is less than the amount we could sell, the opportunity loss is the amount of extra profit we could have made (equal to 10 p. for every loaf we could have sold and did not).

Sample calculation
If none is stocked and 50 could have been sold, the opportunity loss = profit forgone = 50 × 10 p. = £5, whereas if 50 are stocked, and none is sold, opportunity loss = 50 × 10 p. = £5.
If 100 are stocked and sales are 50, actual profit = revenue − cost = 50 × 20 − 100 (10) = £0.
The best decision (stocking 50) would have led to a profit of £5. Therefore, if 100 stocked and sales are 50, opportunity loss = £5 (i.e. 50 unsold @ 10 p. each = £5).
If 150 stocked and 200 could have been sold, opportunity loss = 10 p. for every extra loaf we could have sold = 50 × 10 p. = £5.
We arrive at the conditional opportunity loss from the following table (in £s)

Opportunity loss table

		Stock (act)					
		0	50	100	150	200	Prob.
	0	0	5	10	15	20	0.2
	50	5	0	5	10	15	0.2
Sales	100	10	5	0	5	10	0.2
(Event)	150	15	10	5	0	5	0.2
	200	20	15	10	5	0	0.2

From this we can find the expected opportunity loss of each decision.

	Decision	Expected opportunity loss
Stock	0	£10
	50	£ 7
	100	£ 6
	150	£ 7
	200	£10

Therefore, to minimise expected opportunity loss we stock 100 loaves.

Question

What would be the best decision, to minimise expected opportunity losses, if loaves left unsold could be sold to a piggery for 5 p. each?

Further reading

W. J. Baumol, *Economic Theory and Operations Analysis*, 3rd ed. (London: Prentice-Hall International, 1972) chap. 22.

A. Egerton, 'Acceptable Risk', in *Uncertainty and Expectations in Economics*, ed. C. F. Carter and J. L. Ford (Oxford: Blackwell, 1972) pp. 58–73.

H. Raiffa, *Decision Theory* (Reading, Mass.: Addison-Wesley, 1968).

J. Wiseman, 'Cost and Decisions'. Paper presented at the Association of University Teachers of Economics, at York 1978 (forthcoming).

Questions

1 APEC Ltd, well-known publishers of economic textbooks, are considering the publication of a new book, *Managerial Economics for Beginners*. If the book is produced it will cost £1000 to set up by the printing press and £2.00 for every copy made, and will sell for £5.00 per copy. APEC have studied the market and derived the following probability distribution of potential sales:

Market reception	Sales	Probability
Good	2000	0.2
Average	1000	0.5
Poor	500	0.2
Bad	0	0.1

Once the decision to produce is made, the firm can produce any of the above amounts (0, 500, 1000, 2000), but must produce all the books in one production run because the press is needed for something else (i.e. the firm cannot initially produce 500 books and then produce more if sales are good).

(i) Should APEC produce the book, and, if so, how many copies to *maximise expected profits*?

(ii) Suppose any unsold books can be exported, at a reduced price of £3.00 per copy. What will be the new optimal decision, to *minimise expected opportunity losses*?

(iii) How will the decision be influenced by the fact that APEC is experiencing a financial crisis, so that any losses could be disastrous?

(iv) What assumptions are made throughout?

2 (i) An engineering firm about to undertake a production run of 1000 units must decide whether to overhaul the production machinery. The machinery has a failure rate given by the following probability distribution.

Failure rate	Probability
0.01	0.5
0.02	0.3
0.03	0.2

Each defective unit costs £20 to replace. An overhaul would set the failure rate to 0.01 but would cost £200. Given that the firm's objective is to minimise expected cost, should the firm overhaul?

(ii) How is the decision affected by the further information that a sample run of 5 units produced one defective?

Examine how the decision would be influenced by:

(a) attitudes towards risk

(b) the precarious financial position of the firm.

4
Profits

Defining profit – economist *v*. accountant

The term 'profit' is used by a wide number of different people in a number of
different senses. In many of these uses it has acquired an emotive character, in
either a positive or negative sense. This plurality of meaning has led to the
danger of possible confusion or difficulty in any analysis involving profit. It is
therefore the concern of this chapter to investigate the economist's view of
profit, stripped of any outside connotations. In this respect we shall be particularly interested in how the economic concept of profit differs from its use in
conventional accounting terms. Before embarking on these fundamental differences a few preliminary comments are perhaps in order.

First, the accountant himself may use the term in a number of senses. For
example, profit may be qualified in a number of ways – e.g. gross profit, net
profit, pre-tax profit, post-tax profit, profit before adjustments for exceptional
items[1] profit after adjustment for execptional items, etc. Each of these concepts
themselves will have their special uses in particular circumstances. For the
purpose of the discussion which follows we shall be looking at the accounting
concept of net profit before taxation, making no distinction for exceptional
items. The term 'net' here refers to the profit received on the sale of goods or
services net of the cost of all inputs.

As far as the economist is concerned the term 'profit' receives less qualification, although an important distinction is made between 'normal' and 'abnormal'
profits. In the process of competition any 'abnormal' profits disappear by the
entry of new competitors and the adjustment of production levels of existing
firms. If competition is less fierce then 'abnormal' profits may remain over
longer periods of time. Thus the distinction between normal and abnormal
profits is an important one in the analysis of price and output decisions under
various market conditions. We shall return to this distinction when we investigate
the various market structures in more detail.

We now turn to investigate the accounting and economic concepts of profit
at greater length.

We should note at the outset that profit is a *flow* concept – it has a value
which is only meaningful when expressed as so many units per time period. This
contrasts with *stocks* which can only be measured at an instant of time (e.g. the
value of a firm's capital resources).

The fact that profit is a flow concept leads us to look first at the time period
in which it is measured. In theoretical terms there is no particular unit which we

must use. However, from institutional and convenience standpoints there is much to commend the measurement of profit on an annual basis. For example, taxes, rents and rates are often levied on an annual basis, and this strengthens the argument for making up annual accounts. The choice of the year as the unit of time also serves to smooth out any seasonal factors which may distort the picture in particular months.

While all companies present accounts on an annual basis, many now present interim results for shorter periods – perhaps half-year performance, or three months' results. Such information gives a more up-to-date picture of the company concerned, and may be useful both to managers and investors in the company. To managers the shorter time base may give a better insight into current policy and how this should be changed. To investors it again gives extra information on performance, and enables better decisions to be made in comparing one company with another.

The use of a shorter time base is not, however, without its disadvantages. Annual payments must necessarily fall into one sub-period rather than another and so introduce a distortive element. Also, trades which are subject to wide seasonal movements will give widely differing profit levels for the sub-periods. Hence these factors will have to be allowed for in the interpretation of half-year or quarter-year results.

There remains the reverse case that in certain situations the annual time base may be too short. If one is concerned with looking at the long-term performance of a company, then the averaging of results over several years may be desirable. This would be particularly so if the firm concerned temporarily underwent a particularly good, or bad, trading period for some years and then resumed another path. This pattern is likely to be observed in industries prone to intense cyclical movements – e.g. steel-making.

We therefore see that while accounts are generally presented on an annual basis there may be good reasons in particular circumstances for departing from this convention. In general, we conclude the time period chosen depends upon the purpose for which we define it.

Having decided upon the time period to be adopted the next step is to define what is meant by profits.

It is necessary to distinguish between two concepts of profit: the rate of profit, and the absolute amount of profit.

It is useful to regard the firm, which is our central concern, as a means of transforming inputs into outputs. The inputs comprise labour, capital, land, management, fuel, power, etc., which are used to produce the outputs of goods or services. The rate at which the inputs are transformed into output we may term 'efficiency'. If we value inputs in terms of money (and denote the value by C_t), and value the revenue from the outputs (and denote by R_t) then the rate of profit (Π) in time t becomes

$$\text{rate of } \Pi = \frac{R_t - C_t}{C_t}$$

$$= E_t \text{ (where } E_t \text{ denotes efficiency).}$$

The rate of profit will depend partially on *technical* factors which determine the possible ways of converting inputs into outputs. It will also depend on *economic* decisions such as the technique of production to be chosen, the rate of output and price charged for the product. We will return to discuss these decisions in more detail in other chapters.

A second possibility is to regard profit as an absolute amount, rather than a rate of return. This is generally defined as the residual between total revenue and total costs in the time period, so

$$\Pi_t = R_t - C_t.$$

In both its ratio form $(R_t - C_t)/C_t$ and its absolute form $R_t - C_t$, we have now derived concepts which the entrepreneur will use as a measure of the efficiency of his enterprise. Both of these concepts would appear at first sight to be extremely easy and unambiguous. Unfortunately, this is not the case since there is considerable debate about one particular item in the equations, namely what should be included in total cost. At this point we reach the differences between accountants and economists in their definition of profits.

Up to very recently, accounts have been prepared for firms almost exclusively using the so-called *historic-cost convention*. That is to say, the accountant is concerned with the actual costs incurred in earning the actual revenues for the particular firm in the time period selected. He is *not* concerned whether the value of money has changed during the period over which he has presented the accounts.[2] In times when inflation rates were low generally, then changes in the purchasing power of money were of little significance in their impact on the accounts. However with the onset of higher inflation rates, the historic-cost convention has become less satisfactory in that it is measuring with a unit (money) which is highly variable over time. In consequence much recent debate has concerned alternative techniques of accounting which allow for changes in the value of money. We shall discuss such inflation accounting techniques later on, but here confine ourselves to the historic-cost convention and its basic features.

As we noted above, the accountant is mainly concerned with providing an accurate record of costs and revenues incurred and received by the firm over a period. The economist, however, has a rather differing objective in that he wants to identify that concept of profit which provides the best basis for making decisions relating to the future. In this respect he will often employ the concept of *opportunity cost* to a particular item – namely the return which could have been obtained had the item been put to its next best alternative use. The accountant, however, is concerned with what actually *did* happen rather than what *might* have happened. This then is at the heart of the difference between the two viewpoints.

The differences in practice are crystallised into two major areas in the accounts.

(1) The treatment of managerial earnings and management capital.
(2) The treatment of depreciation.

We deal with these below.

Managerial earnings and management capital

The differences of treatment are perhaps best illustrated by an example. Suppose that firm X is owned by a single proprietor and he acts as manager of the firm. In such circumstances the profits of the firm constitute the income of the owner – if profit is high his income is high, if it is low then income is low. Let us assume for example that profit is £5000 in a given year, and so the £5000 becomes the income of the manager.

Let us also assume that the owner sinks some of his own capital, say £1000 into the firm. He views this as an investment which will later be repaid – he can buy stock, parts, components, labour, etc., with the £1000 to generate goods and services which will be (hopefully) profitably sold in future years.

How is the above situation treated by the accountant? There may be no item of cash outlay for the owner's management services, so no figure is recorded. There is no expense of interest on the £1000 invested by the owner in his own firm – hence no interest cost to be entered.

The economist looking at the same situation would see things rather differently. The owner/manager could have worked elsewhere had he not worked for firm X. He might have got, say £3000 in the next best alternative open to him. As regards the £1000 of his own funds, this could perhaps have earned him £100 interest in the most profitable outlet of comparable risk. The economist would then include these two imputed costs as extra items into the accounting framework. The result would be to reduce the balance of £5000, first by £3000 in respect of forgone management income and, second, by £100 for forgone interest on capital. Profits would then be £1900 on the firm's operations, rather than the £5000 as recorded by the accountant.

The above example is naturally over-simplified, and in particular neglects the complexities of the taxation system. In practice various regulations, conventions and tax factors will govern the way in which owners charge for their services to their own firms. It is not within the compass of this chapter to look at such factors in detail. Suffice to say that the management expenses recorded in the accounts of owner-controlled firms may well be the result of such factors and be constructed to minimise overall tax liability given certain constraints. The wages of managers thus shown should not be construed to indicate the true value of their worth to the company for the services rendered to it in the period considered.

How serious is the above problem likely to be in practice? It obviously only applies to the case where a firm's owner is also the manager, and hence mainly applies to small-sized firms. In such firms it can be a highly distortive factor in assessing the economic performance of the firm. This is especially so in the early years of a small business's life where the manager supplies large amounts of effort and capital 'free' to the firm to give it a reasonable start. He may also 'subsidise' the firm in other ways – e.g. allow it to trade from the owner's own property and charge the firm a nominal rent considerably below the market value.

The problems in this section have far less impact in the larger companies. This is because ownership is generally divorced from control. Ownership usually lies with a wide spectrum of small shareholders, together with larger holdings by financial institutions and other companies. In contrast, management tends to be an executive function in which the individual persons concerned do not have large shareholdings. In consequence the identity of purpose between owners and managers, which existed in the small firm, is broken in the large company. The result of this is that managers get paid in ways which are similar to other workers employed by the company. They therefore represent an identifiable cost item to be automatically included in the accounts. In addition they are never called upon to 'subsidise' the firm in any way – such as investing money in the firm without interest, etc.

In consequence the complications we have mentioned in this section are usually confined to smaller enterprises. In terms of *numbers* of companies to which this applies, this factor could, however, be of considerable significance.

Depreciation

To the economist the value of a fixed asset will depend on its potential earning power over the rest of its life. This will depend partly on the capacity of the asset for producing goods and partly upon the markets for the goods it is capable of producing. The latter is extremely important in that the demand for particular goods, especially non-staple goods, is subject to changes in consumer tastes or the introduction of technically superior new inventions. Thus, quite apart from the physical wearing out of fixed assets through use, and the mere passage of time, there are forces at work which will alter the earning capacity of the assets, and hence their value.

A special type of fixed asset, the sunken asset, is worthy of particular mention. This special case has the peculiarity that the asset has no alternative use – in the economist's terms it has *no opportunity cost*. An example of this would be a particular machine which can make only one product, and is incapable of being transformed into producing anything else. In this case the value of the asset is solely determined by demand factors relating to the product being made.

The depreciation of an asset can therefore be seen as the change in the earning power of the asset over time. In consequence depreciation is not an actual cost item, but a book value estimated by the accountant or economist. The general aim of the depreciation cost is to set aside an amount of money each time period towards the eventual replacement of the asset at the end of its useful life.

The major difference between economists and accountants in this respect concerns the way in which this is to be done. The accountant uses for the basis of his calculations the actual cost incurred in buying the asset in the first place (the *historic cost*). He then estimates the useful life of the asset and from these two figures he sets aside each year a sum, so that at the end of the life of the asset an amount equal to the original cost of the asset has been accumulated. There are a number of different patterns or conventions in which this historic cost can be apportioned over the years (e.g. straight-line basis, reducing-balance method, etc.), but these details do not concern us here.

The economist, however, is not particularly interested in the historic cost of the asset, but sees the *replacement cost* as of major significance. It may, of course, be the case sometimes that the historic cost and replacement cost are not very different, but this is not likely to be the general rule. There are several reasons for this.

First, technology may change so that the same function in terms of end-use can be achieved via a different method. A classic example of this is that of electronic calculators – whereas they at one period of time were heavy, large, expensive and mains-operated, the modern-day equivalent are small, lightweight, battery-operated and available at a fraction of the price. In this case the historic cost of the original item will bear little or no resemblance to its replacement cost.

Second, even with fairly constant technology, relative prices may change significantly over time. An asset which is made using highly specialised factors of production (e.g. particular raw materials, highly skilled labour, etc.) may be highly susceptible to this. For example, if a particular raw material becomes in very short supply, then this will have an effect on the price of the asset, especially if there is no readily available substitute material. Again, we see that for this reason historic cost may not correspond very closely to replacement cost.

A third factor concerns the impact of inflation. Even though relative prices may not change much, and perhaps technology also remains stable, there is a high probability that the general price level will alter. If there is considerable inflation, for example, the result will be that the sum set aside on an historic-cost basis will be insufficient to buy the new asset which replaces the old at the end of its life. The severity of this problem depends on the rate of inflation and the length of the useful life of the asset concerned.

In practice, however, all three factors are likely to be in operation simultaneously – i.e. technology will be changing, relative prices altering and the general price level moving. This may make the historic-cost method inadequate in measuring the actual depreciation of the asset concerned.

In view of the above remarks it would seem that there is a strong case on theoretical grounds for moving over to a replacement-cost basis. In practice, however, the accountancy profession has been very slow to consider doing this. This itself has been the result of certain difficulties in implementing the replacement-cost principle. The main problem here is that a forecast is necessary of the likely replacement cost of the asset at the end of its life. In order to do this correctly one would seemingly have to know in advance how technology was going to change, how relative prices are expected to move and how the general level of prices will change. All of these are, of course, unknown and so accountants have argued that they feel happier working with a figure which is at least known (i.e. the historic cost), rather than indulge in speculation into the future where there is no means (other than the passage of time) for assessing whether the sum set aside was correct. Thus the historic-cost method, despite its deficiencies has still been retained, and has been the exclusive way of presenting accounts until fairly recently.

We have so far concerned ourselves with the major productive assets which are though to depreciate over time. We should, however, at this point note that other assets may also change their value over time, and these may not specifically be measured under the conventional accounting procedures. In particular, certain assets may be subject to windfall gains or losses. For example, a firm may own a piece of freehold property which changes in potential value because of planning decisions on urban redevelopment, changes in demand patterns or speculation on the property market, etc. The conventional accounting procedure would be to value such gains or losses only when they are realised, whereas the economist would be concerned about *all* changes in value, whether realised or not. Such windfall changes in value apply not only to property, but also to financial assets, inventory and even less tangible assets such as goodwill. In theory the economist would want up-to-date valuations of all of these items not subject to depreciation charges. In contrast, under the traditional accounting conventions, they would be valued only at historic cost, unless any change in value of the asset was actually realised by sale of the asset. The extent of *unrealised* holding gains is likely to be far more important when the general price level is rising.

The accelerating inflation rate in the early and mid-1970s introduced strains into the conventional historic-costs basis which had not been experienced before. The danger with such high inflation rates was that the distortions introduced were such that a question mark was raised about the usefulness of conventional accounting practices as a basis for good managerial decisions. In particular, a committee was set up in the United Kingdom to investigate the effects of inflation on accounting procedures[3] – the so-called Sandilands Committee. We now turn to discuss the recommendations of this committee.

Inflation accounting – Sandilands Report

It is not the purpose of this section to discuss this Report in detail. It is a voluminous report on accounting procedures, and the complexities of this belong to a text on accountancy rather than economics. Nevertheless, the proposition for a new method of accounting which allows for inflation has considerable significance for economists, who are also interested in profit as a concept.

The basic problem with a high rate of inflation in the conventional annual accounts is that the £1 measure at the very end of the accounting year is different from the £1 measured at the beginning, in terms of what £1 will purchase. To put items on the same *nominal* basis of £s while the *real* value of the £ is altering through time therefore introduces a distortive element in comparing time periods within the accounting year. Worse still, it makes the comparison of profits, costs and revenues over differing accounting years extremely hazardous.

Mention was made previously of the choice of the year as the period for accounting purposes. In the context of inflation it would therefore appear that a rather shorter time base would be preferable if one is going to stick with the conventional historic-cost method. Cutting down the time interval will tend to lessen the problems of comparing cash flows meaningfully *within* the accounting period. However, this would still not solve the problem of comparison of items between several accounting periods.

As a consequence of these difficulties a new method of accounting was suggested by the Sandilands Committee – known as the current cost accounting. The basic recommendations of the Report can be summarised fairly briefly, although the details of implementation are extremely complex. First, the Report suggests that depreciation estimates should be based on replacement cost rather than historic cost. The method suggested would amount to applying specific price indices to the sort of capital good for which a depreciation charge is required. In effect then, by a process of adjustment year by year through a price index, a reserve is built up over the life of the asset which will approximately equal its replacement cost.

A second recommendation concerns stocks which are influenced in real value by inflation. In effect this amounts to removing from profits an estimate of gains in the nominal value of goods held in stock during the account period. Similarly, other assets, such as land and buildings, should be revalued at regular intervals so as to ascertain an up-to-date figure.

Next all flows of revenues, purchases and all other costs have to be put on a constant real basis. Thus the cash amounts observed in time periods within the accounting period have to be 'corrected' for price movements within that period, again by a process of deflating by an appropriate price index. The actual flows of money, therefore, are replaced by an estimated series of flows which are intended to give an accurate picture in terms of a constant price level.

Finally, the process of linking items in the accounts to price changes has an implication for all monetary debts of firms. In particular, rising prices will diminish the burden of borrowing expressed in money terms (e.g. a mortgage, loan or overdraft). Thus the effect is to add into the profits declared an estimate of the gain accruing to firms as a result of inflation reducing the real burden of its debts.

What effect, in practice, are such changes likely to have? An impression is given in Table 4.1, which gives profits on the standard historic-cost basis and the new current-cost basis for a selection of British companies. It will be seen that the change in basis has a marked effect on the profits measured. In some cases they are increased three- or fourfold, in others reduced by similarly large (and sometimes larger) amounts.

The pattern of rises or falls are the result of the effects of inflation on the various items that we have discussed above. For example, highly capital intensive industries (such as I.C.I., Tube Investments, British Petroleum) tend to report far lower profits on the new basis. This arises because the reduction in profits through larger depreciation costs, and the effect of stock appreciation, far outweigh any gains from the reduction in the real value of debts. However, the reverse is the case for financial and property companies such as Trafalgar House, Grand Metropolitan, etc., which shows that the reduction in the real value of their debts far outweighs any other factor, so that profits rise considerably. It is evident from Table 4.1 that any change away from the historic-cost method would have a profound effect on the level and distribution of profits reported from the various sectors of industry, commerce and finance.

Such a move is as yet some considerable way from implementation, although some companies do report accounts corrected for inflation alongside their normal historic-cost accounts. The implementation is held up by a number of factors, mainly concerning the price indices to be used for 'correcting' the nominal figures for price changes. However, there is also a reluctance among some accountants to depart from hard figures of what actually happened, to the invention of new cash flows based on subjective indices.

From the economist's viewpoint, the suggestions of the Sandilands Report are of considerable interest. The move towards replacement-cost depreciation

Fundamentals of managerial economics

Table 4.1

Profits attributable to ordinary shareholders 1974/5

	Standard historic-cost method (£m)	Current-cost method (£m)
Allbright & Wilson	14.2	9.5
Babcock & Wilcox	4.8	3.4
British Petroleum	475.0	365.0
British Printing Corporation	2.9	3.9
Carpets International	1.7	0.2
Courtaulds	89.1	72.3
Distillers	42.3	34.7
General Electric	71.4	44.9
Glynwed	7.2	5.9
Grand Metropolitan	17.6	85.1
Hawker Siddeley Group	27.1	21.5
I.C.I.	249.0	177.0
London Brick	1.1	0.7
Marks & Spencer	39.3	40.2
Rank Organisation	30.6	65.1
Reckitt & Colman	12.9	10.4
Royal Dutch Shell	1161.0	909.0
Trafalgar House Investments	14.4	46.3
Trust Houses Forte	8.9	29.2
Tube Investments	18.3	8.1
United Biscuits	6.6	9.9

Source: *The Guardian*, 3 Sep 1975, p. 15.

charges, and the emphasis on up-to-date valuation of fixed assets and allowance for stock appreciation are factors which would generally be welcomed. Indeed the general aim of expressing figures on the basis of a unit which has a constant real value through time would also find approval. However, there remains the problem of finding sufficiently good indices for deflating the various items concerned. Finally, it should be noted that the rise in profits reported in some cases on the new basis may not be backed up by comparable liquidity – for example, the larger profits of property companies are mainly in 'book' form rather than ready cash. As a result dividends to shareholders may not move in exactly the way which might be envisaged from the change in profit levels.

It would therefore appear that the recommendations of the Sandilands Committee seem to narrow the gap in the conceptual difference over profit between economists and accountants. There still, however, remain elements in the accounts where the economist would be looking for an estimate of opportunity cost rather than actual cost, as we have illustrated previously in relation to managerial earnings and capital.

Profits and the performance of the firm

We have so far been concerned with the appropriate measure of profits over the conventional time period used by the firm (usually a year). It is these exact figures which will determine certain key characteristics – for example, the tax liability of the firm, the dividends available for shareholders, the valuation of the company shares, etc. Also, the annual accounts, with suitable amendments discussed above, will give an accurate basis on which to make longer-term economic decisions on the direction in which the firm should move.

However, it should be noted that this 'true' picture of the firm is available only once or possibly twice in a year. For the remaining period of time there is no such data available. In consequence, the day-to-day running of the firm involves operations which are to some extent 'in the dark' as far as profitability is concerned. In any firm the daily operations are often done on a 'rule-of-thumb' basis, these rules being devised from actions which have proved successful, or convenient in the past. However, such rules have an inbuilt danger that they may lead the firm into an inflexible policy which is not responsive to changes in the environment. In view of this danger the entrepreneur may at regular intervals within the accounting year make an approximate set of accounts to determine recent progress.

The way in which this is done, and indeed the extent to which it is done, is likely to vary from firm to firm. At the one extreme an owner-manager who is personally in contact with the main financial features of his firm, may have an intuitive 'feel' as to the profit being earned – for example, he may know the level of stocks and changes in recent weeks, the liabilities and credits due to the firm, the balance that he has at the bank, etc. Such items could be kept in his mind so that he has little need to compute actual accounts on a regular basis.

At the other extreme there may be companies where the various financial aspects of the firm are not co-ordinated day to day. For example, the sales, production, inventory and purchasing activities may be delegated to different persons or sections. Under these circumstances a deliberate effort has to be made in order to co-ordinate the various financial flows to arrive at an approximate level of profits (or loss) in the current period. In this situation a formal procedure for presenting approximate accounts for short periods is likely to be instituted. In many cases the time basis used is likely to be a month, as this is often the period used by firms for settlement of purchases and sales.

The making up of such accounts does, of course, require expense and time, and the way in which this is done may reflect a number of factors. For example, a firm which has earned very high profits in the recent past may have less incentive to prepare such accounts than one with a trading record of marginal profitability or loss in recent times. Similarly, a company which is highly motivated towards maximising profit may be more concerned with such progress accounts than another company which merely wishes to attain a satisfactory level of profit. But whatever the differences between firms they all have an objective of avoiding loss, and to that extent would all wish to have as early information as possible when profitable trading turned, for some reason, into a loss-making situation!

Three key variables can be isolated in the preparation of these progress accounts: change in bank balances, changes in level of credits and changes in liabilities. These variables are the ones most likely to indicate changes in profitability, and they have an advantage in being variables which can fairly easily be obtained by the firm at short notice. A change into a loss-making position may be indicated by a fall in the bank balance, coupled with rising liabilities and falling credits. The causes for such a change will then, of course, have to be investigated – for example, is the bank balance down because of falling sales, rising costs, etc.? Or are there other exceptional reasons? The key variables then act as a catalyst to instigate a search operation for the reasons for the apparent change. Once the reason has been ascertained, policy can then be appraised. If the reason is a wholly exceptional item there may be no need for a policy change. If, however, the reason is a drastic fall in a revenue component, or rise in a cost component, then an immediate change in policy may be required.

In the preparation of such progress accounts timing is of crucial importance. The level of liabilities rise through the normal settlement period (usually a month), and so a progress account at the end of such a period will show a high level of liabilities. Similarly, there may be a high level of credits, as other firms will also be delaying payment to the end of the month. In view of such factors the selection of a period midway between settlement dates may be more meaningful. Obviously, this date will have to be kept constant between periods, as otherwise no appropriate measures of performance between months will be possible.

The preparation of such approximate accounts, whatever form they take, serve a useful purpose. They provide the entrepreneur or management with up-to-date information upon which policy changes are made. This is particularly so for firms which are subject to considerable changes in demand or costs over time. The progress accounts, however, do have some disadvantages. First, if the exercise is too approximate, or badly carried out, then the information supplied may be incomplete or misleading. Second, exceptional or periodic items will tend to distort the pattern for particular time intervals, giving rise to irregular effects. Unless the management is aware of such changes, such wrong information could instigate inappropriate decisions.

The source of profits

We have so far been concerned with the definition of profit rather than the reasons why profits arise. A number of different viewpoints have been expressed on this latter subject.

First, we may regard profit as the reward to the entrepreneur for the taking of risks. It is argued that people generally do not like taking risks, especially if the capital commitment involved is substantial and long-term. Therefore in order to induce risk-taking there must be a reward, and this reward is profit. Hence profit arises out of the different attitudes of people to risk – a subject which has been more fully discussed in Chap. 3 (p. 28).

A second approach has been to look at profits as the reward for innovation. This is often taken to mean the production of an entirely new product, although more generally it can be construed as a departure which may involve new marketing techniques, distribution outlets, etc. The advantage conferred on the innovator will result in abnormally high profits, at least in the short run, either through the protection of a patent or a lag before rival firms can mount a responding strategy.

A third approach is to view profits as arising out of the inability of the economic system to compete away any abnormal profits. Such abnormal profits may arise out of innovation or simply a change in consumer tastes, but if the market is not highly competitive these abnormal profits may remain over a considerable period of time. Indeed, in certain cases where a complete monopoly prevails these abnormal profits may continue indefinitely.

Although these three approaches are somewhat different they have a common thread, in that they stem from change within the economy. Instead of the economy being in a steady state of no change, in practice it is subject to continuous movements which disturb the equilibrium. If we removed all change in tastes, all innovation, all risk, and assumed a highly competitive market system abnormal profits would gradually disappear in the economist's sense. It is therefore the dynamic characteristics of the economic system which leads to profit.

Conclusions

We have seen that the concept of profit is an important item to the business firm. It is the main means by which the firm judges its performance, and is an important guide to what actions should be taken in the future.

Two difficulties, however, have been highlighted with respect to the profits. First, the economic concept of profits differs considerably from the standard accounting definition of profit. In consequence, an inspection of net profit in the trading accounts will not necessarily be the best guide to decision-making. We have seen that the main areas of difference between accounting and economic concepts of profit concern three areas: managerial earnings and capital, depreciation and inflation. The debate on the conceptual difference has been highlighted by the Sandilands Report and suggestions for inflation accounting.

Second, there is the problem of information. A complete statement of profit levels is available usually only on an annual basis. In consequence, the day-to-day running of the firm can only be done with incomplete information on current profitability. There are measures which the firm can take to improve this level of information but this naturally involves a cost in terms of data collection.

Further reading

Joel Dean, *Managerial Economics* (Englewood Cliffs, N.J.: Prentice-Hall, 1951) chap. 1.
J. A. Kay, 'Inflation Accounting – A Review Article', *Economic Journal*, vol. 87, no. 346 (June 1977) pp. 300–11.

Questions

1 'Profit is simply the difference between revenue and cost that arises because some firms are more efficient than others.' Discuss.

2 'To an accountant, profit is essentially a historical record of the past. To an economist it is a speculation about the future.' (Joel Dean). Discuss.

3 Profit might be defined as 'the maximum value which the company can distribute during the year, and still expect to be as well off at the end of the year as it was at the beginning' (Sandilands Report). Discuss.

5
Managerial Objectives

Introduction

In Chap. 4 we were concerned with the definition of profit, and it is now the purpose of this chapter to investigate how profit influences the decisions taken by the managers of firms. The decisions we will be concerned with are those which are of particular interest to the economist: the setting of output, the determination of price, optimal advertising, etc.

It should be noted at the outset that these economic decisions are by no means the only decisions managers have to make. They will be concerned with many other areas: industrial relations, marketing, organisational structure, the law relating to commercial activities, methods of financing projects, taxation and the relation to government, public image, etc. These matters are outside the compass of this text, but it should not be assumed that decisions in these other areas are wholly independent of the economic decisions. For example, the state of industrial relations may well be an important factor determining output, or productivity levels, and hence have an impact on generated profit. Conversely, economic decisions may have an impact on other aspects of the firm – for example, a low level of profit, or more especially a trading loss, may have a de-moralising effect on the workforce, giving rise to fears of job insecurity and organisational change. It is perhaps a justifiable criticism of modern economic theory that it tends to ignore the impact of the *whole set* (economic and non-economic) of managerial decisions on the running of the firm.

This said, we now turn to discuss how economists have viewed the ways in which managers take decisions relating to price, output, etc. There have been a number of different approaches which can be conveniently classified under three headings:

(i) Profit-maximising theories.
(ii) Other optimising theories.
(iii) Non-optimising theories.

We will deal with each of these in turn.

Profit-maximising theories

The theories based on an objective of profit maximisation form the basis of a vast literature which may be termed the *traditional marginalist theory of the firm*. The concern here is to predict optimal price and output decisions which will maximise profit of the firm. These decisions are discussed in relation to different forms of competitive structure from perfect competition at one extreme to monopoly at the other.

The central assumption of profit maximisation is of considerable importance, and much work has been done on appraising the realism of such an assumption.[1] Before turning to this issue it is first necessary to define what we mean by profit maximisation. This in turn leads to two questions: What do we mean by 'profit'? and What do we mean by 'maximisation'?

The first question has been discussed at length in Chap. 4 and so there is no need to comment further at this point. Suffice it to say that there are some considerable difficulties in arriving at a consistent and unambiguous definition of this concept. As far as 'maximisation' is concerned, this is generally taken to mean the generation of the largest absolute amount of profits over the time period being analysed. This then throws us a subsidiary question: What time period are we talking about? Two possibilities have been suggested by economists: short-run profit maximisation and long-run profit maximisation.

Again we need to define terms to go any further. The *long* run is a period of time which allows the firm to completely adjust to changed conditions – i.e. it can alter all of its inputs (land, labour, capital, etc.) and effect a complete adaption. The *short* run is a period where adjustment to changed circumstances is only partial – e.g. faced with an increased demand for a product the firm is able to increase output by employing more labour and using its existing machinery more intensively. However, in the short run it cannot alter the capacity of its machines, number of factories, number of highly skilled labour units, etc., in order to optimally adjust to the changed demand. Short-run constraints may be physical or financial. As time passes, these capacity adjustments can gradually be made, and when all are effected the long run is reached.

The reader may be curious as to how these two concepts transform themselves into measured time. No absolute answer can be given, as they will depend upon the individual conditions of the firm and the industry to which it belongs. For a small confectionary shop faced with increased demand (say from the location of a new school near by) it may only be a matter of months before he can find new premises, hire more labour, etc., and effect a complete adjustment. In contrast, a large automobile manufacturer may take years before it can add an extra production line to a factory producing a best-selling car. The skilled labour, specialised tools and scheduling of components from other companies may take a considerable time to organise. Thus the long run may be a matter of weeks for the small-scale enterprise, and perhaps years or even decades for large-scale production processes.

We are now in a position to return to short-run and long-run profit maximisation. How are these two concepts related? Are they consistent or do they conflict? We can see immediately that the long run consists of a number of short-run periods where at least one of the inputs cannot be varied by the firm. If the firm maximises in the short run, then by definition does it not have to maximise in the long run? This indeed will be so, provided one important condition is fulfilled – namely, that the short-run periods can be considered in *isolation* and have no effects which link over from one period to the next. Under this assumption of independence of periods long-run and short-run maximisation of profits are identical, and the problem disappears.

However, if we believe that time periods are linked then the problem re-emerges. An example will illustrate this. Suppose a firm (*X*) dominates a market and has considerable discretion in setting price (and hence output). In the short run it may restrict output, forcing up price so that maximum profits are earned. However, the scarcity of supply coupled with the attraction of considerable profits may cause a rival firm to move into production in a future period, or an existing firm abroad to export to the home market. As far as firm *X* is concerned it will then probably suffer a decline in profits in the future – the competition will lead to a reduction in market price, and hence of profits, in later years. Had firm *X* not maximised profits in the short run it is possible that the competing firm may not be induced to enter the market, and hence future profits for firm *X* would have been higher. In choosing which strategy to pursue, we would have to know the preference of the firm for present against future profits – a topic which will be discussed at greater length in Chap. 13 when we look at investment appraisal.

A number of other circumstances may give rise to dependence between one time period and the next:

(i) A new firm, building up goodwill by efficient operation in its early years, will build a reputation which will affect future profits in years to come. Conversely, the withdrawal, or reduction, of certain levels of service (e.g. delivery of goods by a retailer) may bring a loss of reputation which will reduce further profits.

(ii) Profit maximisation in the short run may generate levels of profit which induce the trade unions to lodge larger wage claims for the future, thus reducing longer-term profits.

(iii) The pursuit of maximum profits may lead to allegations of making excess profits which are deemed against the public interest. Thus government, or quasi-government, organisations (e.g. the Price Commission in the United Kingdom) may take up a case of alleged excess profits, and order a reduction in prices in the future. Thus again short-term maximisation may not be consistent with long-term maximisation.

(iv) The aim of maximising short-run profits may lead to a deterioration of the firm's public image, even if there were no government investigation. Consumer resistance to price levels can be effectively organised and have a devastating effect on sales – for example, the mass reaction by consumers in the United States to exceptionally high prices of coffee in 1976 and 1977. The resistance, which almost amounted to a boycott, was successful in reducing prices considerably.

One aspect of the relationship between the short run and the long run is uncertainty. All of these dependency conditions involve future reactions and are therefore uncertain. One reason for preferring short-run rather than long-run profit maximisation is that uncertainty is an increasing function of the future time projection involved.

If we believe there are links between the short-run periods, then there is a choice to be made between short-run and long-run maximisation. If we opt for long-run maximisation, then while there may be much to commend it as a realistic objective we run into a major difficulty. Namely, that virtually any decision by the firm can be defended on the basis that it contributes to long-run profits. For example, excessive expenditure on reception facilities may be justified as improving the firm's public image, and thus increasing long-run profits. In these circumstances short-run marginal analysis becomes unworkable, and little can be said about economic decisions.

Consequently if there are dependencies between time periods, operational decision criteria are difficult to define. One possible solution is to seek to maximise the discounted present value of the firm, by which future profits are reduced by a discount factor, or weight, to make future profits comparable with present profits. Let *Pvf* refer to the present value of the firm and $\Pi_1 \ldots \Pi_n$ refer to profits in the next n time periods. Then: $Pvf = w_1 \Pi_1 + w_2 \Pi_2 + \ldots w_n \Pi_n$, where $w_1 \ldots w_n$ are the weights attached to enable us to make intertemporal comparisons of money sums.[2] One factor that will influence the choice of weights is how the firm values profits now compared to profits in the future (the firm's rate of time preference).

Present-value maximisation as an objective removes many problems which arise from short-run profit maximisation. Short-run profit maximisation will, if periods are dependent, lead to incorrect decisions because of lack of provision for the future. For example, the firm could generate higher profits now by not replacing capital goods, delaying payment on due accounts, etc., all of which will reduce future profits.

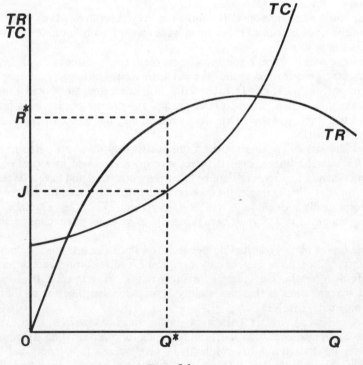

Figure 5.1

However, if profits are independent in different time periods, maximising the series of short-run profits will be equivalent to maximising long-run profit. Unfortunately this is a special case, unlikely to be encountered in practice. All firms with capital equipment, for example, will have profits that are inter-dependent in different time periods. With these complications in mind we now illustrate what the traditional theory has to say about price and output decisions. In essence, the approach is for the firm to compare the cost and revenue implications of different output levels, and to pick the one which maximises the absolute differences between the two.

This is illustrated in Fig. 5.1, where the total cost of revenue curves are drawn for a single firm producing a particular good. Total revenue and total cost curves are shown as non-linear and give rise to an output Q^* which maximises the difference between the two functions, where marginal revenue = marginal cost.

We are not concerned at this point with the shapes of these curves. Suffice it to say that the firm is operating in an imperfect market (so that the total revenue curve is non-linear), and that it has cost curves of the conventional kind.

The reader is referred to Chaps. 7 and 9 for a detailed discussion of the justification of the shape of these curves.

The theory then predicts that the firm will produce an output of $0Q^*$ which will generate a total revenue of $0R^*$. Price can then be determined since:

$$\text{Price} = \frac{\text{total revenue}}{\text{output}}$$

$$= \frac{0R^*}{0Q^*}$$

The profit earned at this output is R^*J, which is the maximum obtainable.

A number of features are important about this analysis. The decision-maker (entrepreneur or manager) is presumed to have relevant information on which to base his decision – i.e. on cost and revenue with respect to output. He is assumed to have the power to make a decision and implement it. It is a simple universal theory applicable to all firms. The main elements and modifications of the theory stem from the competitive environment which the firm is thought to operate in. Hence it is the *external* or market factors which are principally important in determining the optimal decision on price and quantity.

But why does the entrepreneur want to maximise profit? A number of reasons have been suggested, but they fall essentially into two categories:

(i) If the entrepreneur is both owner and manager, maximising profit will maximise his own income. For a given amount of effort this is considered rational behaviour in the same way that maximising utility is rational behaviour by consumers. It should be noted, however, that if the profit varies with the amount of entrepreneurial effort expended and effort has negative utility (dis-utility) for the entrepreneur, rational behaviour will mean that he must find an optimal trade-off between effort and profit to maximise entrepreneural utility which is unlikely to result in maximum profits. Maximising profits for a given amount of effort will be rational behaviour regardless of the nature of com-petition.

(ii) The maximisation of profits is *forced* upon the entrepreneur by the impact of competition from rival firms. In this case it is not a matter of discretion for the entrepreneur what goal he chooses – it is forced upon him simply to survive. It is hence obvious that the strength of this justification for profit maximisation *depends* upon the nature of competition. If competition is absent (e.g. monopoly) then the market is not forcing the entrepreneur into profit maximisation, although he may want to do so along the argument under (i) above. Under highly competitive conditions the entrepreneur has to profit-maximise to survive.

While the above assumption of profit maximisation has formed the basis for the traditional marginalist theory of the firm, it has increasingly been subject to criticism. At this point we look at some alternative suggestions as to which managerial objectives might in fact be pursued.

The rise in popularity of alternatives to profit maximisation stems principally from dissatisfaction with *both* of the justifications used in the preceding section.

First, it was increasingly apparent that the modern economy was dominated by a market structure called *oligopoly*, where competition was confined to a few large firms. In many industries the structure has become gradually more concentrated (mainly through mergers of firms) so that a handful of firms produce the majority of output in each industry. Under these conditions, it is argued, there is less pressure on each firm to independently profit-maximise. Indeed a number of alternative patterns have emerged: collusion among the firms as to what they produce and the prices to be charged, or independent action which was not necessarily designed to maximise profits. The essence of the argument here is that, in these circumstances, the pressure from competitive firms is not strong enough to dictate profit maximisation as an inevitable objective for each firm.

Second, a major challenge was made to the argument that the firm would *want* to maximise profits even though it may not have to due to market conditions. The maximisation of profits was not seen as rational behaviour because of an alleged break in the identity of purpose of the manager and his firm. The essence of this argument stemmed from the pioneering work of Berle and Means in 1932, who discovered an apparent division of ownership and control in many corporations in America.[3] They suggested that in 1929, of the 200 largest non-financial corporations in America, the majority were essentially in the control of the managers rather than the owners (shareholders). This had been brought about by a fragmentation and dispersion of ownership of shares, so that in relatively few cases could a small group of shareholders control the decisions of the corporation. In this situation, with managers typically owning relatively few shares, the identity of purpose of maximising profits and maximising entrepreneurial satisfaction was shattered. Indeed, the notion of the entrepreneur was becoming outmoded with management becoming an executive function taken by a committee, rather than the single decision-taker which had been explicitly (and implicitly) assumed in the traditional marginal approach. The inevitable consequence of this division was that managers may wish to pursue rather different objectives than profit maximisation, and would only take into account the matter of profits to the extent that sufficient had to be generated to pay the shareholders a dividend which would keep them content.

The change in the power structure may be illustrated as in Figs. 5.2 and 5.3, which follows the work of Professor J. K. Galbraith (most notably in his books *The Affluent Society* and *The New Industrial State*[4]).

In Fig. 5.2 we see the traditional viewpoint with shareholders holding the ultimate power and passing their decisions downwards in a chain through the board of directors, management[5] and eventually down to technicians and workers.

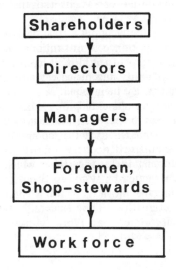

Figure 5.2 Traditional power structure

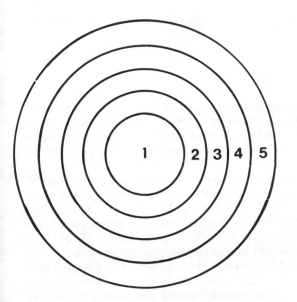

1. Management
2. Scientists and technicians
3. White-collar workers
4. Blue-collar workers
5. Shareholders

Figure 5.3 Modern power structure

In Fig. 5.3 we see the alternative suggested by Galbraith for the modern corporation, consisting of a series of concentric rings. At the centre is management, which controls the firm, and each ring outwards is successively less identified with the objectives of managers. Technicians and scientists are closest, followed by white-collar workers, blue-collar workers and finally shareholders.

Although this change in power is accepted by many economists it is by no means universally held. Defenders of the traditional viewpoint would argue that the shareholders have ultimate power and, if motivated, can wield considerable influence. They cite cases where a few key shareholders, at the annual general meeting of a company, can effectively put a great deal of pressure on managerial decisions. Also the rise in importance of institutional shareholders who depend on profits from companies to pay pensions, insurance payments, etc., will be extremely sensitive to profitability and hence will again be able to put considerable pressure on management. By their expertise and profit motive they can in no sense be considered 'sleeping shareholders'. Additionally, it is suggested that the fact that competition may be between few firms does not necessarily imply that competition is weak. While the extent of competition may depend on the number of firms in the industry it does not *wholly* depend on this. Thus one may get one industry dominated by four firms which is highly competitive, whereas another similarly structured may be less competitive.

Those who believe that the profit-maximising approach is outmoded have suggested a number of alternatives. They essentially fall into two categories: those where something else other than profit is maximised, and those where non-maximising behaviour is postulated.

Other optimising theories

There are a considerable number of alternative approaches suggested, but here we confine our attention to the most important of these.

Baumol - sales revenue maximisation

One alternative to profit maximisation is suggested by Baumol,[6] namely the suggestion that firms operating in oligopoly will seek to maximise sales revenue subject to a profit constraint. The basic argument can be summarised in a simple diagram, Fig. 5.4, where the difference from the profit-maximising solution can easily be seen.

The total cost and revenue curves are normal and the same as in Fig. 5.1. Maximum profit is at Q^* as before where total revenue and total cost show their maximum difference.

Subtracting the total cost curve from total revenue we derive the profit curve Π which cuts the horizontal axis where $TC = TR$. Its maximum level is at Q^*.

If the firm wishes to maximise revenue (without constraint) it will choose output Q'_s, where TR reaches a maximum.[7] However, a constraint is assumed to operate from shareholders – they demand a *level* of absolute profit of some amount which is exogenous (i.e. determined outside this model). If this level

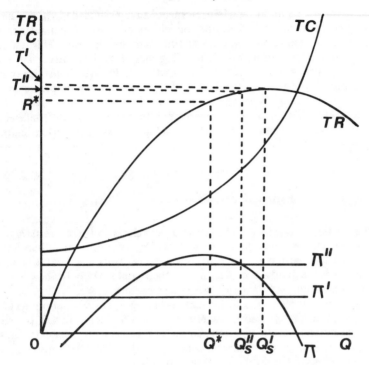

Figure 5.4 Baumol's sales-maximising model

were Π' then the firm could produce Q'_s and still generate profits greater than Π'. Hence in this circumstance it will produce Q'_s.

If, however, the minimum acceptable profit is Π'' then Q'_s will not generate sufficient profits. Output will have to be restricted to generate more profits. Hence we move back along the profit curve until Π'' is generated – i.e. at output Q''_s. Hence this is the optimal output with the profit constraint binding.

The prediction of Baumol's model therefore is that profits will be sacrificed for revenue. The sales-revenue maximising firm will produce more than the profit-maximising firm, and hence sell it at a lower price. The prices may be easily seen from Fig. 5.4. The sales maximiser produces (in the Π'' constrained case) Q''_s and sells at price (= total revenue/output) = $0T''/0Q''_s$. The profit maximiser produces $0Q^*$ and sells at price $0R^*/0Q^*$.

The analysis is based upon the motivation to maximise sales revenue, and this is justified on the basis that the managers of large firms have more to gain from this strategy than profit maximisation. Maximising sales expands the size of the organisation, giving greater status to managers and enhancing their promotion prospects. Also, in terms of salary, payment may be related to responsibility, which is again an increasing function of size. Conversely, Baumol argues that it is irrational for managers to maximise profits for shareholders when they will get little of these extra profits themselves.

The theory as here presented applies at a single moment of time – i.e. it is static in nature. Two important improvements have been made in later development of the basic model. First, the model has been made dynamic, so that combinations of sales and revenues over time can be considered. This is a major improvement in that profits are then endogenous (i.e. determined within the model), since these form the vehicle for growth by reinvested funds. An optimal combination of profits and growth rate of revenue can then be predicted. The exact form of this model is beyond the scope of this chapter.

Second, advertising has been integrated into the model, with subsequent effect on the total revenue curve. This development is taken up in Chap. 10.

Williamson – maximisation of managerial utility

The theory put forward by Williamson[8] again relates to the modern large firm where ownership is divorced from control. He argues that managers of such firms conduct the affairs of the firm to serve their own ends. That is to say, the managers have the goodwill of the firm as their concern only to the extent that it favours their own personal objectives and ambitions.

Williamson conceives of each manager as having a 'utility function' – i.e. a set of factors which give rise to managerial satisfaction. Such utility is thought to stem from certain aspects of the management task – e.g. responsibility, prestige, status, power, salary, etc. These aspects are reduced by Williamson to three component terms in the utility function as follows:

$$U = f(S, MSC, DPI),$$

where U = managerial utility, S = staff, MSC = managerial slack absorbed as a cost, and DPI = discretionary power for investment.

The staff term is designed to cover benefits to the manager of increases in the staffing level. In many cases this will be mainly in the form of salary – for example, a manager in charge of say a team of twenty is often paid more than a manager in charge of a smaller team. However there are other positive aspects to the staff term – the greater status of managing a bigger team, and the increased chance of promotion which comes from greater responsibility and authority. Thus the staff term is a much wider one than simply measuring managerial salary.

The management slack term reflects the utility derived by the manager from being able to authorise expenditure of the firm to serve his own ends. Allowances for the use of a car, expense accounts for entertainment and luxuriously decorated and equipped offices are but a few examples of this concept. In accounting terms they appear as legitimate costs of the firm, whereas they may seem to many as expenditures which have little or no benefits to the firm. If challenged, however, the manager will generally defend such spending on the grounds that it creates the right atmosphere for business and will, in the long run, generate higher profits. However, if such expenditures were removed (as they often have to be in time of austerity), there would be little noticeable effect on productivity in the short run.

The third component term - discretionary power for investment - is somewhat allied to the management slack in that it again involves 'unnecessary' expenditure by the firm to serve the ends of the manager. However, discretionary power for investment refers to investment projects rather than current expenditure items, and reflects the ability of the manager to undertake projects which may not be strictly justified in economic terms. The manager is therefore able to undertake projects which appeal to him in particular but which may not necessarily be the best in terms of generating profits for the firm. Often such investments involve advanced technology - for example, terminals linked to a computer, mini-computers, automated equipment for processing data and keeping records. Projects of this kind may reflect a fascination by the manager for what is 'new', what can be deemed as 'scientific progress' and what may put him above other managerial staff in terms of status and esteem. It may be that such a new investment of this kind may be less efficient than a previous manual system of handling the same problem. The above is not to infer that *all* scientific inventions are of this type, and many may represent an improvement in economic efficiency. It merely reflects that *some* such investments are taken up, not for their efficiency as such, but more on the basis of the favourable light that it throws on the manager.

The utility function is maximised subject to a constraint - that satisfactory profits are earned to meet the expectations of shareholders. Williamson predicts from his model[9] that in the normal situation the firm will act in such a way that management slack and discretionary power for investment are positive amounts, so that strictly 'unnecessary' expenditure is tolerated by the shareholders. The 'normal' situation hence is where the firm has discretion in the setting of price and output and the forces of competition are not thought to be excessively strong. It should be noted that not only do management slack and discretionary power for investment become positive, but also excess staff is built up in the staff component, as this has a positive effect on managerial utility.

When the firm hits harder times, and satisfactory profits are less easy to attain, the components in the utility function are used as a means of reducing costs. Unnecessary prestige investments are cut back or delayed, expense accounts are less generous and some excess staff may have to be shed.

In the limiting case where competition is very fierce the firm will be forced into producing in such a way which implies maximisation of profits. If this were to happen, management slack and discretionary power for investment would fall to zero, and excess staff dispensed with. In such a circumstance the prediction of Williamson's model would be similar to that of the traditional marginal approach.

In general, however, Williamson believes that competitive forces are not as strong as this. In consequence his predictions on what the firm will do vary significantly from the marginal approach.

Marris - growth maximisation

An alternative approach which again stems from the alleged dichotomy between ownership and control, has been developed by Robin Marris.[10] Marris, like Williamson, suggests that managers have a utility function in which salary, prestige, status, power, security, etc., are important. The owners of the firm are, however, likely to be more concerned with profits, market share, output, etc.

In contrast to Williamson, Marris argues that the owners and managers have one aspect of the firm in common; namely, its size. He therefore postulates that managers will be primarily concerned with maximisation of the rate of the growth of size. Size here is defined to mean: 'Corporate capital, that is, the book value of fixed assets, plus inventory, plus net short-term assets, including cash revenue'. The attraction of the growth rate of size is thought to stem from the positive effect growth has upon promotion prospects. Stress is put on an alleged preference of managers for *internal* promotion (rather than promotion through changing firms), and this is made easier if the firm is seen to be expanding rapidly.

This drive for growth is not, however, without constraint. First, the ability of firms to grow will depend on a number of factors – the ability of the management to cope and administer a rapidly growing enterprise without losing control, the ability of managers to find and successfully launch new products to take the place of declining products, the ability of the research and development expenditure to produce an expanding flow of potential new products, etc. Marris suggests that these factors tend to limit the growth process.

Second, there is a deliberate brake on this process coming from the desire of the management for job security. If this is held in high regard the firm must grow in such a way that the financial side is not damaged. For example, growth requires investment and one means of attaining investment funds is to borrow money. But by increasing the rate at which the firm borrows the firm may appear to be moving towards a less prudent financial policy and hence increasing the rate of failure or take-over by another firm. Both of these results would be obviously a very real danger to the job-secure motivation of the manager. Hence there is a desire for growth financed mainly from the profit levels being generated by the present span of products. This is not to say that there will be no external finance, merely that the ratio of external to internal finance should not grow markedly.

There is hence postulated a theory of balanced growth, i.e. growth in demand (arising mainly from new products), matched by growth in capital (providing the finance to launch and make the products). There are risks in expanding too rapidly – in undertaking projects which are more risky, by stretching management capacity beyond its realistic limits, by incurring excessive levels of debt to finance the expansion. On the other hand, there are dangers in not expanding rapidly enough – lack of initiative in not spotting new products or markets, excessive reserves not going into new investment projects, allegations of slack or uninventive management. The effect of the latter characteristics could lead to take-over bids by other firms with more active managers who are aware of the potential in the slow-growing firm which is not being realised.

Again the model is formally presented in mathematical and/or graphical form but the complexities of the model are beyond the scope of this book.[11] Out of the model comes the possibility of an *optimum growth rate* of the firm through time, assuming that the environment in which the firm operates does not alter significantly. In finding this optimum growth rate we have already mentioned a number of constraints – management capacity to successfully generate greater demand, ability of existing products to generate profits to finance investment –

but there is a further constraint, namely profit. As in Williamson's and Baumol's models. Marris also includes a profit constraint so that, if the growth-maximising solution does not generate sufficient profits, growth will have to be sacrificed somewhat to increase current dividend payments to meet shareholders' expectations.

Marris's model is interesting in that it again highlights two important factors as far as management is concerned: the attitude to risk and uncertainty and the desire for utility which may not be maximised by the pursuit of maximum profits.

Non-optimising theories

Under this category we consider theories of the firm which do not hypothesise any optimising behaviour.

SIMON – SATISFICING

An important contributor to this general viewpoint is Herbert Simon.[12] Simon's theory again rests on the basis that firms operated by single entrepreneurs (who are also the owners) are likely to have different objectives from firms operated by modern executives in large firms (who are typically not the owners).

Simon puts forward the idea that firms have an 'aspiration level' which they wish to reach. This aspiration level may be in terms of sales, market share, profits, etc. For any given period actual results are compared with the aspiration level.

If actual performance is *greater* than aspiration then little action is necessary, except perhaps to raise the aspiration level for the next period. If actual performance is *less* than aspiration then the firm tries to find out why its hopes have not been realised. Often it is not immediately apparent why this should be and an investigation is necessary. This requires a 'search' operation which will involve time, effort and money being expended. The result of this search may be to find some sort of answer for the shortfall. Alternatively, it might find no apparent inefficiencies (with the shortfall due to factors beyond its control) and the likely result of this is a downward revision of the aspiration level for the next period. The aspiration level is of course the consensus of what can reasonably be expected in the future period, taking into account past performance.

Simon's theory is therefore of 'satisficing' behaviour rather than optimising behaviour. It forms the basis for a more detailed analysis of the objectives of firms as given by Cyert and March in their behavioural theory of the firm.

Cyert and March – behavioural theory of the firm

Cyert and March[13] go further than Simon in looking in detail at the way decisions are made in the modern firm. They look at the bureaucratic structure of the firm and study the interrelationships of its various parts.

As a starting-point, Cyert and March declare that:

if we wish to develop a theory that predicts and explains business decision making behaviour, we face a problem which can be paraphrased in terms of the following:

(i) people (i.e. individuals) have goals; collectivities of people do not.
(ii) to define a theory of organisational decision making, we need something analogous – at the organisational level – to individual goals at the individual level.

Cyert and March see the formulation of organisational goals through the notion of a coalition.

The coalition consists of the various components or parties associated with the firm: managers, workers, shareholders, customers, suppliers, accountants, lawyers, etc.

The goals change through a process of bargaining, in which 'side payments' are involved (side payments not only involve money, but authority, personal treatment, etc.). Finally a winning coalition forms and the goals are set. However, the position is not static. Circumstances are continually changing and bargaining is going on much of the time so that the coalition and its goals are liable to alter.

Within such a coalition there will be conflict, and it is quite possible that some of the goals may be incompatible. Cyert and March suggest that the organisation gets round this in two ways. First, decisions may be localised into departments and divisions. Hence conflict may be isolated geographically so that all conflicts do not act within the same unit. Second, crises and conflicts are dealt with sequentially; hence they are spaced out over time and can be dealt with as they arise.

Cyert and March argue that the firm may be pursuing a wide variety of goals, but these can generally be classified under five headings:

(1) Production
(2) Inventory
(3) Sales
(4) Market share
(5) Profit.

The *production* goal will be set as a target for the coming period, and this will take on two aspects: *level* and *smoothness*. Hence, for example, a division may set up a goal of say 100 units per time period, with a restriction that output should not deviate by more than x per cent from this figure.

Inventories serve as a buffer between production and sales. It is necessary that sufficient stocks are held to satisfy customers quickly while at the same time not holding excessively large stocks at high cost. Again the inventory goal may be specified in terms of a target level and maximum/minimum.

The *sales goal* may be specified either as a volume or value for the future period; it again may be given in terms of a level and/or range.

As far as *market share* is concerned, the firm may set a target related to its share of industry sales from the product concerned. In some cases this may be a substitute for the sales goal, but in other cases it may be an additional goal.

Finally there is the *profit goal*. The purpose of profit is twofold: as a measure of the effectiveness of management, and as a source of payments of dividends to shareholders.

Cyert and March (like Simon previously) state that firms compare performance with goals. If the goal is met no action is normally taken. If the goal is not met a search activity begins to establish why it has not been met. If the reason is within the firm's compass steps are taken to rectify the non-attainment. If the reason is *outside* the control of the firm (e.g. depressed market conditions due to recession in the economy) a downward revision in the goal is likely for the next period.

Of considerable importance in rectifying the non-attainment of goals is the concept of 'organisational slack'.[14] This is defined as 'payments to members of the coalition in excess of what is required to maintain the organisation'.

For example:

(i) Shareholders paid more than that which is required to keep holding shares.

(ii) Wages in excess of those required to maintain labour.

(iii) Executives provided with luxuries and services in excess of what they really need.

Cyert and March argue that organisation slack grows naturally as the firm prospers; it is not a deliberate objective. When circumstances become more difficult, organisational slack provides the first means of making economies on costs.

The behavioural approach of Cyert and March is a dynamic one. The goals and objectives of a particular firm will emerge from the coalition in existence at any given moment. However, this coalition is likely to change, and with it will change the objectives pursued by the organisation as a whole. Hence, not only will different firms at a single moment have differing objectives, but the same firm at various periods may change in terms of the aims it is pursuing.

Conclusion

In this chapter we have looked at the ways in which managerial objectives have been seen by a number of writers.

The *profit-maximising* approach sees profit as, if not the only goal, certainly the most important goal of the firm. Maximisation of profit is seen as rational behaviour, and as fitting in with most of the other goals pursued by the firm in the long run.

The second approach is that of the various other theories which postulate maximisation of something other than profit. Great stress is placed on the division of ownership and control in large organisation, with power in the hands of managerial staff. It is suggested that they have more to gain by maximising items such as revenue, growth, etc., than maximising profit.

Finally, the third approach suggests that managers do not pursue any maximisation goal; rather they set targets and are simply concerned whether such targets are put into practice.

The second and third approaches depend for their validity upon two important assumptions:

(i) That competition is sufficiently weak to permit managers to decide *not* to profit-maximise.

(ii) That the goal of profit maximisation is *not* consistent with the pursuance of other goals such as the maximisation of growth, total revenue, etc.

The question of which approach is most valid is essentially an empirical one. At the moment evidence is inconclusive, but research in this area is still continuing.

Further reading

C. S. Beed, 'The Separation of Ownership and Control', in *The Modern Business Enterprise*, ed. M. Gilbert (Harmondsworth: Penguin Books, 1972) pp. 137–52.

A. Koutsoyiannis, *Modern Microeconomics*, 2nd ed.(London: Macmillan, 1979) chap. 11.

F. Machlup, 'Theories of the Firm: Marginalist, Managerialist, Behavioral', *American Economic Review* (Mar 1967) pp. 1–33.

G. L. Nordquist, 'The Breakup of the Maximisation Principle', *Quarterly Review of Economics and Business*, vol. 5 (Autumn 1965) pp. 33–46, reprinted in *Readings in Microeconomics*, ed. D. R. Kamershen (New York: Wiley, 1969).

A. Silberston, 'Price Behaviour of Firms', *Economic Journal*, vol. 80, no. 319 (Sep 1970) pp. 511–82.

Questions

1 What are the possible objectives of a modern firm? How far are these *substitutes* for, or *complements* to, profit?

2 'Long-run profit is the sum of successive short-run profits. Therefore the maximisation of short-run profit ensures that profits are also maximised in the long run.' Discuss.

3 Examine the impact of an increase in production costs on price and output decisions if the objective of the firm is to maximise sales revenue.

4 'Since ownership no longer implies control, we can no longer explain business behaviour on the assumption of profit maximisation.' Discuss.

6
Market Structure and Competition

Introduction

An important aspect of decision-making by an entrepreneur concerns the environment within which the firm operates. A number of factors influence this external environment, the principal of which is the extent of competition coming from rival producers of the same product or a close substitute for it. Competition may come from rival producers in the domestic market, or from imports from abroad. The distinction between those two sources is not of critical importance in this chapter, although it may be important in other contexts – for example, balance-of-payments implications of high imports, quotas and controls on imports which do not apply to the home market, etc.

The competitive environment is only part of the external factors influencing the firm. Also important are the laws and regulations governing the product group and its manufacture – for example, quality levels for certain products, controlled or prohibited imports in manufacture (dangerous chemicals), safety and health regulations for manufacture. Similarly, institutional factors will be of importance, particularly those associated with purchase of the product – for example, credit and hire-purchase, banking and loan facilities. Finally, the whole set of economic factors will be of significance – size and structure of population, level and distribution of personal incomes, distribution of wealth, etc. All these factors – legal, institutional and economic – the firm has to take as given and do its best within these circumstances.[1] For the most part the competitive environment is also of this kind; most firms have to accept the present level of competition as given, and then adopt appropriate internal policies which are optimal within these confines. We should, however, add that many firms try to influence the level of competition in the long run, although their ability to do so is rather limited. They may, for example, adopt a pricing policy which effectively bars a new firm from entering the industry – i.e. the practice of limit pricing (see Chap. 11, p. 165). Also they may use legal powers (mainly patents and licences) to prevent rival firms producing particular products. Finally they may put pressure on government agencies or influence public opinion on the level of competition from abroad – for example, an import control or ban on products from abroad, or a tariff on price of these products.

For the most part, however, in the short run, the firm has to accept the competitive environment as given. Its decisions therefore have to be made within this framework. The extent to which the competitive environment influences decision-making depends on the existing form of competition. For this purpose markets are classified into different structures, reflecting the degree of control that the firm has over price. It should not be thought that these structures are of a rigid compartmentalised form, but rather they form a continuum where one type of structure gradually shades into the next. The continuum is represented in Fig. 6.1, where we see that market structures range between two extremes: monopoly and perfect competition. In between are the structures of pure competition, monopolistic competition and oligopoly, each of which will be discussed below. Before discussing these, however, we must first consider the two extremes of monopoly and perfect competition.

Continuum of market structures

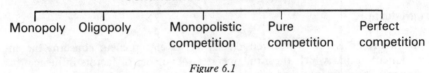

| Monopoly | Oligopoly | Monopolistic competition | Pure competition | Perfect competition |

Figure 6.1

Monopoly

A monopoly is usually conceived of as a condition when there is only a single producer of a particular product, i.e. no rival exists either in the domestic market, nor are there any imports. In this situation the firm and the industry (defined as the collection of firms producing the product) become one and the same thing.

Because of the simplicity of the assumption of only one producer the prediction of price and output in the short run is relatively simple (see Fig. 6.2). The firm is assumed to face a normal downward-sloping demand curve (*DD*) for its product, i.e. more is bought at a lower price than at a higher price. Also associated with this is a downward-sloping marginal revenue curve (*MR*), which lies consistently below it (see Chap. 2 on relationship of marginals and averages for proof of this). On the cost side the functions are of the conventional *U* shape with both average and marginal curves of this shape. Profit maximisation will occur at the output where marginal revenue equals marginal cost, with the marginal cost function in its rising section. Output is then optimally at Q^* in the short run, with the associated price of P^* coming from the demand curve. We should note that this diagram is identical with Fig. 5.1 except that the presentation here is in the form of averages and marginals rather than totals. The analysis here has the merit of simplicity, but is it useful when applied to real-world situations?

One difficulty concerns the concept of the product being made. If we define a product by its physical characteristics then we should soon find that many products fall into this category – the Parker Pen Company is the sole producer of the Parker 61 pen, the Ford Motor Company is the sole producer of the Ford Cortina saloon, Procter & Gamble are the sole producers of Daz soap powder, etc. However, if we asked the management of any of these companies whether they considered themselves as monopolists, the answer would certainly be

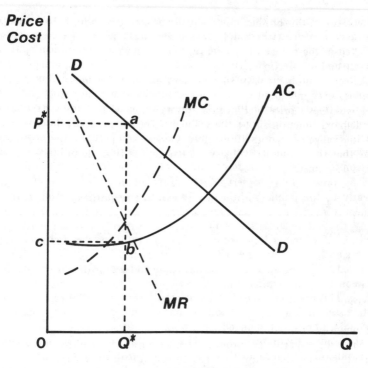

Figure 6.2

negative. They would cite the presence of other brands which they regarded as close substitutes - for example, Unilever's Persil as a competitor with Procter & Gamble's Daz. Hence the definition of product used has to be in the form of the degree of substitution of brands for a certain use - i.e. the formation of a *product category*.[2] For example, for the Ford Cortina the product category would presumably contain the characteristics of the good: size of engine, overall dimension, seating capacity, luggage space, performance, accessories, etc. On this definition a whole list of other vehicles would then enter into the category depending on the degree of substitution with the product in question - here the Ford Cortina.

The difficulty arises that the product group is itself a value judgement. In the last resort almost all goods are potential substitutes; for example, when incomes are low, many very different categories of goods become substitutes for one another. However, we have seen that the notion of the product category, despite its difficulty in exact definition, is a useful way of looking at branded items.

The problems for non-branded items is less acute. For example, if we take the product oxygen this is chemically definable, and hence if there were only a single producer of oxygen, we would have an example of a monopoly.

However, again there remains a problem of the degree of substitution with other goods - for example, imagine a rival chemical which is as effective as oxygen in 90 per cent or so of its uses and is competitive in price. Would it be useful then to classify the oxygen producer as a monopolist despite the fact that the end-use of this product could equally be served by a rival chemical? One way out of this difficulty is simply to let the close rivalry of another product be reflected in the nature of the demand curve; it will be that much more sensitive to price and will become flatter.

A second problem with the standard monopoly model in Fig. 6.2 concerns what is being measured on the vertical axis – i.e. the price (and cost axis). The model defines a price of $P*$ being optimal – but what is this price? Presumably the demand function shows the willingness of consumers to buy the product at a whole range of hypothetical prices. Hence the optimal price of $P*$ shows the price that the consumer will pay, which implies that the producer sells directly to the consumer.

This presumption is very rarely mirrored in reality – very few firms sell directly to the public without a wholesaler, distributor or retailer. In order to make the model more applicable we should therefore make the demand curve apply to that organisation which is purchasing the product from the manufacturer. If a retailer buys from the manufacturer the demand curve represents the prices that the retailer is willing to buy the product for. The retailer will then be faced with the consumer demand curve and get his profit on the difference between the selling price and the cost price of the article, less his expenses in selling. This brings us immediately into the complications of retail pricing, which is discussed in Chap. 11. The point to note at this stage is *what* demand curve we are talking about – i.e. demand from whom.[3]

The standard monopoly model in Fig. 6.2 predicts profits in the short run as optimum output multiplied by the average profit margin – i.e. the box $P*abc$. Again we should take care in relating this to the real world. The businessman would argue that what we have omitted is any mention of taxes. First, almost all goods will be subject to a value-added tax (or in some countries a sales tax). Hence the demand curve (in the case of value-added tax) includes the tax element – i.e. it is the price which the demander (whether it is consumer, retailer or wholesaler) is willing to pay for the good. Part of what the producer adds to the value of the product, i.e. in transforming it from a raw or semi-finished state into a more refined form, is taxed away. Hence part of the box disappears in respect of value-added tax, the amount depending on the amount of value added and the rate of tax applicable. It is not the purpose here to go into the complexities of the value-added tax system, but merely to point out some businessmen's potential objections to an analysis of the firm which does not even mention taxes.

A second element of tax which has to be deducted from the box $P*abc$ is in respect of taxes on corporate profits (corporation tax in the United Kingdom). The system is complicated in practice by the fact that these taxes are collected in arrears. Thus, a company in 1980 will pay the taxes for its trading in 1979. It reports in its 1980 accounts what it believes it is liable to pay on 1980 trading; this, however, will not actually be paid until 1981. Hence the deduction in respect of current taxes from the box $P*abc$ will be a book item forecasting liability in the next year. However, there will be a deduction from current profit to pay last year's taxes.

The above complication is peculiarly difficult to present on the diagram Fig. 6.2 because this refers to 'the short period', which is most unlikely to exactly equal a calendar year. Suffice it to say that there will be a payment out of gross profit in respect of a previous time period's taxes on profits, and a liability on this period's trading which will be delayed in payment to a further period.[4]

We therefore find that the profits box *P*abc* is *before* liability to value-added tax and *before* corporation tax. The above discussion on taxes has been presented with reference to monopoly, but is obviously also applicable to all firms paying taxes under other market structures. We have briefly outlined the issue at this point as a matter of convenience.

A final complication of the monopoly model is whether we wish to apply strictly to a *single* producer. In the real world it is rare to find a firm with a complete monopoly of production of a certain commodity that remains in the private sector. Most of the single producers have been nationalised and brought into the public sector. There may be occasional examples of private firms with exclusive rights to extract minerals, chemicals, etc., in a certain area, but again this is often under government supervision or licence.[5]

In order to make the model more applicable we may relax the 'single-producer' assumption a little, and count a firm (*X*) which produced say 95 per cent of industry output as a monopoly, with a handful of small firms producing the residual 5 per cent. In these circumstances we would use the model and predict the price and output of firm *X* 'as if' it were a monopolist. This makes the assumption that the 5 per cent residual can be regarded as being of negligible importance. But again one is faced with a value judgement. Should the cut-off figure of 95 per cent not be 99 per cent or 90 per cent or 80 per cent, etc.? Should one decide on a single percentage figure for all industries, or should one take each case on its own merit and investigate the actions of the residual firms? Such decisions are by no means easy or without dispute. Nevertheless, it obviously makes the monopoly model more powerful if we can investigate such cases of *almost* total market coverage by a single firm.

We have so far been concerned with the price and output decision in the short run, and have noted the discretion which the monopolist has in this regard. In the long run, however, he is able to alter all his inputs and will be replacing his plant and equipment and skilled labour with new units. The long-run output and price decision is far more complex,[6] but will centre around the way in which the demand function is expected to move and the cost structure associated with different scales of operation. If the monopolist can block entry of rivals then again he will have considerable discretion in the price/output decision, and will continued to enjoy profits above what would prevail if more competition was present.

Perfect competition

Perfect competition is at the other end of the market structure spectrum from monopoly. The formal analysis of perfect competition involves a number of assumptions. Specifically these are:

(i) A large number of sellers of the product, each seller small in size so that no firm can materially affect market price by alteration of its output level.

(ii) A large number of buyers of the product, with each buyer being small so that no individual can materially affect the market price by alteration of purchase level.

(iii) Free entry and exit of firms, i.e. there are no barriers (other than time) which prevent entry and exit of firms.

(iv) Product homogeneity – the output of each firm is identical, so that purchasers are unable to recognise output from a specific firm.

(v) Perfect knowledge on the part of buyers and sellers so that they are fully aware of all transactions (and potential transactions) that are being carried out by other buyers and sellers.

(vi) Perfect mobility of factors of production (labour, land, capital, etc.) into firms.

(vii) No outside interference with the free working of the market mechanism, i.e. prices are set by the unimpeded working of the forces of supply and demand. Specifically excluded are government practices such as guaranteed minimum prices, or regulations on price increases as part of anti-inflation policy.

Added to this list we have the motivational assumption of profit maximisation by each firm, but this clearly becomes a decision by the firm for survival rather than a matter of discretion.

For perfect competition to exist each and every one of the above assumptions outlined must hold concurrently. Marginal analysis can then predict price and output decisions for the firm in the short and long run. This is briefly summarised in Fig. 6.3 and Fig. 6.4.

In perfect competition it is necessary to look at the typical firm and the industry to which it belongs. In Fig. 6.3 the consumer market demand function is DD and the industry supply curve is $S_1 S_1$.[7] An equilibrium price of P_1 results which clears the market. From the firm's viewpoint it *takes* the price of P_1 as given – it can by definition do nothing about it. The only decision to be made is how much to produce given this market price. Assuming that the firm has a plant whose average cost structure is SAC_1, and associated marginal cost MC_1,

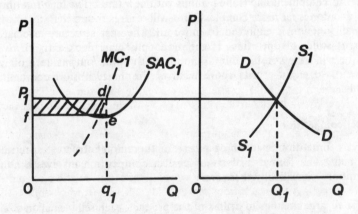

Figure 6.3 Perfect competition – short-run

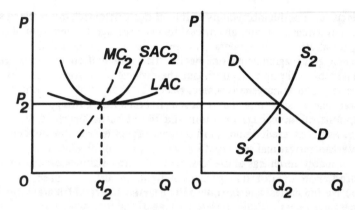

Figure 6.4 Perfect competition – long-run

then the firm will profit-maximise at the point where $MC = MR$. In this case marginal revenue (MR) equals average revenue (AR) equals price (P_1), so that the firm optimally produces q_1. The profits earned are $P_1 def$.

The term 'profit' is here used in its economic sense, taking into account opportunity costs. If management earns a return equal to that which could be obtained elsewhere (this being imputed into the cost structure[8]) the profit $P_1 def$ reflects a return over and above the next-best alternative. Hence it is excess in form and sometimes referred to as 'abnormal' or 'supernormal' profits.

The short-run picture of Fig. 6.3 cannot hold for very long since the abnormal profits will attract other firms into the industry. In consequence the industry supply curve will shift downwards to the right to $S_2 S_2$ in Fig. 6.4. Assuming demand to be unchanged as DD, then equilibrium price drops to P_2. This is taken by the firm and it is evident that only one cost structure (SAC_2 at the bottom of the long-run cost curve LAC)[9] will generate normal profits.

As far as the industry is concerned, output rises from Q_1 in Fig. 6.3 to Q_2 in Fig. 6.4. From the firm's viewpoint output rises from q_1 in Fig. 6.3 to q_2 in Fig. 6.4. The output q_2 is determined by the intersection of MC with the marginal (= average) revenue curve, which in this case is the price P_2.

In this long-run equilibrium we note that average revenue = average cost, so the supernormal profits have disappeared. Only when each of the firms is of this size (cost structure 2 at point of minimum LAC) will a normal return be generated. In all other cases losses will be incurred. We therefore see that when the price line becomes tangential to the LAC curve the long-run equilibrium price has been reached, and any further shift of $S_2 S_2$ to the right would necessarily incur industry losses.

It can be seen that the assumptions of this form of market structure allow an analysis to be developed which successfully predicts price and output decisions. The analysis has, however, come under attack on the ground that its assumptions are totally unrealistic in the real world. While one might discover examples where some of the assumptions are upheld, it is almost impossible to find cases where all assumptions hold. In the past, fruit, vegetable, basic commodity, and metal markets have been cited as examples, but more recently these markets have incurred considerable intervention in the price mechanism. For example, agreed government minimum prices for certain agricultural products (milk, meat), international agreements on commodity prices (cocoa, coffee, tea), and producers' price agreements on metals. The intervention has been generally stimulated by a desire to smooth out the cyclical or seasonal fluctuations that such basic products have been subject to.

Nevertheless there may be certain markets which still approximate to the assumptions of perfect competition, and to this situation the term *pure competition* has been used. Hence perfect competition is now generally accepted as a purely theoretical market structure which is useful for analytical purposes but which probably never has existed, or will exist, in reality. Pure competition, as its nearest approximator, may perhaps be found in certain small-scale service and distributive industries, and in some agricultural markets which are not protected by price agreements.

We have seen above that perfect competition requires product homogeneity as one of its assumptions. One of the major limitations of the model is the rise in importance of branded products, which by definition are differentiated one from another. A specific market structure which deals with competition embracing branded products, but still retaining the assumption of competition amongst the many, has been constructed. This is *monopolistic competition*, to which we now turn.

Monopolistic competition

Monopolistic competition essentially retains the assumptions of perfect competition, but dispenses with assumption (v) and allows for differentiation of products by brand. Hence the structure consists of a large number of small firms competing with one another producing branded items which are differentiated, but have a large degree of substitution one with another. As a result of the differentiation of product the firm again has discretion over price – it can now decide on price, rather than have to accept one market price.

The short-run equilibrium for the firm is shown in Fig. 6.5, which assumes profit maximisation as the objective being pursued.

Fig. 6.5 is very similar to the standard monopoly diagram of Fig. 6.1, with the exception that the demand curve is typically much flatter, reflecting the large number of close substitutes for the rival products.

Output (q_3) is determined where $MC = MR$, resulting in a price of P_3, and abnormal profits of $P_3 hiK$. However, theses abnormal profits attract new potential entrants, and these emerge in the long run as there is no barrier to entry.

The effect of the entry is to shift the demand schedule $D_1 D_1$ inwards for each firm. Market demand for the product range remains unchanged, but has to be shared out among a larger number of firms. The effect of the shifting demand curve is to gradually diminish the amount of abnormal profits so that the limiting long-run case of Fig. 6.6 is achieved.

Here a tangency solution of the average revenue curve and the average cost solution emerges, as it did in Fig. 6.4 for perfect competition, but here the tangency solution is on a downward-sloping part of the short-run average cost

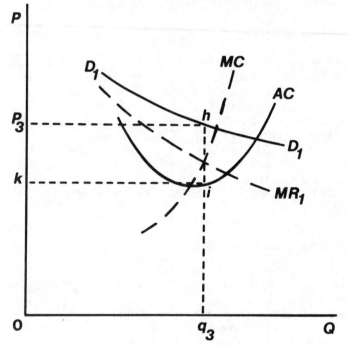

Figure 6.5 Monopolistic competition – short-run

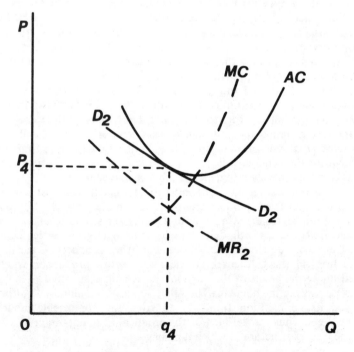

Figure 6.6 Monopolistic competition – long-run

curve. Profits are maximised where $MC = MR_2$, and profits return to zero as average cost = average revenue.

It should be noted that we have made no mention of the industry situation – in fact it is extremely difficult to do so, since the products are branded and we have a product category rather than a product.[10] As far as the firm is concerned we have also assumed identical cost structures despite the fact that products are assumed differentiated – thus the situations in Fig. 6.5 and 6.6 are of the typical firm in the industry, rather than of firm X producing brand A.

Despite its deficiencies this market structure has been seen by many as a useful adaptation of the perfectly competitive case to the situations most likely to be encountered in the real world.

There remains one category left for consideration, namely that of oligopoly, which we now discuss.

Oligopoly: collusive and non-collusive

The market structure of oligopoly covers the case where competition is restricted to relatively few firms. The product concerned may be homogeneous or differentiated.

Emphasis is usually put on the number of firms in the industry in this market structure, but often of more importance is the concentration of the industry and the way in which firms react one to another. Thus two industries, both consisting of 100 firms, may vary considerably in competitive conditions. In one the structure may be of 100 firms of roughly the same size in which competition may be more of the type discussed in the section on Monopolistic Competition, above. In the other industry the top four or five firms may dominate 80–90 per cent of the market, with the remaining 95 or 96 firms producing only a very small proportion of the total. In this situation, despite the large number of firms, competition is really between the few large firms which dominate the industry. In this case we have an oligopolistic market.

The market structure of oligopoly is an extremely difficult situation to handle conceptually. The main problem arises from the fact that individual firms take decisions on the basis of anticipated reactions of their rivals. Each firm, in the case of non-branded products, has discretion over price and output, but each knows that any action taken by it will bring some reaction from a rival. The problem for the economist is therefore to try to model the situation when decision-taking is essentially interdependent between rival firms.

We noted in the section on Monopoly, above, that it was most sensible to view branded products in 'product groups'. Thus, in one example, the production of the Ford Cortina moved out of the market structure of monopoly, because there were several other elements in its product group which could be considered as close substitutes. As the number of car producers is small (only four large firms in the U.K. market), the Ford Cortina production would be considered under the ambit of the oligopolistic structure. It would be looked at relative to its rivals in the home market – BL Marina, Vauxhall Cavalier, Chrysler Alpine – and its competition from abroad from the comparable models of Datsun, Fiat, etc. Thus the defining of the product has an important bearing on defining the market structure to which it belongs.

There are a large number of models which have been developed to analyse oligopoly, but they can broadly be divided into two categories:

(i) Collusive oligopoly
(ii) Non-collusive oligopoly

COLLUSIVE OLIGOPOLY

The category of collusive models works on the assumption that the rival firms come together either formally or in secret to decide common strategy for the industry. This ensures survival for each firm and a reduction in risk, in that it knows generally some of the actions that rivals will take. Usually agreement refers to price of the product (although sometimes it can refer to output). With price agreed, competition between firms takes place in 'safer' areas: advertising, promotion, distribution, marketing techniques, etc.

A simple example of a collusive oligopoly is a price cartel. Here the constituent firms delegate the settting of industry price, and the way it is produced, to a separate organisation (presumably consisting of representatives of each of the rivals). The cartel then decides how to adjust the activities of the *industry* to secure highest possible profits. This is depicted in Fig. 6.7, where for simplicity two firms (A and B) are assumed to comprise the industry.

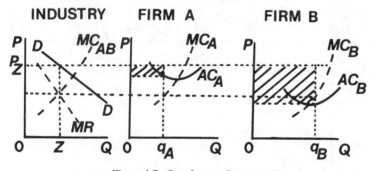

Figure 6.7 Cartel – two-firm example

The industry position is shown on the left with demand as DD and marginal cost (combined) of the two firms as MC_{AB}. The profit-maximising position is where $MC_{AB} = MR$, i.e. at output Z. The optimum way of producing this is by equating the MR to the *individual* marginal costs of each firm. If the cost structures are identical, each firm will produce exactly half of the optimum quantity produced. If, however, cost structures are different, as they are in Fig. 6.7 with firm A a high-cost producer and firm B a low-cost, then the allocation will be different. In this case production will be concentrated on the most efficient (lowest-cost) producer (B) producing q_B, and less produced from (A), producing q_A. Total industry profits will be the sum of the shaded areas in Fig. 6.7. These profits will then be shared out between the two firms on some agreed basis, defined presumably when the cartel was set up.

Formal agreements of this kind are relatively rare because they are considered by governments as undesirable in that they exploit the consumer. Often, there-fore, such collusive agreements become secret, with an 'understanding' between the firms on price. Alternatively, firms within the industry may elect one firm (often the largest, or lowest-cost producer) as a 'price leader'. In this situation the price leader takes decisions on price which reflect the industries' interests and not merely his own. Then the rival firms come quickly into line thus preserv-ing the same price relatives at a different level.

Non-collusive oligopoly

Where collusion does not exist between the firms then each decision-maker has to act on the basis of rivals' anticipated reactions. A common feature of non-collusive oligopoly models is the notion of a specific form of reaction being assumed.

One example of this is the kinked demand model shown in Fig. 6.8.

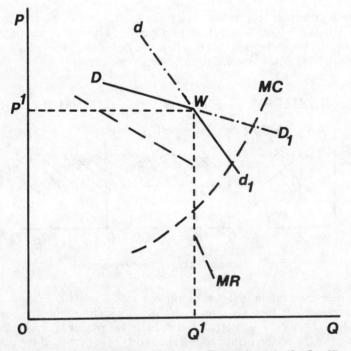

Figure 6.8   Kinked demand model of non-collusive oligopoly (for firm X)

The kinked demand model rests on a particular type of demand function, which alters at a critical point. It is assumed in Fig. 6.8 that there are two demand curves: DD_1, which assumes that rivals do *not* match a price change by a particular firm concerned, and dd_1, which presumes that they do match. If firm X decides to raise price it is thought rivals will not match it, but if it lowers price then others will follow. Hence the demand curve is DWd_1 in Fig. 6.8. The associated marginal revenue curve is MR, which has a discontinuity, as the slope of the demand curve suddenly changes.

The assumption is that if X raises his price no one follows and hence he loses to his rivals because demand is elastic along DW. If, however, he lowers price then rivals match his cut, and he gains little since demand is inelastic along Wd_1.

In consequence there is a desire to stay at price P_1 where the slope alters. It will be noted that because of the discontinuity in MR, a substantial alteration of costs (MC) will not bring about a change in output from Q_1. Thus the theory purports to show why prices do not alter rapidly under non-collusive oligopolistic conditions.

The kinked demand theory is but one of a number of theories dealing with anticipated reactions of rivals. None of them has yet reached a stage of refinement that it can be said to constitute a comprehensive model of non-collusive behaviour. Indeed the market structure is so complex and varied that it is doubtful whether any model will achieve such a status.

Conclusion

Market structures set the environment in which the firm makes it price and output decisions. These structures vary along a continuum from monopoly at one extreme to perfect competition at the other. Neither of the extremes is usually found in practice, so increasingly attention has been focused on the intermediate structures. Of particular importance in the modern economy is oligopoly, which generally involves competition among the few. Despite its paramount importance, this situation has yet to be successfully incorporated in a model of the traditional marginal kind. However, we have already seen that other writers (see Chap. 5) have put forward some interesting alternatives in analysing this situation.

Appendix Oligopoly and Game Theory

The theory of games has been developed to analyse action in competitive situations, where outcomes depend on the behaviour of all competitors. We are here interested in games of strategy rather than chance, where the competitor has control over his actions but not those of his competitors.

To illustrate the usefulness of game theory for oligopoly behaviour consider the duopoly (two-firm) situation. Suppose both firms A and B have the objective of maximising their own market share, and each have three possible courses of action (different possible combinations of decision variables; for example, strategy 1 may be high-price and aggressive marketing). Using the terminology of

Chap. 3 (p. 24) we can construct a pay-off matrix, showing the market share of firm A resulting from different combinations of strategies.

		B		
	1	2	3	min.
1	50	65	45	45
A 2	55	60	65	55 ←
3	45	50	60	45
max.	55	65	65	
	↑			

The problem for both A and B is to choose that strategy to maximise market share. Remember that the total market share is 100 per cent, so that if A gets X per cent B must get $(100 - X)$ per cent.[1] A knows that B is also trying to maximise his market share, so A expects that, whichever choice he makes, B will react to minimise the market share of A. This offers a clue to solving the problem. Since A expects the worst possible reaction from B, A adopts a *maximin* criteria. To do this A considers what is the worst that could happen for each choice. If he chooses strategy 1, his worst possible market share is 45 per cent, for strategy 2, 55 per cent and for 3, 45 per cent. Reasoning that B will do his worst, A would choose strategy 2, where the worst that can happen is a 55 per cent share.

B decides in the same manner, only now a *minimax* strategy is adopted, since B wishes to minimise the market share of A (and therefore maximise his own share). He therefore looks down the columns of the pay-off matrix, selecting the least of the column maximums. If he chooses strategy 1, the worst that can happen is that A gets a 55 per cent share, for column 2 65 per cent, and column 3 also 65 per cent. B therefore chooses strategy 1.

In this situation both strategies result in the same expected outcome, a market share for A of 55 per cent. This equilibrium is called a *saddle-point*, and represents a position where neither A nor B would wish to change their minds. Pure saddle-points, where the row minimum equals the column maximum need not occur. In this situation the optimal choice will be a mix of strategies, where different choices are made in fixed proportion.

Before considering this situation we can see that the choice of strategy could have been simplified. However B reacts, choice 2 is always better than choice 3 (results in a higher market share). Therefore A will never choose action 3, and it is said to be *dominated* by 2. From B's point of view, strategy 1 is always better than strategy 2, since 1 always results in a lower market share for A (higher share for B).

To calculate the optimum strategy when there is no saddle-point, consider the general 2 x 2 pay-off matrix shown below.

		B	
		I	II
	I	a_1	a_2
A II		b_1	b_2

Let the proportion of times A plays strategy I be p_1. Then if p_2 is the proportion of times A plays II, $p_2 = 1 - p_1$. Similarly, let p_3 and p_4 represent the mixed proportions for B playing I and II, and therefore $p_3 + p_4 = 1$.

The problem is then to find $p_1 \ldots p_4$. To do this we need the concept of the *value* of a game (V). This is simply the net result of the game if optimum strategies are adopted. Therefore the expected value of the game $(E/(V))$ is

$$E(V) = a_1 p_1 p_3 + a_2 p_1 p_4 + b_1 p_2 p_4 + b_2 p_2 p_4.$$

The problem can now be written as

Max $E(V)$.

subject to the constraints $p_1 + p_2 = 1$; $p_3 + p_4 = 1$.

This can of course be solved by the method of Lagrangean multipliers (Chap. 2, p. 19) by adding the artificial variables λ_1 and λ_2, and forming the Lagrangean function with constraints in implicit form.[2]
i.e.

$$\text{Max } L = E(V) + \lambda_1 (p_1 + p_2 - 1) + \lambda_2 (p_3 + p_4 - 1).$$

We take the partial derivatives with respect to $p_1 \ldots p_4$ and set equal to zero.

$$\frac{\partial L}{\partial p_1} = a_1 p_3 + a_2 p_4 + \lambda_1 = 0. \tag{6A.1}$$

$$\frac{\partial L}{\partial p_2} = b_1 p_3 + b_2 p_4 + \lambda_1 = 0. \tag{6A.2}$$

$$\frac{\partial L}{\partial p_3} = a_1 p_1 + b_1 p_2 + \lambda_2 = 0. \tag{6A.3}$$

$$\frac{\partial L}{\partial p_4} = a_2 p_1 + b_2 p_2 + \lambda_2 = 0. \tag{6A.4}$$

$$\frac{\partial L}{\partial \lambda_1} = p_1 + p_2 - 1 = 0. \tag{6A.5}$$

$$\frac{\partial L}{\partial \lambda_2} = p_3 + p_4 - 1 = 0. \tag{6A.6}$$

The six simultaneous equations can now be manipulated to solve for $p_1 \ldots p_4$ and λ_1, λ_2 (we have six equations and six unknown variables).

For example, if equation (6A.1) is multiplied by b_1 and equation (6A.2) by a_1 we get:

$$a_1 b_1 p_3 + a_2 b_1 p_4 + b_1 \lambda_1 = 0$$

and $\quad a_1 b_1 p_3 + a_1 b_2 p_4 + a_1 \lambda_1 = 0.$

Subtracting

$$p_4 (a_2 b_1 - a_1 b_2) + \lambda_1 (b_1 - a_1) = 0$$

$$p_4 = \frac{\lambda_1 (a_1 - b_1)}{(a_2 b_1 - a_1 b_2)} .$$

Similarly, for p_3

$$p_3 = \frac{\lambda_1 (b_2 - a_2)}{(a_2 b_1 - a_1 b_2)} .$$

Now let $C = \dfrac{\lambda_1}{a_2 b_1 - a_1 b_2}$

then $p_4 = C(a_1 - b_1)$

               $p_3 = C(b_2 - a_2).$

Now, from equation (6A.6), $p_3 + p_4 = 1$

   Therefore $C(a_1 - b_1) + C(b_2 - a_2) = 1$

$$C = \frac{1}{(a_1 - b_1) + (b_2 - a_2)}$$

and $$p_3 = \frac{(b_2 - a_2)}{(a_1 - b_1) + (b_2 - a_2)}$$

$$p_4 = \frac{(a_1 - b_1)}{(a_1 - b_1) + (b_2 - a_2)}$$

Using similar reasoning,

$$p_1 = \frac{(b_2 - b_1)}{(a_1 - a_2) + (b_2 - b_1)}$$

$$p_2 = \frac{(a_1 - a_2)}{(a_1 - a_2) + (b_2 - b_1)}$$

This is the method of oddments, with results very simple to calculate. The proportion of times A plays strategy I is simply the ratio of the absolute value of the other row difference to the absolute value of *that row* difference (note that if A plays I and II in the ratio $x:y$, $p_1 = x/x + y$ and $p_2 = y/x + y$).

The proportion of times B plays his strategy I is the ratio of the absolute value of the *other column* difference to the absolute value of *that column* difference.

Example
Suppose we have the following pay-off matrix, with figures referring to the pay-off to A.

$$
\begin{array}{ccc}
 & & B \\
 & \text{I} & \text{II} \\
\end{array}
$$

		I	II
A	I	2	-1
	II	-2	3

$|b_1 - b_2| = 5$

$|a_1 - a_2| = 3$

$|a_2 - b_2| = 4$ $|a_1 - b_1| = 4$

Since A's maximin does not equal B's minimax we have no saddle-point, and a mixed strategy must be used. We calculate the absolute value[3] of the row and column differences, $|b_1 - b_2|$, etc. Then A will play strategies I and II in the ratio 5:3, i.e. $p_1 = \frac{5}{8}$, $p_2 = \frac{3}{8}$, and B will play strategies in the ratio 4:4, i.e. $p_3 = \frac{4}{8}$, $p_4 = \frac{4}{8}$. This is not to infer that of eight games B will follow strategy I for the first four games, and strategy II for the next four. If this were to occur, player A would soon deduce B's strategy and react accordingly. Rather B will play I and II, so that these occur equally, thus for each game B's choice will be random, but over a series of games the ratio of choices is given. B could achieve this by *simulation*; for example, by tossing a fair coin before each game to determine choice of actions. Then for each game A cannot determine what B's move will be, but over a series of games B will make the choice in the proportion 4:4.

Since $p_1 \ldots p_4$ are now known we can find the expected value of the game, using the formula given above, i.e.

$$E(V) = a_1 p_1 p_3 + a_2 p_1 p_4 + b_1 p_2 p_3 + b_2 p_2 p_4.$$
$$E(V) = 2 \cdot \tfrac{5}{8} \cdot \tfrac{4}{8} + -1 \cdot \tfrac{5}{8} \cdot \tfrac{4}{8} + -2 \cdot \tfrac{3}{8} \cdot \tfrac{4}{8} + 3 \cdot \tfrac{3}{8} \cdot \tfrac{5}{8}$$
$$= \tfrac{4}{8} = \tfrac{1}{2}.$$

Therefore, following these strategies, A will have an expected pay-off of $\frac{1}{2}$ per game (and B will have an expected loss of $\frac{1}{2}$ per game).

We seem to have come a long way from oligopoly behaviour. Perhaps the greatest advantage of game theory in competitive situations is the clarification of ideas.[4] We are not suggesting that game theory offers unique solutions to practical competitive situations. Rather it is our premise that the concepts of game theory, players' strategies, the pay-off matrix, the conflict of interests and the process of maximising, all provide a rational way of thinking in competitive situations. In particular there are two major difficulties in the application of game theory. The first is that we have assumed a single pair of moves, whereas in real situations behaviour may be a series of moves and counter-moves. In this case, although an optimal strategy may exist theoretically, finding it may involve greater costs than the benefit of the strategy provide. Second, we have assumed rational behaviour. In practice competitive situations are likely to be full of misleading information with moves made solely with the purpose of disguising intentions. Paradoxically it may even be rational to behave irrationally. By being seen to be capable of reacting in the most aggressive manner, even if this is self-harming, the need for such a reaction may be reduced.

Further reading

B. S. Kierstead, 'Decision-taking and the Theory of Games', in *Uncertainty and Expectations in Economics*, ed. C. F. Carter and J. L. Ford (Oxford: Blackwell, 1972) pp. 160–74.

A. Koutsoyiannis, *Modern Microeconomics*, 2nd ed. (London: Macmillan, 1979) part 2.

D. Needham, *Economic Analysis and Industrial Structure*, 2nd ed. (New York: Holt, Rinehart & Winston, 1978), esp. chap. 3.

F. M. Scherer, *Industrial Pricing* (Chicago: Rand McNally, 1970) chap. 1.

Questions

1 Examine how the market structure within which the firm operates delineates the discretion which managers have to make decisions.

2 'The market uncertainty which a firm has to face varies inversely with the number of firms in the industry.' Discuss.

3 'Product differentiation is of greater importance than the number and size of firms in determining the extent of competition in an industry.' Discuss.

4 Determine the optimal strategies for each player in the following games. What is the value of each game to player A? Each table shows the pay-off to player A.

(i)

		I	II	B III	IV	V
	I	3	0	1	4	−2
	II	1	−4	0	−7	4
A	III	5	2	3	4	6
	IV	−4	1	−1	3	5
	V	2	−1	−3	0	1

(ii)

		B			
		I	II	III	IV
	I	2	−2	6	3
	II	4	−2	4	5
A	III	−2	0	0	0
	IV	−4	0	8	4

7
Demand Analysis

Introduction

Because decisions have to be made about an uncertain future, part of the manager's task is to estimate what the value of a particular variable will be. This process of estimation is a recurring problem for managers, and thus the description and evaluation of various estimation techniques form a crucial part of managerial economics. We have seen that any action will be undertaken if its benefit is greater than its cost. An intrinsic part of this calculation is the estimation of returns from any particular action. Most often this involves calculating what the level of sales will be for various combinations of the decision variables under the manager's control. Consequently it is relevant to inquire what factors influence the level of sales, and what impact changes in decision variables will have upon sales. Before considering in detail the empirical relationship between sales and other variables it is worth while to devote some attention to those parts of demand theory which are most relevant to the task of managerial decision-making.

The first premise of demand theory is that goods are demanded, not for their own sake, but for the satisfaction that they yield. The good will possess a number of attributes or characteristics which give rise to satisfaction, such as size, design quality, brand image, etc. Such attributes vary in importance between products. We can then see competition as the availability of goods of similar attributes or characteristics, capable of satisfying similar wants or desires.

Demand functions

A general demand function is an unspecified function relating the quantity of a good that consumers wish to purchase to those variables that determine demand. Mathematically, we write:

$$Da = f(X_1, X_2 \ldots X_n).$$

Where Da is demand for good a and the X_i are the n variables that determine demand. The variables to be included and their relative importance will depend on the nature of the good in question. For example, the availability and cost of credit will be an important determinant of the demand for new cars, while being of negligible effect on the sales of cigarettes.

The sensitivity of demand to changes in the determining variables can be measured by the sign and magnitude of the partial derivatives $\partial Da/\partial X_i$. If an increase in X_i increases demand then $\partial Da/\partial X_i$ will be positive, and conversely if an increase in X_i decreases demand then $\partial Da/\partial X_i$ will be negative.

Microeconomics lays most emphasis on the relationship between price (Pa) and demand, and tells us that normally $\partial Da/\partial Pa < 0$. The simple demand function relates demand solely to price, holding all other variables constant. This can be summarised in a demand curve which is then downward-sloping. When the price of a particular good changes the impact on demand can be divided into two parts. First, there is an *income effect*, because the amount of money the consumer is able to spend, in real terms, on all goods changes. Second, there is a *substitution effect* because the change in price of a particular good changes its price relative to other goods, i.e. if its price increases other goods become relatively cheaper. The net effect on sales depends on the direction and magnitude of the income and substitution effects. Using the substitution effect, less of the good whose price increases and more of the other goods will be demanded. If the good is *normal* the income effect will be negative, i.e. as real income decreases less of that good will be purchased. Only if the good is *inferior* will the reduction in real income associated with a price increase cause more of it to be purchased. Only if the good is inferior, and the positive income effect is greater than the negative substitution effect, will an increase in price lead to an increase in quantity demanded.

While price is undoubtedly a significant factor determining demand it is often only one of several influences and may not be the most important. Thus for the managerial economist the simple demand function is inadequate, and can be replaced by the demand function consisting of several variables which are particularly important for the good in question.

One of these factors is likely to be income (Y). As we have seen, for normal goods $\partial Da/\partial Y > 0$. Advertising, both by the firm producing the good (Aa) and by competitors (Ac), will influence demand and we expect $\partial Da/\partial Aa > 0$, and $\partial Da/\partial Ac < 0$. This brings us to the price of other goods which is likely to be significant. If $\partial Da/\partial Pc < 0$, so that an increase in the price of good C leads to a fall in the demand for A, then A and C are complements (for example, bread and butter). If $\partial Da/\partial Ps > 0$, then A and S are substitute goods.

We have seen that the demand for a good will be influenced by the nature of the good in question; it is useful to make two distinctions between types of goods. The first distinction is between durable and non-durable goods. Durable goods yield a flow of services or satisfaction over time. Then the demand for these goods is particularly sensitive to the existing stock of the product held by consumers. There are many durable goods (such as telephones and electric irons) where each household ordinarily only demands one item of the product. Then the demand for the product will depend on the number of households as yet without it, and the net rate of new household formation. We should note that for many durable goods, seen as luxuries, the market may well be saturated well below the point where each household owns one unit of the good. Conversely the market may not be saturated even when ownership levels approach 100 per cent. This is the case where multiple ownership may be increasing; for example, in the car market. One qualification is that where a household holds more than one unit of a consumer durable of similar characteristics, these are unlikely to be seen as close substitutes, i.e. the multi-car family is likely to own cars of different brands and sizes.

We have seen that existing levels of ownership will be an important influence on demand. However, the existing stock of the product will not all have been bought at the same time, used to the same degree, or be maintained and serviced equally. Thus apart from the ownership extension market there will be a market of *replacement demand*. The desire for replacement will depend on two factors, the physical condition of the good, from a technical and economic point of view, and the attitude of the consumer to the product regardless of its physical condition. Although functioning adequately the good may be perceived to be out of date, or old-fashioned. The degree of psychological obsolescence depends on the good in question and is capable of being influenced by the manufacturer by way of model changes, advertising etc.

Many durable goods are expensive and bought on credit. Thus the availability and cost of credit will influence demand. This effect is increased by the ability to postpone purchase, often by retaining the older unit, until credit becomes easier or cheaper.

Non-durable goods are those that are consumed either immediately or over a short space of time. Purchase is often repetitive, involving a pattern of behaviour, in contrast to the one-off decision to purchase a consumer durable. Because of this producers seek to establish brand loyalty; for example, to ensure that the same brand of coffee is purchased weekly.

Because purchase of non-durables is likely to be repetitive, the consumer tends to devote little thought to their purchase, first because non-durable goods are usually cheaper and thus the cost of mistaken purchase is low, and, second, because the consumer does not have to live with his mistaken purchase for long. As a result many non-durables are bought on impulse and the manufacturers lay great emphasis on packaging design and colour.

The second distinction that can be made is between consumer goods and producer goods. Consumer goods are purchased for the satisfaction or services they yield to the purchaser, whereas producer goods are bought to make other goods.

The demand for producer goods is derived from the demand for the goods they produce. The decision to purchase will depend on the expected profit derived from the products made by the producer good over its economic life. The purchase of producer goods is a type of investment decision (see Chap. 13, p. 205). The major influence on the demand for producer goods will be the expectation of demand for the goods they produce. Thus the decision to purchase a producer good will depend on an estimate of the demand for the final good.

Elasticity

The general demand function can now be rewritten in more explicit form, identifying the major influences on demand.

$$Da = f(Pa, Pi, Y, Aa, Ai).$$

Here Pi refers to the price of other goods, Y is income and $Aa(i)$ denotes advertising by the firm (and other firms). We have seen that the partial derivatives are one measure of the sensitivity of demand to changes in these variables. A more common but related measure is the *elasticity of demand*, defined as the percentage change in demand divided by the percentage change in the relevant variable. So for any variable X, elasticity equals:

$$E = \frac{\Delta D/D}{\Delta X/X} \cdot \frac{100}{100} = \frac{\Delta D}{\Delta X} \cdot \frac{X}{D},$$

with D referring to a change in demand. Even if $\Delta D/\Delta X$ is constant, elasticity varies with the magnitude of X and D. Thus the elasticity with respect to X depends on the size and direction of the change in X. This means that between two values of X elasticities will differ depending on the direction of movement. Consider a linear demand function, represented by Fig. 7.1:

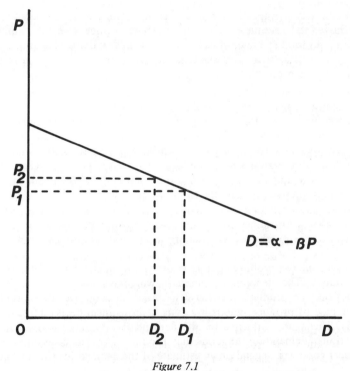

Figure 7.1

For a price increase from P_1 to P_2 elasticity of demand will be

$$E_1 = \frac{(D_2 - D_1)/D_1}{(P_2 - P_1)/P_1},$$

while for a price decrease from P_2 to P_1 elasticity will be

$$E_2 = \frac{(D_1 - D_2)/D_2}{(P_1 - P_2)/P_2} .$$

Because different basis are used, $E_1 \neq E_2$. The normal procedure is to measure the arc elasticity of demand, averaging elasticity over the range.

Then $\quad E_a = \dfrac{E_1 + E_2}{2} = \dfrac{\Delta D}{\Delta X} \cdot \dfrac{X_2 + X_1}{D_2 + D_1}.$

For very small changes $\Delta D/\Delta X$ will tend to the partial derivative $\partial D/\partial X$. This enables us to calculate elasticity at a point, i.e. $E_p = \partial D/\partial X \cdot X/D$.

The most common elasticity measure is, of course, price elasticity (Ep). In absolute terms, if $Ep < 1$ demand is referred to as inelastic, and if $Ep > 1$ then demand is elastic.

Price elasticity is important from a decision-making point of view because it tells us how total revenue responds to a change in price. If $Ep > 1$, increasing price decreases total revenue, while the converse holds if demand is price inelastic. In fact price elasticity of demand tells us how marginal revenue is related to price. It can be proved[1] that

$$MR = P(1 + \frac{1}{Ep}) .$$

Several generalisations about behaviour can be made on the basis of price elasticity. If demand is inelastic it would never be profitable to decrease price, for although more would be sold total revenue would fall. With inelastic demand if price was increased less would be sold but total revenue would rise. Then as long as marginal cost is non-negative, increasing price would increase profit. If demand is elastic profit strategy depends on the nature of costs. A price decrease would increase revenue, but this would need to be compared to the cost of producing the extra units sold. A price increase would reduce total revenue, but may increase profit if costs are reduced by a greater amount.[2]

However, we should be aware of the tautological nature of these statements. Price elasticity of demand is calculated as a *result* of price changes, and therefore cannot be used to *predict* the effects of price changes without some assumption; for example, that elasticity is constant over the price range being considered.

Thus to know the true elasticity of demand, price changes must be made. However, to make decisions we must estimate the effects of changes and therefore we use estimates of elasticity[3]. To estimate arc elasticity we need sales information at different prices, while to estimate point elasticity we need some estimate of the specified demand function at that point.

There are a number of other elasticity measures of interest to the managerial economist. Income elasticity of demand relates changes in demand to changes in income. It will be positive for normal goods and negative for inferior goods. The casual distinction between luxuries and necessities can be formalised in terms of income elasticity of demand, because luxury goods will have a high income elasticity, while the demand for necessary goods will be invariant with respect to income.

We have seen that the degree of competition is important in forming the decision environment. One useful indicator of the extent of competition is the cross-elasticity of demand, relating the demand for one product to the price of others, in the familiar elasticity format, i.e.

$$Ec = \frac{\partial Da}{\partial Pb} \cdot \frac{Pb}{Da}.$$

The cross-elasticity of demand will be positive for substitute goods, with its magnitude indicating the closeness of substitution. For complementary goods cross-elasticity of demand will be negative.

So far we have only considered product demand. Firms demand and industry demand may also be of interest. Only if the firm is a monopolist producing a single homogeneous good will the three coincide.

For the multi-product firm there will often be demand interrelationships because of competition or complementarity between different members of the firms' product lines. Then a change in the price of one product will affect the demand for others.[4]

The relationship between firms demand and industry demand will depend on the nature of competition between firms in the industry. For example, in perfect competition an increase in industry demand will have its major impact on the number of firms in the industry. In oligopoly how an increase in industry demand is accommodated depends on the extent of collusion and how the rivals react to each other's behaviour.

Before considering demand estimation one further factor affecting the demand for many goods must be discussed. In a variety of situations time is an important influence on demand. There may be seasonal differences in demand due to climate or custom, or there may be cyclical variations in demand due to movements in macroeconomic variables such as unemployment. These influences may be accommodated by the inclusion of a time variable in the demand function to be estimated.[5]

Demand estimation

In estimating demand we are attempting to predict future consumer behaviour. There are a number of possible ways of proceeding, none of which will give reliable estimates in all circumstances. What we must do is consider the cost and benefits of alternative approaches. For example, if a particular decision is crucial to the firm's survival we will be prepared to spend considerable effort to produce accurate estimates.

Information about the future is normally expensive, difficult to obtain and unlikely to be accurate. However, some kind of prediction is essential to decision-making and efficient estimation is usually superior to the next best alternatives, intuition or guess-work. However, it should be emphasised that estimation can never be mechanical but relies heavily on the forecaster's experience and judgement; for example, in deciding what variables to include in a demand function estimate.

There are basically two kinds of estimation procedure. The first attempts to explain variations in the predicted variable; for example, by estimating a demand function consisting of variables the economist would expect to be important. The second procedure relies on empirical relationships, and consists of extrapolating from past behaviour, without being too concerned about why variation occurs. Both procedures have advantages and disadvantages. Using the first method, it may be possible, for example, to establish that demand varies in a particular way with advertising, price and consumer income. However, to be able to successfully predict future demand we then need reliable estimates of future price advertising and income. While the first two of these variables are to a large extent within the control of the firm and therefore relatively easy to predict, the third is not. Then the reliability of the demand estimate will be largely determined by the accuracy of the income prediction. The second procedure is not without difficulty. Empirical evidence of a strong past relationship between demand and another variable is not conclusive evidence that this will be continued in future. The particular circumstances that affected the relationship in the past may not be continued in the future.

The problems can only be overcome by the exercise of forecasting judgement. Often the appropriate method is a combination of the two approaches, combining explanatory power with strong empirical relationships.

Methods of demand estimation

There are two stages in the estimation of demand. The first is the collection of data, while the second is the processing of that data to provide a demand estimate. There are two types of demand information that can be collected: the first is time-series data, and refers to the behaviour of consumers over time while the second is cross-sectional data referring to the behaviour of different consumers at the same moment in time. Both of these kinds of information provide sufficient basis for the estimation of demand. The following section discusses means of collecting information, and the subsequent section describes ways of generating demand estimates from this information.

Survey approaches

The most obvious way to find out what consumers would buy at different prices in the future is to ask them. Unfortunately this is unlikely to provide reliable estimates because of the hypothetical nature of the question. There is always the risk that the consumer does not know what he would do or that he will give the answer he thinks the questioner wants. One possibility is to ask about past behaviour patterns. This information can be collated and assessed in the light of knowledge about income movements, advertising levels, product design, price relative to competitors, etc. From this information future levels of demand may be predicted, given assumptions about the future levels of other factors such as advertising.

A second approach is to inquire about consumers' attitudes to the product such as its design, attractiveness, price, etc. This may indicate why consumers make particular purchases and how they react to changes in the product's characteristics. Sometimes a lack of knowledge may provide insight. For example, a consumer's ignorance of the price of a frequently purchased good may indicate that for that good price is not too important, i.e. demand is inelastic.

Surveys are most likely to be useful where attitudes are important in determining demand. For example, industry associations often survey management opinion of future output because these opinions have a very real impact on investment decisions. A variant of this approach is to survey sales staff in the belief that these people are 'closest' to the market and therefore most able to estimate future demand. The problem here, as with all survey methods, is that answers are inevitably subjective. The sales force may generally be over-pessimistic to avoid the problem of their performance not living up to expectations.

Direct market experiments

These involve selling the product at different prices in different markets, in the expectation that the answers generated would be representative of the full market. This method overcomes the problem of subjectivity by providing actual answers to previously hypothetical questions. However, there are again a formidable array of potential problems.

It is often very difficult to find a market segment with similar characteristics to the total market. Because of their uniqueness such 'micromarkets' are likely to be used to such an extent that consumers become aware that they are being used for market experiments, so that reactions become distorted.

Market experiments are generally expensive, so that only a small sample is used. This leads to statistical problems (sampling errors) so that predictions can only be made with a low degree of confidence. There are many instances where competitors have become aware of the existence of market experiments and have acted to distort the results.[6] Market experiments are not controlled experiments, so that other factors affecting demand may change during the duration of the experiment.

Market experiments are particularly frequent for new products, but there are special dangers here. The market experiment should be conducted for a sufficient period to complete the repurchase cycle, otherwise the results will be distorted by the novelty impact of the new good. Of course for certain goods (especially consumer durables) the repurchase cycle may be lengthy, making the market experiment impracticable.

We have discussed means of collecting information about consumer demand. Another approach favoured by applied economists is to gather historical data about the past levels of sales and explanatory variables. This information can be used to generate demand estimates in the manner outlined below.

Statistical approaches

We may again make a division between empirical approaches, where a pattern of past behaviour is identified and extrapolated, and explanatory approaches where we seek a specific demand function. The second approach is particularly useful when we wish to consider the impact of control variable (e.g. price, advertising) changes on demand and therefore on total revenue. Consequently we shall proceed by considering means of finding specific demand functions and then progressing to examination of the purely empirical relationship between demand and time.

In attempting to find an appropriate specified demand function, the first problem we encounter is that of choosing the functional form. Consider a simple linear demand function

$$D = \alpha + \beta P.$$

Given observations on D and P, a line can be fitted to the data (i.e. α and β estimates) by the method of ordinary least squares.[7] To do this let $\hat{D}$ represent our estimate of demand. Then we find the estimates of α and β ($\hat{\alpha}, \hat{\beta}$) that minimises the sum of the squares of the prediction errors $D - \hat{D}$. Squared errors are minimised because of the possibility that even for an obviously ill-fitting line prediction errors may be sufficiently positively and negatively distributed to sum to zero.

Consider an illustration. Suppose we have the scatter of observations in Fig. 7.2 and the ill-fitting line *ab*:

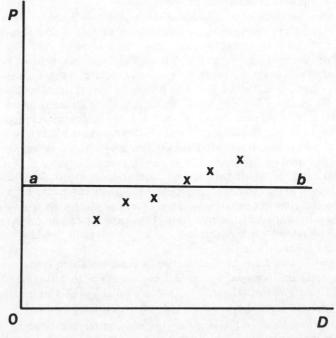

Figure 7.2

The line of best fit obviously slopes upward, yet for the line *ab* the sum of prediction errors will be near to zero, because positive and negative errors are equally distributed. Thus the problem we have is to find $\hat{\alpha}$ and $\hat{\beta}$ to minimise

$\Sigma (D - \hat{D})^2$. This is an ordinary unconstrained minimisation problem, solved by finding partial derivatives with respect to α and β and setting equal to zero to get the following simultaneous equations, referred to as the *normal* regression equations.

$$\hat{\alpha} = \bar{D} - \hat{\beta}\bar{P}$$

$$\hat{\beta} = \frac{\Sigma DP - n\bar{D}\bar{P}}{\Sigma P^2 - n\bar{P}^2}$$

where n is the number of pairs of observations and $\bar{D}$ and $\bar{P}$ are the mean quantity demanded and price respectively.[8]

For example, suppose we had the following empirical observations:

when
$$P = 5, \quad \text{demand} = 10$$
$$4 \qquad\qquad 12$$
$$3 \qquad\qquad 14$$
$$2 \qquad\qquad 16$$

Then we find $\Sigma DP = 172$, $\Sigma P^2 = 54$, $\bar{P} = 3.5$ and $\bar{D} = 13$.

Substituting into the simple regression equations,

$$\hat{\beta} = \frac{172 - 4.13(3.5)}{54 - 4(3.5)^2}$$

$$\therefore \quad \hat{\beta} = -2$$

$$\hat{\alpha} = 13 - (-2)(3.5)$$

$$= 20$$

Therefore the relationship we find is that $D = 20 - 2P$. Given this equation we can estimate what demand would be at various prices. For example if price is six units, we would estimate demand to be eight units. Also from the estimated equation point or arc elasticity can also be estimated.

The goodness of fit of the line is indicated by the coefficient of determination (R^2) which measures proportion of total variation explained by the estimated equation, i.e.

$$R^2 = \frac{\Sigma(\hat{D} - \bar{D})}{\Sigma D - \bar{D}}.$$

As R^2 approaches unity the equation becomes better and better in terms of explaining variations in demand. It likewise has a value of zero when none of the variation in demand is explained by the equation.

The estimate can often be improved, even in simple linear form, by the inclusion of other explanatory variables. For example, we may wish to estimate the demand function

$$D = \alpha + \beta_1 P + \beta_2 P + \beta_3 Y,$$

including both advertising and income as demand determinants. This can be estimated by multiple regression, in essentially the same manner as the simple regression.[9]

In the linear regression form, the β parameters measure the partial derivative with respect to the relevant variable and can be interpreted as the marginal impact of a change in that variable upon demand. It is a property of the linear form that these are independent of both the magnitude of that variable and the size of the other variables. In some situations this is an unrealistic assumption, and can be removed by estimating other functional forms.

Often the most satisfactory demand function form is the logarithmic or exponential form, i.e.

$$D = \alpha P^{\beta_1} A^{\beta_2} Y^{\beta_3}.$$

This form has several useful properties. The most important is that the marginal impact of a unit change in one of the explanatory variables is no longer constant, but depends on both the magnitude of that variable and the size of the other explanatory variables. A related property is that the β coefficients can be interpreted as the elasticity of demand with respect to the relevant variable. Remember the (point) price elasticity of demand was defined as $\partial D / \partial P \cdot P/D$.

Now if $\quad D = \alpha P^{\beta_1} A^{\beta_2} Y^{\beta_3}$

then $\qquad \dfrac{\partial D}{\partial P} = \beta_1 (\alpha P^{\beta_1 - 1} A^{\beta_2} Y^{\beta_3})$

(this demonstrates that the marginal impact of a change in price on demand depends on the size of P and the other variables).

Now price elasticity $= \beta_1 (\alpha P^{\beta_1 - 1} A^{\beta_2} Y^{\beta_2}) \cdot \dfrac{P}{D}$

$$= \beta_1 \cdot \dfrac{D}{D} = \beta_1$$

Correspondingly β_2 and β_3 measure advertising and income elasticity respectively.

The final property of the power function is that it is *intrinsically linear* and can therefore be estimated by ordinary least squares. We have:

$$D = \alpha P^{\beta_1} A^{\beta_2} Y^{\beta_3}.$$

Now take logarithms of both sides to get:

$$\log D = \log \alpha + \beta_1 \log P + \beta_2 \log A + \beta_3 \log Y.$$

All we need to do now is let $D' = \log D$, $\alpha' = \log \alpha$, etc., to get

$$D' = \alpha' + \beta_1 P' + \beta_2 A' + \beta_3 Y'$$

which can be estimated by ordinary least squares as before.

Statistical problems

Whatever the functional form chosen, there is the serious problem of what variables to include or exclude. Economic theory is the main guideline with the provision that for particular goods, as we have seen, particular variables may be important demand determinants (for example, the availability of credit and the demand for automobiles). The more variables are sensibly included the greater the explanatory power of the resulting estimated equation. However, the more variables are included, the more complex the analysis becomes and more observations are needed to get significant results. Also if more than one variable is included in the estimated demand equation, then the possibility arises that these variables may not be independent of each other. For example there may be positive correlation between advertising and price. Then our estimation procedure will divide the total impact of these variables on demand in some arbitrary way which is unlikely to correspond to the true situation.

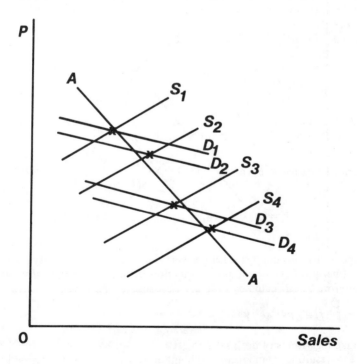

Figure 7.3

A further potential problem is that of *identification*. Microeconomic theory tells us that equilibrium prices are determined by supply and demand operating simultaneously. The difficulty is then to separate out the relationships from the observed statistics. We may have data on price and sales over a period, but we do not know if price changes are the result of demand or supply changes, or even both changing simultaneously.

Suppose we observe price and sales combinations represented by the above scatter diagram (Fig. 7.3). If we regress sales we would estimate a line AA, which slopes down and gives the impression of being a demand curve. But it may be that over the observation period, both the true demand and supply curves ($D_1 \ldots D_4$ and S_1 to S_4) have shifted and that the *Mongrel* curve AA adequately represents neither. This particular difficulty is called the 'identification problem' because it is due to our inability to identify the separate functions.

The only solution to this problem is further knowledge. Suppose we know that the demand function has remained stationary while the supply curve has shifted (for example, due to technological changes in production):

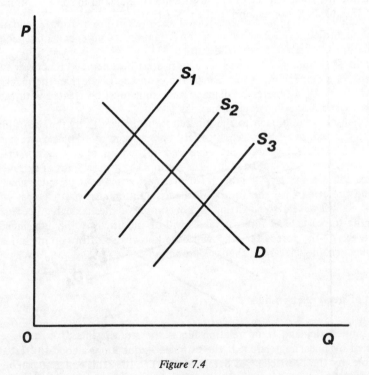

Figure 7.4

Then the resulting equilibrium combinations trace out the demand curve. Conversely if the supply function remains stationary while the demand curve shifts, the supply curve can be identified.

However, in practice it is unusual to know if the demand or supply curves have moved. Ordinarily only if both have shifted can they both be identified, but the task of unscrambling the simultaneous relationships is complex.

The identification problem can be illustrated by a three-equation model,

$$S = f(P)$$
$$D = g(P)$$

with the equilibrium condition $S = D$.

As they stand, neither the demand nor supply curves can be estimated. Suppose, however, that demand was known to vary with income, while this had no effect on supply, i.e.

$$D = g(P, Y).$$

Then we know that movements in income will shift the demand curve and therefore if income changes we can find the supply curve. This offers the clue to the identification problems solution.

More formally, in a two-equation model, if equation 1 contains an independent variable (with non-zero coefficient) not present in equation 2, equation 2 can be identified. Conversely, if equation 2 contains an independent variable not in equation 1, equation 1 can be identified.[10]

There are a number of other problems in statistical demand-functions estimation that are perhaps more relevant to the econometrician than the managerial economist.[11] All estimates of demand functions must be treated with caution and seen as no more than approximations.

An alternative approach to the prediction of demand is by the use of mathematically fitted *trend curves*. Historical observations of demand are plotted against time, and the relationship expressed in the form of an equation or curve which can then be extrapolated into the future. The general basis of this method is to establish a pattern of growth (or decline) over recent periods, which can then be projected into the future on the assumption that past changes will be continued. However, trend-fitting is not simply a mechanical procedure for obtaining forecasts. The forecast values will be modified by the judgement and experience of the forecaster who will have knowledge of important influences that may become relevant in the forecast period.

Types of trend relationships

The simplest demand trend relationship is the straight line $D = a + bt$ easily obtained by linear regression. If the estimated equation is a good fit (tested, for example, by the coefficient of determination),[12] then this equation can be used for demand prediction by substituting the relevant value for t. If the straight line is a good fit then demand will change in successive periods by the same absolute amount (indicated by the size of the coefficient b). The simple exponential function $D = ab^t$ is often a better representation of the relationship between demand and time. This is illustrated in Fig. 7.5, and shows demand increasing by a constant proportion each period (the slope of the curve increases at a constant rate).

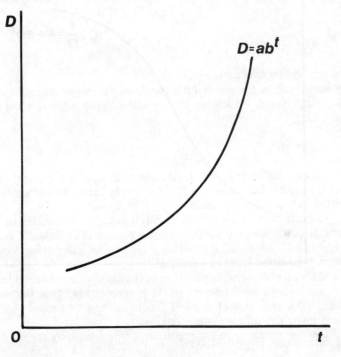

Figure 7.5

This function can be estimated by way of linear regression simply by taking the logarithms of both sides, i.e.

if $\quad\quad D_t = ab^t$

then $\quad\quad \log D_t = \log a + t \log b.$

The final functional trend form we shall consider is the logistic function, taking the general form

$$\frac{1}{D_t} = k + ab^t$$

where k, a and b are constant.[13]

This curve is particularly useful because it defines a three-phase relationship of slow, rapid and slow growth illustrated in Fig. 7.6.

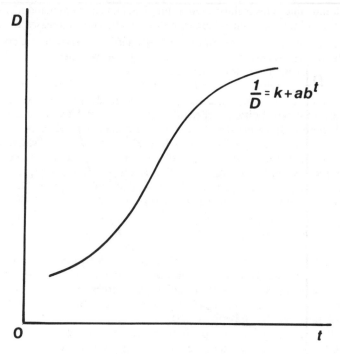

$$\frac{1}{D} = k + ab^t$$

Figure 7.6

This three-phase growth is typical of many products, particularly durable goods. During the period of introduction, when the product is unfamiliar, growth is slow. Then the product 'takes off' and moves into rapid growth. Finally, growth tails off as saturation levels are approached.[14]

The use of an appropriate trend curve may generate reasonable forecasts of product demand. However, the use of these curves on their own is not a sufficient basis for forecasting, as considered judgement is needed to support the hypothesis that past movements will be continued into the future. Without this support the trend-fitting technique degenerates into mathematical exercise with little practical application.

Sometimes the two statistical approaches of estimating demand curves and trend-fitting may be combined by the estimation of a demand function that includes time as an argument, for example:

$$D = a + bP + cA + dY + eT.$$

This function states that, with price, advertising and income constant demand varies proportionally with time. The inclusion of the time term has the advantage that it is not subject to prediction error, because we know the value it will take in the future.

Forecast assessment

The final question that arises in demand estimation is: How do we appraise the estimate we have achieved? How are we to judge whether a given forecasting method is successful or not? The obvious answer is to compare the predicted value of demand with the value that actually occurs. The problem with this is that it may be too late; decisions have to be made and mistakes may prove expensive. One possibility for checking the predictive ability of our forecasting method, before decisions about the future are made on the basis of these estimates, is to divide the available data into two parts, one of which is used to generate estimates, and the other used to test for prediction errors. Suppose, for example, we have twenty pairs of observations on price $(P_1 \ldots P_{20})$ and sales $(S_1 \ldots S_{20})$. Then the first fifteen pairs of observations could be used to estimate the values of a and b in the equation:

$$S = a + bP.$$

The remaining five observations on price can be substituted into the estimated equation to generate forecasts for sales which can then be compared to observed sales at these prices. The series of prediction errors $S - \hat{S}$ can be calculated. These prediction errors can then be expressed as a percentage of sales by dividing by actual sales and multiplying by 100.

Let P equal the percentage prediction error, $P = S - \hat{S}.100/S$. The sign and magnitude of P indicates the accuracy of the prediction. If the percentage prediction errors are all positive, forecast sales are consistently lower than actual sales, and conversely. The actual forecast can be revised in the light of this information.

Whether the forecasting procedure is good enough to provide information for decision-making depends on the degree of tolerance we are prepared to accept. In some circumstances $P = 0 \pm 5$ per cent may be acceptable, whereas in others the tolerance limits may be much smaller. Thus we are able to make some evaluation of the reliability of our estimates before they are used in practice.[15]

While the above method gives an indication of the accuracy of a forecasting method, the real test is in comparing future estimates with actual future values. Also the forecast must be correct for the right reasons. For example, if we were using an estimated demand function and predicted demand was close to actual result, this may occur because the forecast values assigned to the explanatory variables happened by chance to yield the correct result. However, if we substituted actual values in the demand equation the forecast may differ from the observed value. It is important to discover whether the forecasting method is yielding correct values by a mixture of chance events, or whether it is a true indication of the market situation.

The forecasting methods discussed in this chapter are neither exclusive or exhaustive. For example, the firm may prefer to use indicator forecasts, whereby certain series are known to be good predictors of future demand conditions (for example, an increase in stocks held by manufacturers may indicate a future decrease in the demand for investment goods). Finally, some firms may prefer to rely on the intuition and experience of the decision-maker. However, such judgements often involve informal assessment of the approaches outlined in this chapter, consumer reaction to the product's attributes, the main economic factors determining demand for the product and recent trends in sales.

Further reading

W. J. Baumol, *Economic Theory and Operations Analysis*, 3rd ed. (London: Prentice-Hall International, 1972) chaps 9 and 10.

Joel Dean, *Managerial Economics* (Englewood Cliffs, N.J.: Prentice-Hall, 1951) chap. 4.

J. M. Heineke, *Microeconomics for Business Decisions: Theory and Applications* (Englewood Cliffs, N.J.: Prentice-Hall, 1976) chaps 1 and 2.

A. Koutsoyiannis, *Theory of Econometrics*, 2nd ed. (London: Macmillan, 1977) chap. 5.

For an interesting case study of demand estimation, using the logarithmic demand function approach, see T. McGuinness and K. Cowling, 'Advertising and the Aggregate Demand for Cigarettes', *European Economic Review*, vol. 6 (1975) 311-28.

Questions

1 APEC Ltd, well-known publishers of textbooks, are considering production of a new book, *A Popular Guide to Demand Analysis*.

  (i) Indicate how APEC may estimate the demand for this book.

  (ii) If a demand function is to be estimated, what explanatory variables should be included?

  (iii) How should the forecast be judged?

2 'The best way to prepare short-term forecasts of product demand is to ask potential customers about their buying intentions'. Discuss.

3 'All that is required of a forecast is accuracy. The reason why it is accurate is not only unimportant, it is irrelevant'. Discuss.

4 Indicate the statistical problems associated with the estimation of a linear demand function from time series data on past prices and quantity sold.

5 To generate data for demand estimation oranges are sold in four supermarkets at different prices for one week.

	Price	*Number sold*
Supermarket *A*	3	65
B	5	55
C	7	45
D	9	35

From these observations, estimate demand as a linear function of price. Using this estimated function:

(i)   Find the total, average and marginal revenue functions.
(ii) Graph the functions in question (i), and comment on their interrelation.
(iii) Estimate demand when price equals 6. Find the point elasticity of demand at this price.
(iv) Measure the arc elasticity of demand between a price of 6 and 8 units.
(v)   At what price is demand of unit elasticity?

Given the form of the experiment, comment on the likely reliability of the demand estimates.

8
Production

Introduction - the production function

While individual firms may differ in their objectives the main activity of all firms is the production of commodities – either goods or services. The production activity consists of a variety of tasks and operations of varying complexity depending on the nature of the product and the size of the firm.

The analysis of production of commodities normally makes little or no distinction between goods and services. Yet there remains in practice an essential difference between the two categories. The production of goods has the feature that the physical end-product can be held in the form of *stocks*. In contrast the production of services cannot be stockpiled, but is only possible when there is a demand for these services. A simple example will illustrate. A firm producing component parts for computers can stockpile its output, whereas a firm selling computer services (computer time) can only effect production if there is a demand for it – if there is no demand the service remains potential rather than actual. It may be, of course, that the producer of a service is able to overcome this difficulty – for example, ordering demand by an appointment or allocation of the service time available. The particular problems of stockpiling goods under conditions of uncertain demand are discussed in Chap. 14.

The starting-point for any analysis of production is generally the *production function*, which takes the general form:

$$Q = f(X_1, X_2, \ldots, X_n),$$

where Q = level of output of commodity, and

           X_i = quantity of input i used in production.

We may define the level of output per time period as Q, measured in physical rather than value terms. This is made an unspecified function of the constituent inputs (or factors of production) which give rise to this output. The inputs are generally conceived to be labour, management, capital, land, buildings, fuel, part-finished products, raw materials, etc. As the production process is a flow over a period, the inputs also have to be specified in terms of units available per period of time. Thus while a machine exists for production, the appropriate concept in the production function is the machine hours which are available.

Production

Similarly with labour, it is the number of labour hours of a particular type of labour which is of significance.

Almost all production situations involve the combination of more than one input. It is indeed rare to find a commodity produced only by labour (perhaps personal valet services is an example) or only by capital (e.g. a transport service such as an underpass under a road system). In consequence a major part of the analysis of production is concerned with the way in which factors are combined. A number of possibilities exist, depending on the degree to which inputs are substitutable for one another.

At one extreme there may be *zero* substitution possible. If we limit ourselves, for simplicity, to two inputs, labour (L) and capital (K), output can only be increased by combining the two inputs in a specific way. This is illustrated by Fig. 8.1.

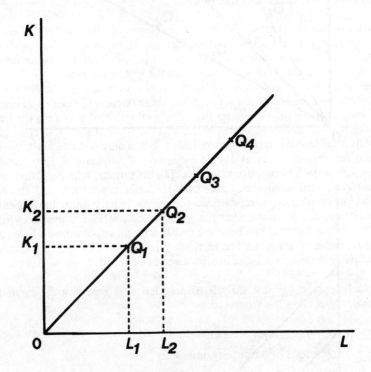

Figure 8.1

Output level Q_1 can only be produced using K_1 machine hours and L_1 labour hours, and Q_2 only by combining K_2 and L_2. If we add more labour than L_1 to K_1 we get no more output than Q_1; similarly, if we add more K_1 to L_1 then we get no more output than Q_1.

A variant of the above is the possibility of a limited number of alternative techniques, each of which when chosen has the characteristic of zero substitution between K and L. This is illustrated by Fig. 8.2.

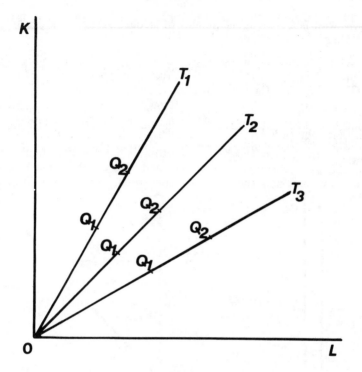

Figure 8.2

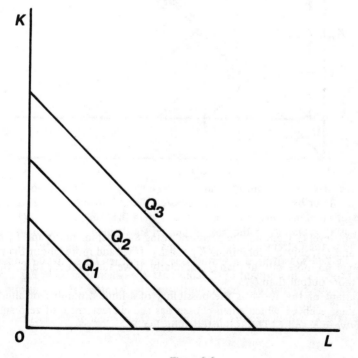

Figure 8.3

In this case there are three distinct techniques: T_1, T_2 and T_3. T_1 is relatively capital intensive, T_2 relatively labour intensive, and T_2 intermediate between the two.

At the other extreme in the production spectrum is the possibility of *perfect* substitution between the inputs. In this situation it is possible to produce an output (Q^*) either with (in the two-factor K and L case) all L, or all K, for any linear combination of K and L, substituting for each other at a constant rate. This is illustrated in Fig. 8.3, where the production function becomes a series of parallel lines outwards for outputs, respectively Q_1, Q_2 and Q_3. This is perhaps more clearly illustrated by Fig. 8.4, where output Q is taken on to the third dimension.

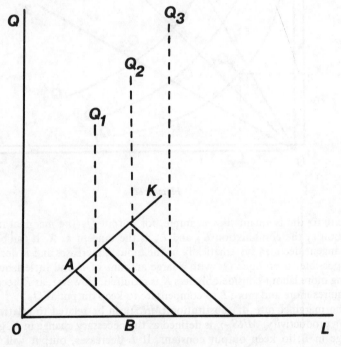

Figure 8.4

We see here that output Q_1 can be produced by $0A$ of K and no L, or $0B$ of L and no K; or by any combination of capital and labour on AB. Thus we have a series of combinations of K and L which yield the same output of Q_1 – this is known as an *isoquant*. In the case of perfect substitutably of factors it is linear.

Between the extremes of zero substitution and perfect substitution is a wide area of limited substitution of inputs one for another. Of particular importance in this respect is an isoquant of the convex-to-the-origin form as in Fig. 8.5. This has the property that one input substitutes for another at a continuous and diminishing rate.

The rate at which factors substitute at the margin is represented by the

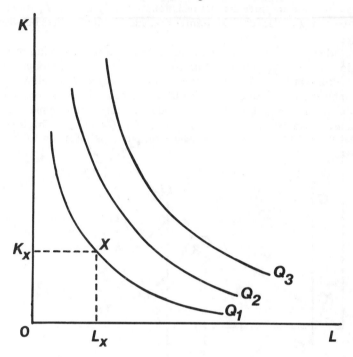

Figure 8.5

tangent to the isoquant. For example, for output Q_1 the marginal rate of substitution at the combination K_x and L_x is the tangent at X. It can be seen that the tangent declines systematically as the input L increases and K declines. Thus it is possible to produce Q_1 with a large amount of K and little labour, but by adding more labour considerably less K is required. However, as K becomes small it requires more and more L to compensate to keep output at Q_1.

The marginal rate of substitution (*MRS*) can be related to relative marginal factor productivity. MRS_{KL} is defined as the necessary change in K, given a unit change in L, to keep output constant. If L decreases, output will fall by the change in L (ΔL) times the marginal product of L (MP_L). To keep output constant, K must then be increased so that this is equal to the change in K times its marginal product. Therefore along the isoquant

$$MP_L \Delta L = -MP_K \cdot \Delta K.$$

$$\therefore \frac{\Delta L}{\Delta K} = -\frac{MP_K}{MP_L}$$

Therefore the slope of the isoquant is equal to the ratio of factor marginal productivity.

The isoquant can be derived from the production surface by passing a series

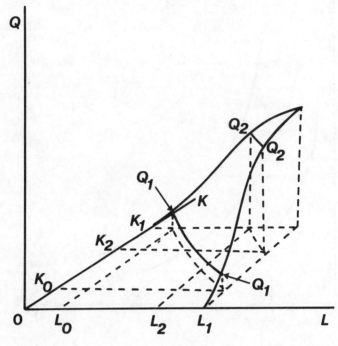

Figure 8.6

of planes horizontal to the input plane at various heights. Each plane then represents a different level of production.

To produce Q_1 we could use $L_1 K_0$ or $K_1 L_0$. If we use $L_1 K_2$, maximum output is Q_2, which is the same as if we use $K_1 L_2$.

The concept of an isoquant may be clarified if the production surface is seen in geographical terms as a hill. The isoquant is then a contour line, with different isoquants corresponding to different heights (levels of production).

Before proceeding to discuss which combination of K and L the firm should choose we should perhaps say a little more about the actual process of substitution. If we retain the example of two-input production the units are labour hours and machine hours. If more labour is added to the same amount of machine time, in the case of Fig. 8.1, nothing will happen to output. The labour units will simply remain idle in terms of production. The position here must be that the machine has no spare capacity, and is being fully operated before the additional labour is added. Similarly, there is no opportunity for increasing output by reorganising labour into different tasks – e.g. more division of labour.

If we contrast this with Fig. 8.5 then by adding more L to a given level of K will increase output (so that a reduced amount of K with the new L will retain the same output). This is equivalent to saying that, for a given level of capital K^*, adding more L means progressively moving on to higher isoquants Q', Q'', etc., as in Fig. 8.7.

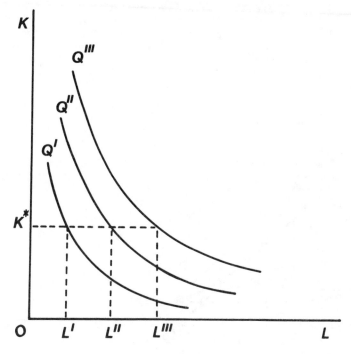

Figure 8.7

How does the higher output emerge? Presumably the answer lies in a form of excess capacity on the machine time K^*. Adding more labour takes up the slack, and more output emerges. Excess capacity on K can take several forms - working at below physical *maximum load*, running below maximum *speed*, or running below the maximum *number of machine hours* available in any given day - or any combination of these three aspects. The increased labour content is able, by reallocation of the labour duties, and by increasing overall labour time, to exploit these capacity reserves. We therefore see that the difference between Fig. 8.1 and Fig. 8.5 depends in practice on the extent to which labour is able to extract potential from the capital - in some circumstances the nature of the capital good will be such that it is very limited, while in other cases it may be much wider in scope.

Efficient production

Given the techniques available, how does the decision-taker find the most efficient way of producing a given output level? Using Fig. 8.5, the possible techniques for producing Q_1 are shown on the isoquant. The additional information we require is the relative price of K and L. If, for example, K is expensive and L cheap, the decision taken will concentrate on labour intensive methods of production.

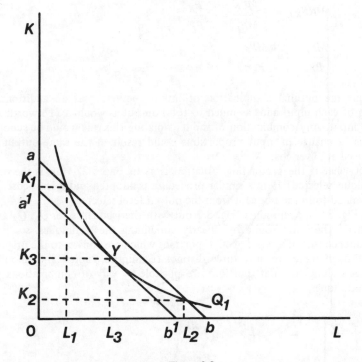

Figure 8.8

If K and L are available at a constant price per unit, then for a given outlay A, the combination of K and L available will be the straight line ab, as in Fig. 8.8.

All of A spent on K gives $0a$ units of K, where $0a = A/P_K$, while all of A spent on L buys $0b$ units of labour ($0b = A/P_L$). The slope of ab is equal to the factor price ratio, $-P_K/P_L$. It is possible to produce Q_1 with K_2 of K and L_2 of L, or with K_1 of K and L_1 of L. But both of these are needlessly expensive as the same output can be produced more cheaply. A lower expenditure than A will result in a set of purchases represented by a parallel line to ab nearer the origin. The optimal least-cost solution is with an outlay represented by $a^1 b^1$ where only one combination of K and L brings output Q_1 - the solution is at a point of tangency (Y) between the outlay line and the isoquant for Q_1. The technique chosen is then K_3 of K and L_3 of L. This technique is efficient in the sense that no other technique will bring an output Q_1 at lower outlay.

Optimal input combinations

At the point of tangency the marginal rate of substitution is equal to factor-price ratio. As we have seen, the marginal rate of substitution can be expressed as the ratio of marginal products. Therefore the rule for optimum input combinations can be rewritten as

$$MRS_{KL} = -\frac{MP_K}{MP_L} = -\frac{P_K}{P_L}$$

or $$\frac{MP_L}{P_L} = \frac{MP_K}{P_K}.$$

Thus the optimal combination of inputs requires that an additional £1's worth of each input adds as much to total output as would a £1's worth of any other input. Any combination of inputs violating this rule would be suboptimal because a change in input proportions could result in the same output being produced at lower cost.

But what if the production situation is as in Fig. 8.2? How is the optimal technique selected? Here a similar procedure is adopted and a least-cost outlay determined from the isoquant from the output level selected.

In Fig. 8.9 we reproduce Fig. 8.2 but with the isoquants for Q_1, Q_2 and Q_3 included. These are found by linearly combining the techniques, so that the isoquants consist of a series of 'flat' portions which are convex to the origin.[1]

Although there are only three distinct techniques, capital and labour combinations along the 'flat' portions are possible by way of combinations of the two techniques.[2]

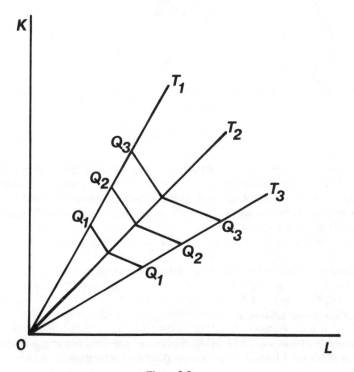

Figure 8.9

The least-cost solution is then obtained by observing the relative labour and capital costs, selecting an arbitrary outlay, and drawing the line of combinations of K and L which will use up this outlay (an *isocost* line). Such a line is ab in Fig. 8.10.

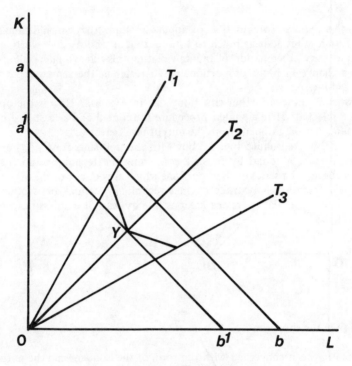

Figure 8.10

The line ab is then moved parallel to itself towards the origin until it just reaches the edge of the isoquant. This occurs at a corner point[3] with this sort of production situation – at Y in the diagram with an outlay represented by the isocost line $a^1 b^1$. Here technique T_2 is optimal and will be chosen given this relative cost of labour relative to capital.

In fact the technique we have just used is an elementary use of linear programming – which we will return to in more detail in Chap. 12.

For completeness we should note that if production is as in Fig. 8.1 with zero substitution, there is only one way of producing a given output, and so whatever the factor prices only one technique can be chosen.

In the case of perfect substitutability, either a labour only, or capital only technique will be chosen depending on the relative prices of labour and capital.[4] This is illustrated in Fig. 8.11 below where a labour only technique is chosen by bringing the isocost line ab to its nearest point to the origin at $a^1 b^1$.

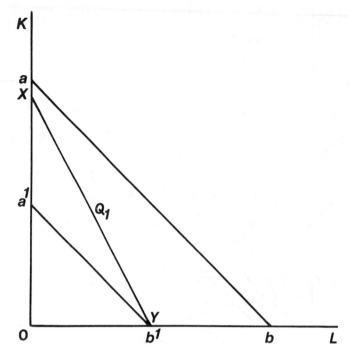

Figure 8.11

Production in the short run

We have so far been concerned with the form of the isoquant and the notion of efficiency in production. We now turn to look at the way output varies with input use. This is taken in two stages: first, when only some of the inputs are able to be varied, and, second, when all inputs are variable. As indicated in previous chapters this is essentially the distinction between the short and long time period.

The analysis is again easiest explained using the two-input example of capital (K) and labour (L). If we assume isoquants of the convex-to-the-origin type and hold capital at a constant K^*, we are interested in the output levels associated with varying degrees of labour added to this capital. This situation was exhibited in Fig. 8.7 (above, p. 119). If we then plot the output levels Q', Q'', Q''', etc., against their corresponding labour inputs L', L'' and L''', we get a relationship between variable input (L) and output (Q), holding capital (K) constant at K^*. This is shown in Fig. 8.12.

The short-run production function generally takes the form of Fig. 8.12. This shows production rising at an increasing rate in the initial stages as small amounts of labour are added to the fixed capital K^*. This however gradually becomes less distinct until eventually the rate of increase changes from positive to negative at the point of inflexion (at D). The tangent to the curve in fact represents the

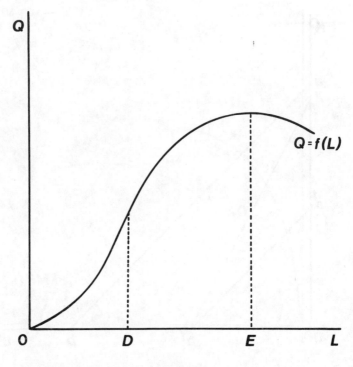

Figure 8.12

marginal contribution that labour is making to output (the marginal product of labour). From *D* onwards, diminishing marginal returns set in with the marginal unit of labour adding progressively less and less to total output. Finally, at *E* the tangent becomes horizontal, the marginal unit of labour adds nothing and total output reaches a maximum. Thereafter the marginal contribution of labour is negative and total output starts to fall.

The corresponding marginal and average product curves are shown in Fig. 8.13.

The marginal product may also be represented in algebraic terms. If we took a particular production function, for example the Cobb-Douglas production function, of the form[5]

$$Q = aK^b L^c$$

then the marginal product of labour is the partial derivative of *Q* with respect to *L*:

$$\frac{\partial Q}{\partial L} = aK^b cL^{c-1}$$

$$= c\,\frac{Q}{L}.$$

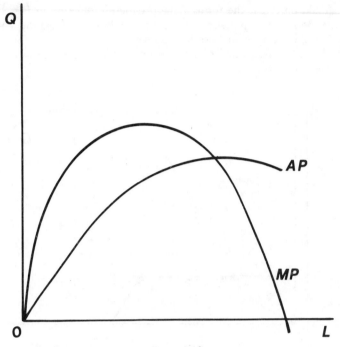

Figure 8.13

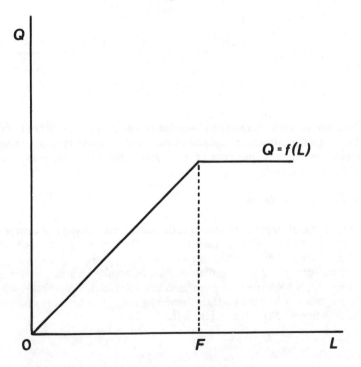

Figure 8.14

We should note that the form of the production function in Fig. 8.11 is not necessarily the case in practice. One alternative is given in Fig. 8.14 with total product rising linearly with L up to capacity F, and thereafter adding no output at all, and this has the associated marginal and average curves in Fig. 8.15.

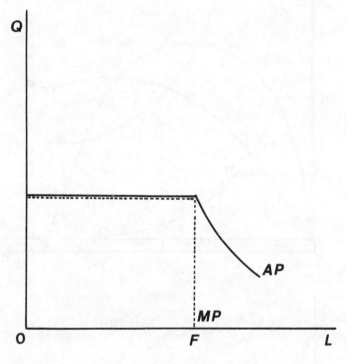

Figure 8.15

While the increase in output is attributed to adding more labour we should not forget that in most practical cases this is only possible because labour is able to extract some spare capacity from the capital K^*.

Production in the long run

In the long run all inputs are variable, so that in our two-input example both K and L can be varied. What is then of interest is how output varies when both factors are increased by a certain proportion – say α.

If output increases by more than α, then *increasing* returns to scale exist. If output increases by exactly α, then *constant* returns to scale obtain. Finally if output increases by less than α then *decreasing* returns to scale are observed.

The situation is illustrated in Fig. 8.16.

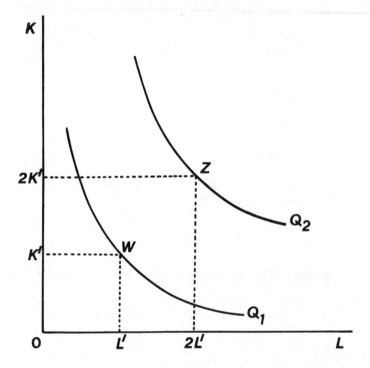

Figure 8.16

If $\alpha = 2$, then the combination Z represents inputs of twice as much labour and capital as combination W. Then, *increasing* returns to scale exist if

$$Q_2 > 2Q_1$$

constant returns if

$$Q_2 = 2Q_1$$

and *decreasing* returns if

$$Q_2 < 2Q_1.$$

The reasons which give rise to varying returns to scale are discussed more fully in Chap. 9 (p. 138).

The impact of returns to scale can again be traced with relation to certain production functions. Taking the Cobb–Douglas production function,

$$Q = aK^b L^c,$$

increase both K and L by a proportion α so that increase in output (ΔQ) is

$$\Delta Q = a(\alpha K)^b (\alpha L)^c$$
$$= a\alpha^b K^b \alpha^c L^c$$
$$= \alpha^b \alpha^c (aK^b L^c)$$
$$= \alpha^b \alpha^c Q.$$

Now if $c = 1 - b$ then

$$\Delta Q = \alpha^b \alpha^{1-b} Q$$
$$= \alpha Q$$

Hence the Cobb–Douglas production function exhibits constant returns to scale if it is of the form

$$Q = aK^b L^{1-b}$$

i.e. sum of powers on K and L is unity.

Decreasing returns to scale are observed if the sum of the powers $(b + c) < 1$, and increasing returns if $(b + c) > 1$.

Production functions are generalisations about production at a certain moment of time. They represent what is possible in terms of output given the inputs which are available and technical knowledge which is current at that time. We should note that these factors are liable to alter substantially in different periods. The advance of technology in particular will have a marked effect, with the same output level being possible with a reduced amount of inputs. In geometric terms the isoquants all move nearer to the origin.

From the decision-taker's viewpoint the *actual* state of production rather than the *ideal potential* production is of greatest importance. In real life, problems arise day in day out in the production line – a machine breaks down, key workers are ill, vital components may be in short supply, fuel deliveries may be awaited. If all these problems were removed the actual production level could probably be raised significantly, but the periods when all such problems disappear are comparatively rare. In order to utilise say 100 units of labour hours on an average week it may be necessary to employ a labour force capable of significantly more than 100 units if all problems such as sickness, holidays, strikes, etc., were removed.

The actual quantity of labour employed will depend on the probability distribution of absence and the cost associated with having less than the desired amount of labour available. For example, suppose each man works 10 hours per week, and has a probability of 0.1 of being absent in a given week, then if 11 men are employed, there will be a probability of 0.7 of having at least 100 hours labour available in any week. This probability rises to 0.9 if 12 men are employed.[6]

The nature of the production function is crucial in determining the cost functions of the firm. These are discussed in the following chapter.

Further reading

A. Koutsoyiannis, *Modern Microeconomics*, 2nd ed. (London: Macmillan, 1979) chap. 3.
J. M. Heineke, *Microeconomics for Business Decisions: Theory and Applications* (Englewood Cliffs, N.J.: Prentice-Hall, 1976) chaps. 3 and 4.

Questions

1 'The value of output per man in industry A is £5000. In industry B it is £4000. Therefore industry A is more efficient than B.' Discuss. What can we say about relative efficiency if A and B are two firms in the same industry?

2 As a result of innovation it is possible to produce the same level of output with 10 per cent less capital and 5 per cent less labour. Analyse the effect of this change on

  (i) the isoquants for the good;
  (ii) the production function.

3 Determine the marginal product of capital and labour in the following production function:

$$Q = 5L - 2LK + 2LK^2 - 5K^2.$$

  (i) Do the factors exhibit diminishing returns? (*hint* – returns to the factors are indicated by the sign of the second derivatives – why?)
  (ii) What is the nature of returns to scale?

9
Costs

The expansion path and cost functions

In the preceding chapter we saw that economically efficient production occurred where the isocost is tangential to the isoquant. The *expansion path* of the firm traces the locus of these points and illustrates the optimum input combinations for different output levels. If we retain the assumptions of a two-input production function, $Q = f(K, L)$ and constant input prices, we may readily move from the expansion path to the cost function, relating the level of costs to the level of output.

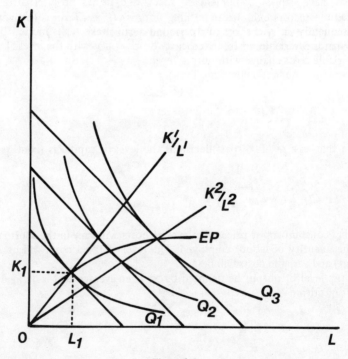

Figure 9.1

The expansion path for a set of concave production functions is illustrated in Fig. 9.1.

Output Q_1 would be produced with inputs K_1, L_1. The cost of this output level can be found by multiplying the input quantities by their respective prices and summing. If the cost per unit of capital is r, and that of labour w, then, if C_1 is the cost of producing output level Q_1,

$$C_1 = K_1 r + L_1 w.$$

The optimal input proportion for a given output level is illustrated by the slope of a ray from the origin to the tangency of the isocost with the isoquant at that output level. The capital–labour ratio of output Q_1 is K'/L' while that of Q_2 is K^2/L^2. Thus in this case we can see that as output expands production becomes more labour intensive.

Short-run cost functions

The short run is defined as the period of time in which some factor of production is fixed in quantity. The fixity of factors depends on both the contractual obligations of the firm and the degree of input specialisation. The firm may have contracted to employ x men during the decision period with unacceptably high costs of contract non-fulfilment. Alternatively, as a result of past decisions, the firm may have capital equipment so specialised it has no alternative use or resale value.

Consequently in the short-run period we can make a distinction between fixed costs and variable costs. Fixed costs do not vary with the level of output, while variable costs change with output level.

Returning to our total cost function

$$C_i = K_i r + L_i w, \text{ for output level } i.$$

Assume that as a result of past decisions the level of capital is fixed, say at $\bar{K}$. Then

$$C_i = \bar{K} r + L_i w.$$

Assuming constant input prices the level of costs will vary in the short run only with the quantity of labour employed. The level of fixed costs will be $\bar{K} r$ ($= d$ constant) and variable costs will be $L_i w$.

Let the level of output be denoted by x. Then average cost is defined as cost per unit of output

$$\frac{C_x}{x} = \frac{d}{x} + \frac{L_x w}{x}.$$

We can then see that average total cost is the sum of average fixed costs (d/x) and average variable costs $L_x w/x$.

The relationship between total cost and the level of output in the short run can now be graphed (in Fig. 9.2):

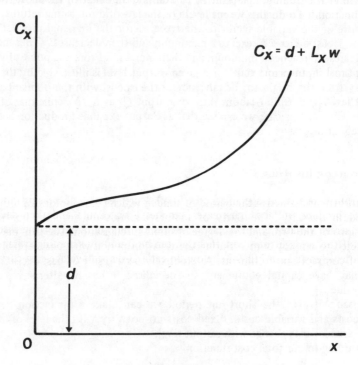

Figure 9.2

The level of fixed costs determines the location of the total cost curve, while the level of variable costs determines the shape of the curve. If fixed costs were higher (d larger) the total cost curve would move upwards.

In Chap. 2 (p. 10) we encountered the concept of marginal cost (MC) defined as the change in total cost associated with a unit change in output. This may be represented by the derivative of costs with respect to output. We have the total cost function

$$C = \bar{K}r + L_x w$$

and the production function

$$x = f(L, \bar{K}), \text{ where } \bar{K} \text{ is our fixed quantity of capital.}$$

Then:

$$\frac{dC}{dx} = w \cdot \frac{dL}{dx}$$

In Chap. 8 (p. 124) the marginal product of labour was defined as dx/dL. Thus we have the relationship that $MC = w/MPL$, and with constant wages, the marginal cost of production varies inversely with the marginal product of labour. Therefore if the marginal product of labour rises, marginal cost must fall, and conversely. We are now in a position to examine the shape of the short-run total cost function.[1] To do this we make use of the law of diminishing returns. As we add more of the variable factor to the fixed factor the marginal product of the variable factor increases, reaches a maximum and then decreases.[2] Thus marginal cost decreases, reaches a minimum and then increases. From the point of view of average cost, in the short run:

$$AC = \frac{C}{x} = \frac{L_x}{x} + \frac{d}{x}.$$

Therefore $AC = \dfrac{w}{APL} + \dfrac{d}{x}$, where APL = average product of labour.

As output expands average fixed cost (d/x) decreases at a decreasing rate.[3] The average product of labour increases, reaches a maximum and then decreases. Thus average variable cost decreases, reaches a minimum and then increases. The shape of the average total cost function can be found by summing average fixed and variable costs as in Fig. 9.3, below, to get a U-shaped average cost curve.

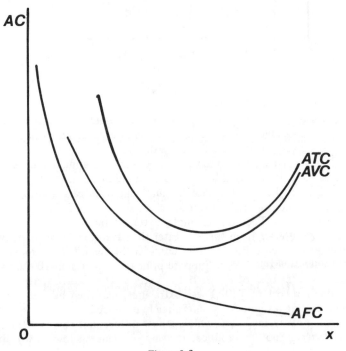

Figure 9.3

As we have seen earlier, average cost can be measured by the slope of a line from the origin to the total cost curve at that point. Thus, if average cost is U-shaped, the total cost curve must have the following shape (Fig. 9.4):

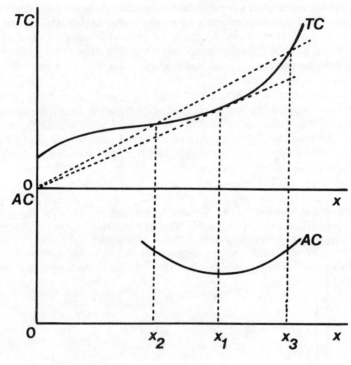

Figure 9.4

At output level x_1 the slope of a line from the origin to the total cost curve is at a minimum so average cost is at a minimum (and equal to marginal cost). At output levels x_2 and x_3 average costs are equal.

Short-run cost curves are used for day-to-day operating decisions. Generally only those variables affected by a decision should be considered in making the decision. Thus if the firm has capital equipment from past decisions, its cost is fixed and need not enter short-run decisions about production (since its opportunity cost is zero). Then, for example, extra production should be undertaken if the average revenue from this is greater than average variable cost, even if less than average total cost. For example, consider the decision to introduce an extra shift to meet an extra order. Suppose prior to the decision 100 units are produced for a total cost of £840. If the extra shift is worked, 10 units will be produced for a cost of £40. These extra units can then be sold for £6 each, without affecting revenue from units already produced.

Reasoning by average cost, which is now £8 per unit $(840 + 40)/(100 + 10)$, we would decide not to produce, as average revenue is lower (£6). But this is incorrect decision-making. The cost of producing the previous 100 units has already been incurred, and should not enter our decision about extra units. By producing the extra units a surplus of revenue over costs of £60–£40 will be made and consequently profit will be increased by £20. This is because average revenue for the extra units (£6) is greater than the average variable cost (£4) of these units. Fixed costs have already been paid and need not enter our decision.

The long-run cost curve

So far we have considered decision-making, with some factor fixity, from the point of view of operating decisions. For the purposes of long-run planning the requisite of factor fixity can be dropped, as the firm is able to alter the use of all inputs in the long run. Thus the firm can choose the optimal level of plant, equipment, etc., to determine the *capacity* of the firm. We are now considering changes in the scale of the firm.

In Chap. 8 (p. 126) the concept of returns to scale was examined, by asking the question how output changes if inputs all change in proportion (say α). If output changes by more (less) than α, returns to scale are increasing (decreasing). We can now examine the relationship between the long-run total cost curve, returns to scale and input prices.

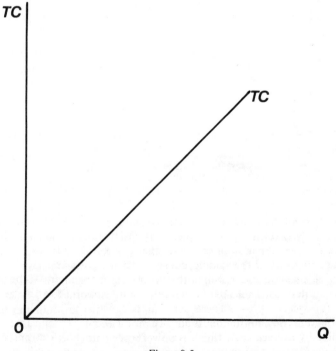

Figure 9.5

First we shall proceed with an assumption of constant input prices. Then the shape of the total cost function depends only on the nature of returns to scale.

If we have constant returns to scale, increasing output by α per cent will require all inputs to be increased by α per cent. Under our assumption of constant input prices, total cost must also increase by α per cent. Thus with constant returns to scale total cost is a linear function of output level (Fig. 9.5).

If we have decreasing returns to scale more than an α per cent increase in inputs will be needed to increase output by α per cent. Thus the total cost function increases at an increasing rate. Similarly, with increasing returns to scale, total cost increases at a decreasing rate.

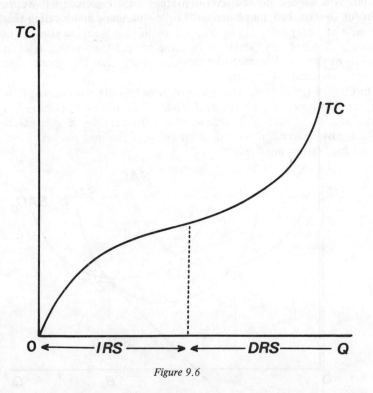

Figure 9.6

Generally if we have increasing returns to scale over a small output range and then decreasing returns to scale, the total cost function will have the above shape, under the assumption of constant input prices (Fig. 9.6).

We can now examine the assumption of constant input prices more closely. In particular this assumption requires the supply curve for inputs to be perfectly elastic. Only then will increased demand for inputs not lead to a change in input prices.

If we have an upward-sloping supply curve for inputs, an increase in demand will increase input prices. With constant returns to scale, this means that total cost increases at an increasing rate. The converse, of course, holds for a downward-sloping input supply curve. Thus, while the production function and total cost function are related by way of returns to scale, input supply curves must be examined before the relationship can be specified.

The relationship between short- and long-run average cost curves
Long-run cost curves are constructed on the assumption that an optimal plant is used to produce any given output level. The range of possible plant sizes is not continuous but discrete, that is to say, each plant size can produce a range of output. Associated with each plant size will be a short-run average cost curve. Suppose there are three possible plant sizes, *a*, *b* and *c*. Associated with each plant size is its corresponding short-run average cost curve. Which plant is optimal will depend on the level of output we are considering. Suppose the short-run average cost curves have the following shape and location (Fig. 9.7):

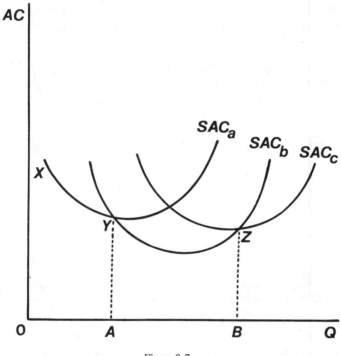

Figure 9.7

If desired output is in the range *0A* plant *a* will be used, in the range *AB* plant *b* will be used, etc.

Then the *LRAC* curve is the envelope of these curves, line *XYZ*. If we assume a large number of possible plant sizes, then the *LRAC* curve becomes smooth. Note that with a U-shaped *LRAC* curve, the most efficient plant for each output level will not necessarily be operating at the point where average cost is minimised for that plant. This means that with increasing returns to scale the least-cost plant will typically operate at less than full capacity.

Economies and diseconomies of scale

Economies of scale provide us with the explanation of the downward-sloping part of the long-run average cost curve. The most obvious economy of scale is the division of labour and increased specialisation that accompanies high output levels. Stochastic economies of scale result from the reduction of uncertainty achieved by being able to hold stocks of raw materials, spare parts, etc. Some economies result from the purely technical aspects of increased dimensions. For example, the cost of containers increases with the dimensions of surface area while volume increases geometrically. Large firms find finance easier, often at lower interest rates and may be able to influence external decisions through political power. Perhaps the most important economy of scale is the learning effect of greater production. Because of learning effects it may take new plants time to work up to production efficiency and therefore there exists a family of scale curves for a new plant relating to successive points in time. External economies may be realised; for example, economies of scale in manufacturing may lead to greater factor demand and consequent economies of scale in factor production.

However, at some output level long-run average cost may begin to rise, perhaps due to managerial diseconomies – the loss of control in large organisations. Diseconomies can often be avoided by duplication of efficient plant size.

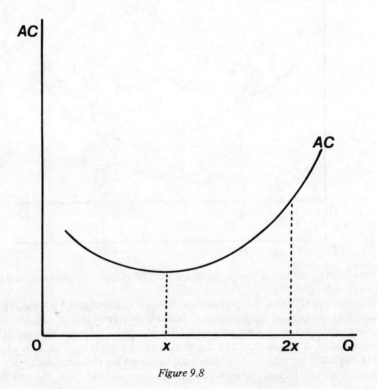

Figure 9.8

For example, if we have the following long-run average cost curve and seek to produce output level 2x, the most obvious way to minimise this output cost is to have two plants, both producing 0x (Fig. 9.8).

This enables us to make a distinction between different levels of aggregation. Duplication may prevent diseconomies at plant level, but cannot prevent them at firm level.

Plant size and flexibility

The plant size producing a given output level at lowest cost may not be optimal if demand is uncertain. The low-cost plant may be inflexible, so that if demand is different to efficient output level, costs increase rapidly. Consider two plants, x and y, with the following average cost curves (Fig. 9.9):

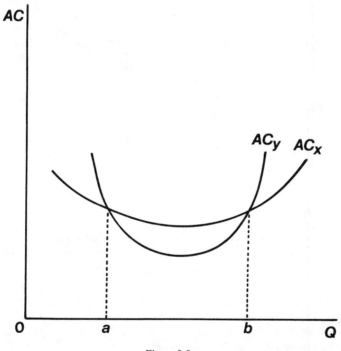

Figure 9.9

Plant y is most efficient between output levels ab, but plant x is most efficient outside that range. The optimal plant choice will depend on the risk attitude of the decision-maker and the probability distribution of future demand. If the decision-maker is risk-neutral the decision could be made on the basis of minimising expected average cost, which would depend on the probability distribution of demand. If both plants had the same expected cost the risk-averse decision-maker would choose plant x as average cost has lower variability. Different solutions would occur for different combinations of expected average costs and different attitudes toward risk.

Break-even analysis

This presents a useful tool for summarising the relationship between the level of output and the costs and revenues associated with that output. The firm's total revenue function and total cost function are plotted on the same graph (Fig. 9.10).

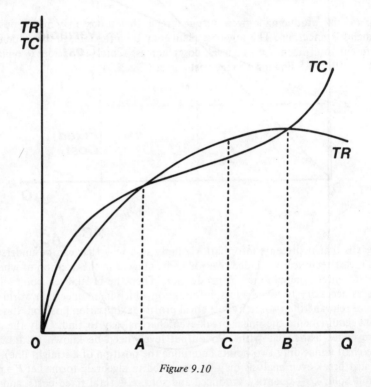

Figure 9.10

The profit associated with each output level can then be directly read from the graph. The output levels A and B indicate the range of output necessary if a loss is to be avoided (they are the break-even points). Point C corresponds to the position of maximum profit.

The obvious difficulty is that of estimating total cost and revenue functions. For short-run operating decisions linear break-even analysis may be more useful (Fig. 9.11).

The sales/output level x represents the break-even point. Beyond x a profit is made, at output less than x the firm operates at a loss. The concept of a break-even point is one much used in business. For example, a cinema manager may claim that he needs 120 customers per night to break even and that every customer beyond that represents a profit. The major benefit of break-even

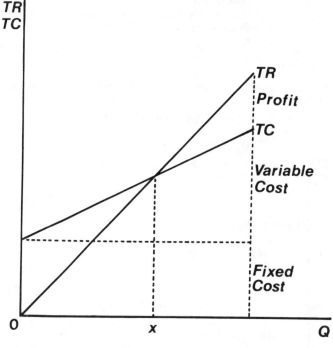

Figure 9.11

analysis is that it presents information simply in a way that can be understood by the least technically minded. Another advantage is in the decision of whether or not to enter a new branch of production. Then the break-even point tells us the sales necessary to avoid a loss, information which in an uncertain world may be more relevant than some hypothetical profit-maximisation position. In terms of data requirements the linear break-even chart is easy to find. Only the costs and revenues associated with two output levels need be known to draw the whole chart (since only two points determine the position of a straight line).

Linear break-even analysis may be expressed in algebraic form. Let P = price per unit sold, Q = quantity produced and sold, F = total fixed costs, and V = variable cost per unit. Under the linearity assumption P and V are constants (do not vary with Q).

The break-even point is defined where total revenue equals total cost, i.e.

where $\quad PQ = F + VQ$

then $\qquad Q^* = \dfrac{F}{P - V}$, Q^* is the break-even quantity.

This form is particularly useful for items with a high fixed cost. For example, suppose an airline wishes to discover its break-even point for a particular flight and has the following information on costs, with the price of a ticket at £128.00.

	Fixed costs	
Cost of aeroplane		£10,000
Fuel		5,000
Staff		2,000
Airport fees		1,000
	Total fixed cost	£18,000

	Variable costs (unit)	
In-flight entertainment		£2.00
Food on board		£4.00
Airport tax		£2.00
		£8.00

Then using the above fomula

$$Q^* = \frac{F}{P-V} = \frac{18,000}{128-8} = 150.$$

Thus the flight needs 150 passengers to break even.[4]

A technique related to break-even analysis is that of *profit-contribution analysis*. In the short run, when many costs are fixed, management is often interested in the effect of a specific action on profit. Profit-contribution analysis attempts to provide that information. The profit contribution per unit is defined as the per unit difference between price and average variable cost. This provides a convenient method of analysing price–output decisions. Returning to our aeroplane example, suppose that instead of finding the break-even point we wished to know how many seats must be sold to make £2000 profit. The sales volume required is given by the formula:

$$Q^1 = \frac{\text{Fixed costs plus profit requirement}}{\text{Profit contribution per unit}} .$$

Therefore $Q^1 = \dfrac{18,000 + 2000}{128 - 8} = 167$ passengers.

This answer could have been found from break-even analysis. If 150 passengers are required to break even, and profit contribution is £120, an extra 17 passengers are needed to make £2000 profit.

The major limitation of this kind of analysis is that we have assumed a constant output price and constant input price (to ensure linearity). The analysis could be extended to reflect varying input or output price, but only at the cost of considerable complexity.

Dimensions of output

So far we have examined the relationship between costs and the rate of output. It has been point out by A. A. Alchian[5] that output is a many-dimensional concept and that concentration on the *rate of output alone* 'has led to serious error'. According to Alchian there are three dimensions of output that are important for costs:

(1) The rate of output.
(2) Total contemplated volume of output.
(3) Programmed delivery time schedule.

The relationship between these can be summarised in an equation

$$V = \sum_{T}^{T+m} x(t)dt,$$

where V = total contemplated volume of output, $x(t)$ is output rate at time t, T is the moment the first unit of output is completed and m is the length of the time interval over which output is made available. Once three of these values are determined the fourth is also determined.

The cost output relationship $C = f(x)$ is now replaced by $C' = g(V, x, T, m)$.

In this formulation economies of scale are not the results of higher rates of output, but due to higher contemplated volume of output. The relationship between cost and output can be summarised in terms of the partial derivatives of C with respect to x and v.

Alchian suggests four basic propositions:

Proposition 1. $\quad \dfrac{\partial C}{\partial x(t)} > 0.$

This states that the faster the rate of output, the higher the total cost of that output.

Proposition 2. $\quad \dfrac{\partial^2 C}{\partial x^2} > 0.$

As the rate of output increases, total cost increases at an increasing rate.

Proposition 3. $\quad \dfrac{\partial C}{\partial V} > 0.$

Total costs increase with total contemplated volume of output, for a given rate of output and date of initial output.

Proposition 4. $\quad \dfrac{\partial^2 C}{\partial V^2} < 0.$

For any given rate of output, as total planned output increases, total cost increases at a decreasing rate.

A numerical example will illustrate the relation of costs to its determining factors. Alchian provides the following arithmetic illustration:[6]

COST, VOLUME OF OUTPUT AND RATES OF OUTPUT

Rate of output x (per year)	Volume of output (V)			
	1	2	3	4
1	100	180	255	325
2	120	195	265	330
3	145	215	280	340
4	175	240	300	355

The table shows the way in which V and x determine costs.[7] Production starts at time T and proceeds for a period m. If, for example, we are interested in producing 3 units of output, we could choose a rate of output of 1 and run this technique for 3 time periods (years) - the associated cost is \$255. Alternatively, we could choose a rate of output x of 3, and run it for one period - in this case the associated cost would be less - in fact only \$145. Thus the choice of a higher capacity technique run for a shorter time is in this case less costly.

The four propositions of Alchian are shown by the table:

Proposition 1
As we move down the *columns* costs increase.

Proposition 2
The difference in total cost between successive rates of output increases as the rate of output increases. For example, costs increase from 100 to 120 between output rates 1 and 2, but from 120 to 145 between output rates 2 and 3.

Proposition 3
Costs increase as we move from left to right along rows of the table.

Proposition 4
As V increases, total cost increases at a decreasing rate (keeping x constant). Thus for $x = 1$ the difference in cost between $V = 1$ and $V = 2$ is $180 - 100$, whereas the difference in cost between $V = 2$ and $V = 3$ is only $255 - 180$.

Confusion about the relationship between costs and output arises because greater output is associated with both a higher rate of output and a larger planned volume of output. A larger planned volume of output increases costs at a decreasing rate because of the opportunity to use different production techniques, usually involving production facilities with longer productive duration. With modern techniques of production it is often difficult (expensive) to vary the rate of output.

Before leaving the contribution of Alchian, one further proposition is of interest: 'As the total quantity of units produced increases, the cost of *future* output declines.'[8] This was referred to earlier as the *learning* economy of scale, and is distinct from proposition 4 above. This learning effect is not due to the opportunity to switch techniques, but rather to new technology. In other words, future output is cheaper as present output expands because knowledge increases as a result of production.

Empirical cost analysis

Empirical cost analysis is important both from the firm's point of view and that of society. Empirical cost studies provide essential information about cost conditions for price and output decisions. From a social point of view empirical studies go far in explaining market concentration as a result of significant economies of scale. For decision-making purposes cost studies can be divided into the estimation of short-run cost curves for operating decisions and the estimation of long-run cost curves for planning purposes.

Short-run cost estimation

Utilising economic analysis we have seen that in the short run changes in output lead to changes in factor proportions, so that marginal product falls and therefore marginal cost rises. Following from this we expect short-run average-cost curves to be U-shaped.

The most common estimation method is to regress total variable cost on output using historical data and ordinary least squares to estimate the relationship between cost and output. Alternatively cross-sectional data may be used so that an estimate of the cost–output relationship is generated by attributing inter-firm differences in costs to differences in output.

There are a number of problems associated with these approaches. In particular for decision-making purposes we are interested in how costs *will* behave at future output levels, which may not be closely related to how costs behaved in the past, or to present inter-firm differences in costs. In dealing with costs for decision-making it is important to remember that records of firm's activities are generally provided by accountants and that accounting convention may not reflect the appropriate cost concept for decision-making.[9] Accounting systems normally fail to record opportunity cost. According to Joel Dean, 'In business problems the message of opportunity costs is that it is dangerous to confine cost knowledge to what the firm is doing. What the firm is not doing but could do is frequently the critical cost consideration, which it is perilous but easy to ignore.'[10]

Even for a single-product firm, it may be very difficult to relate particular costs to particular outputs. In short-run cost studies only those costs which vary with output should be included, but it may be difficult to determine which costs are, and which are not, related to output. For example, consider the problem of depreciation. Depreciation due to obsolescence is a fixed cost but difficult to distinguish from depreciation due to use (user cost), which is a variable cost. This problem is acute if there are time lags between input purchase and output production. Production may necessitate expenditure on maintenance, but how do maintenance costs vary with output? Often maintenance costs are a contractual obligation, and therefore properly belong under fixed costs.

Short-run cost estimation using cross-sectional data suffers from the problem that inter-firm differences in costs may be due to factors other than differences in output levels. Historical data in an inflationary period suffer from the same problem of dividing increasing costs into that due to inflation and that due to changes in scale. Increased input prices may be due to increased demand for inputs by the firm or may be due to changes elsewhere in the economy. Only those input price increases independent of the firm should be excluded from the data for cost analysis.

The estimated short-run average-cost curve should relate costs to output at a given scale of production. Often in modern business enterprises plant facilities are changing continuously. Decreasing the observation period reduces the probability of scale changes in the observation period distorting the curve estimates, but also restricts the size of the sample on which estimates are based.

Functional form
Having overcome the problems of data collection, we must decide the appropriate functional form to transform the general cost function $C = f(Q)$ into specific form. A variety of linear, or intrinsically linear, functions can be estimated

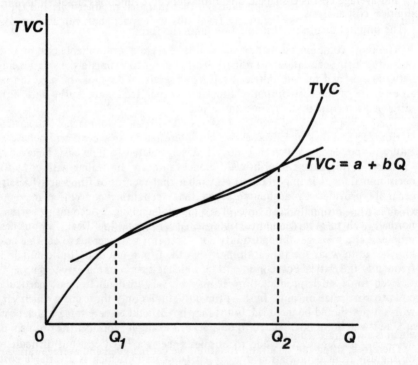

Figure 9.12

simply, using ordinary least-square regression. If there are no *a priori* reasons for choosing, the normal procedure is to estimate several forms to see which gives *best fit*, usually as measured by the coefficient of determination.

The simplest cost function estimated is the linear function $Y = a + bQ$, where Y is total variable cost and Q is output level; a and b are then the estimated parameters of the model. The intercept a is theoretically irrelevant and cannot be interpreted as fixed costs (cost when output equals zero) because these are by definition excluded from the short-run model. Also zero output is normally beyond the range of observed output values. This emphasises the point that extrapolating the results beyond the observed range may be misleading and result in incorrect decisions. For example, suppose the true variable cost curve has the above form (Fig. 9.12). If the range of actual observations is from Q_1 to Q_2, the straight line $TVC = a + bQ$ may be estimated, and gives a reasonable fit between these output levels. However, outside the observed interval the fit is poor, and estimates may be misleading.

The parameter b provides an estimate of both marginal and average variable cost within the relevant range. From the equation if output changes by one unit, total cost changes by b units (thus b estimates marginal cost). If the output level is large, b can also be used as an estimate of average variable cost (since marginal cost is constant).

Because of the inference from economic analysis that marginal cost is increasing and average cost is U-shaped, quadratic and cubic functions are often used in empirical cost analysis.

The simplest quadratic cost function takes the form:

$$TVC = a + bQ + cQ^2,$$

where a, b and c are the estimated parameters. Since marginal cost is the derivative of total cost with respect to quantity, we find:

$$MC = b + 2cQ,$$

which is a linear function and upward-sloping if $c > 0$.

Average cost can be found by dividing total cost by output,

$$AVC = \frac{TVC}{Q} = \frac{a}{Q} + b + cQ,$$

which is a quadratic functon.

Therefore, using the quadratic function, we get marginal and average variable cost functions of the following shapes (Fig. 9.13):

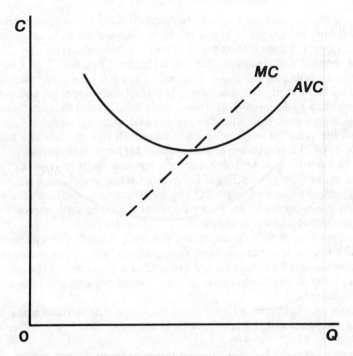

Figure 9.13

The cubic cost function of simplest form is:

$$TVC = a + bQ - cQ^2 + dQ^3.$$

By similar reasoning to the above,

$$MC = b - 2cQ + 3dQ^2$$

and

$$AC = \frac{a}{Q} + b - cQ + dQ^2.$$

Graphically:

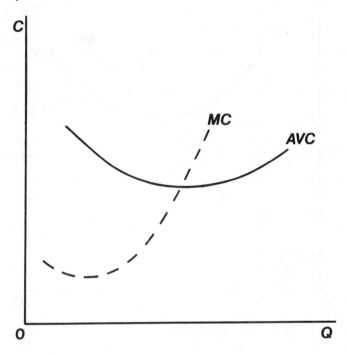

Figure 9.14

Empirical evidence of short-run cost curves are generally inconclusive, permitting whatever relationship is preferred by the analyst. The definitive study was by Johnston,[11] who found approximately linear short-run average-cost curves, suggesting that marginal cost is constant over a substantial output range.

Estimating long-run cost curves

The estimation of long-run cost curves is essential for the determination of optimal plant. Due to their usefulness in this area, long-run cost curves are often called 'planning curves'.

In addition as we have mentioned, long-run cost curves are important from a social point of view because the proportion of total output which a firm must produce to be reasonably efficient determines the extent to which concentration is favoured by the pursuit of minimum costs. The relation of productive efficiency to the proportion of the market supplied by a plant or firm will have an effect on potential competition. Economies of scale may provide a deterrent to entry, and enable firms to raise prices above competitive levels.

Thus we can see that accurate estimates of long-run cost curves are essential for decision-making, both by the firm itself and by society as a whole.

Whether time-series or cross-sectional data is used the basic problem is again that of separating changes in costs due to scale from changes because of other factors. There are a variety of other influences, both inter-firm and for the same firm over time, that may influence the level of cost. These include the stability of demand, the homogeneity of output, technological and location differences, and differences in accounting convention and procedures. Surveying empirical studies, C. A. Smith observes: 'In practice we do not find either plants or firms which, during a period of growth from small-scale to large-scale, produced one homogeneous product, nor do we find a group of plants or firms of widely different size which produce a single homogeneous product'.[12] Statistical estimates of long-run average-cost curves suggest that these are L-shaped rather than the U shape anticipated by economic theory. Thus there is a little evidence of the existence of significant diseconomies of scale, up to the levels of output actually observed.

Because of the empirical difficulties referred to in the statistical estimation of long run average cost curves two alternative approaches have been developed. These are referred to as the survivor technique and the engineering approach.

1. The survivor technique

The rationale behind this technique is that efficient firms (those with lowest average cost) will survive over time. Then, by examining changes in the structure of industry, we can infer the nature of the cost–output relationship. The precise method is to classify firms by size and to calculate the share of industry output provided by each size class over time. If the share of one class rises over time it is inferred to be relatively efficient, and conversely. Thus the shape of the long-run average-cost curve can be inferred (usually in qualitative rather than quantitative terms). This method has been applied to several industries, notably by Stigler, with the general result of U-shaped long-run average-cost curves. The main difficulty with this approach is that the argument that survival is dependent on minimising long-run average cost is far from convincing, because it assumes the existence of strong competition and is therefore inappropriate in a modern industrial structure.

2. The engineering approach

This method is based on the relationship between production and cost functions. Using information on production technology (usually from engineers), the optimal input combinations for any output level are found. The total cost curve is then found by multiplying each input quantity by its price and summing.

This is probably the most intellectually satisfying approach because the influence of other variables on cost can be eliminated, but it is essentially subjective, relying on opinions about future production functions and input prices. Thus this method is most useful for industries with clearly defined technology, such as the oil industry.

Further reading

A. A. Alchian, 'Costs and Outputs': see note 5, p. 244 below.

Joel Dean, *Managerial Economics* (Englewood Cliffs, N.J.: Prentice-Hall, 1951) chap. 5.

Milton Friedman, 'The Theory and Measurement of Long Run Cost', reprinted in *The Theory of the Firm*, ed. G. C. Archibald (Harmondsworth: Penguin Books, 1973). pp. 44–52.

G. J. Stigler, 'The Economies of Scale', *Journal of Law and Economics*, vol. 1 (1958) 54–71.

For an empirical study of the cost–output relationship see L. Cookenboo Jr, 'Costs of Operation of Crude Oil Trunk Lines', in *Crude Oil Pipelines and Competition in the Oil Industry* (Cambridge, Mass.: Harvard University Press, 1955) pp. 8–32, reprinted in *Price Theory*, ed. H. Townsend (Harmondsworth: Penguin Books, 1971) pp. 193–215.

Questions

1 Explain how the shape of the total cost function is related to:

  (i) the firm's production function;
  (ii) the supply curve for inputs.

2 'Neither logic nor appeal to any facts at present available makes possible the estimation of the benefits of competition relative to economies of scale'. (C. F. Pratten.) Discuss.

3 To what extent does the opportunity for duplication eliminate the possibility of diseconomies of scale?

4 'Since it is impossible to identify the relationship between cost and output in practice, intuition is likely to be a more reliable guide than empirical investigation.' Discuss.

10
Advertising

Introduction

The twentieth century has seen advertising grow from a peripheral activity to one of the main features of economic life. This growth of advertising is due to a number of factors: increased concentration, the growth of products susceptible to advertising, increased media importance and the creation of brand loyalty, until advertising accounts for about $1\frac{1}{2}$ per cent of consumer expenditure in most European economies, and almost double this in the United States.

In this chapter we are concerned with advertising from a decision-making point of view. Consequently we shall consider the relationship of advertising to other economic variables and the determination of the advertising budget.

Advertising is undertaken in the expectation of increased revenue. This may be due to higher sales at given prices, the same sales at higher prices or higher sales at increased prices. Immediately we can see the relationship between advertising and price as demand determinants. In a similar way to price, advertising elasticity can be defined as the percentage change in demand over the percentage change in advertising expense. Using the notation of Chap. 7.

$$E_a = \frac{\%\Delta D}{\%\Delta A}$$

and at the limit

$$E_a = \frac{\delta D}{\delta A} \cdot \frac{A}{D}.$$

The most important determinant of this advertising elasticity is the nature of the product. In particular the effectiveness of advertising is determined by the opportunity for product differentiation. Thus, for example, toothpaste is susceptible to advertising because of the nature of the product, while nuts and bolts are not. The distinction seems to be dependent upon consumer ignorance: where products are different or may appear different, the opportunity for advertising emerges. This argument goes a long way in explaining the *distribution*

Table 10.1

Food	0.82
Clothing	0.22
Automobiles	1.11
Drink and tobacco	1.05
Toiletries and medical	6.23
Household and leisure	1.55
Publishing, books	1.74
Tourism, entertainment, foreign	0.75

of advertising in an economy between different products. Table 10.1 shows advertising expenditure in the United Kingdom as a percentage of consumer expenditure for different product groups in 1974.[1]

In the past, economists have made a distinction between informative and persuasive advertising, in terms of the content of the advertisement. At one end of the spectrum informative advertisements contain only factual information about a product's characteristics. The nearest example is probably the newspaper classified advertisement. At the other end of the spectrum is the purely persuasive advertisement, containing no reference to product characteristics, but attempting to promote an image of life associated with the product. This distinction is generally disregarded nowadays because most advertisements contain elements of both approaches.

A more useful distinction is in terms of the effect that advertising can have upon sales. This can be broken down into a *market expansion* effect and a *market redistribution* effect. Advertising has a market expansion effect if demand for the industries product expands (normally at the expense of other products). The market redistribution effect occurs when advertising reallocates demand between different firms within an industry.

This distinction is useful in terms of the market structure of an industry. For the monopolist only the market expansion effect is relevant, as there are no other producers from whom sales may be gained. On the other hand, in monopolistic competition the market expansion effect of advertising by a particular firm is likely to be distributed among all producers, so that the original advertiser gains little. Here it is the market redistribution effect that is important to the firm. In the extreme market situation of perfect competition there will be no advertising by individual firms, because output cannot be differentiated and each firm can sell as much as it can produce at the given price.

Another feature of advertising is that it is often said to be wasteful in oligopoly, since mutually high advertising by individual firms offsets each other in market redistribution terms. However, even offsetting advertising may be beneficial without any market expansion effects because advertising can create high barriers to entry, enabling existing firms to enjoy high profits for a long period.

As we have seen, oligopoly is characterised by price stability, i.e. lack of price competition. In this situation advertising may provide an outlet for competitive pressures which is less risky than price changes because advertising changes cannot be reacted to by competitors without time lags, especially if the advertising campaign rests upon some successful gimmick.

Advertising as a cost of production

While the role of advertising is to influence demand, the expenditure so incurred enters into costs of production. The extent of advertising depends on many factors (the nature of the product, market concentration, etc,) and in some situations advertising and other promotional expenditure may form a very high proportion of total cost. Table 10.2 shows a breakdown of the retail price of a particular group of products (dental preparations).

Table 10.2

Price of a dental preparation – by cost components

	% of retail price
Materials – product	6
packaging	13
Factory labour	3
Advertising and promotion	18
Selling and distribution	6
Other overheads[2]	8
Profit	6
Manufacturer's price	60
Tax	22
TOTAL wholesale price	82
Retail marign	18
TOTAL retail price	100[3]

It is apparent that the cost of labour and raw materials are of little significance compared to advertising, sales promotion and packaging. While this single example may not be representative[4] it does indicate that promotion costs may be an extremely important component part of total costs.

Advertising and size

There is some evidence that, as the quantity of advertising increases, the cost per unit of advertising decreases (economies of advertising), but that the return per unit of advertising also falls (decreasing returns to advertising). The cost per unit of advertising may fall because of quantity discounts, and the discontinuous nature of advertising 'reach'. For example, a one-minute advertisement on local television may cost £2000 and reach five million potential customers, making a cost per potential customer of 0.4 p., while the same one-minute advertisement may cost £5000 on national television and reach twenty-five million potential customers (0.2 p. per potential customer). There is some suggestion that advertising effectiveness may be subject to thresholds so that a low advertising budget hardly attracts customer attention, while a medium budget receives far more notice. There is little doubt, however, that beyond a certain point each successive advertisement has a decreasing marginal effect on the consumer, and there may even be a point where customer resistance to advertising develops, so that the marginal effect is negative.

The result of these factors is that the sales-revenue function associated with advertising expenditure is likely to have an elongated S shape as shown in Fig. 10.1, below.

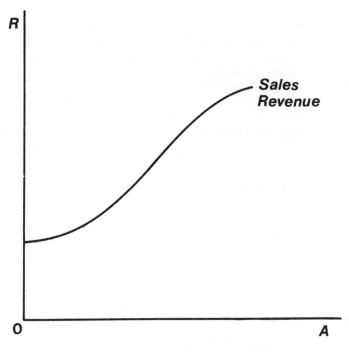

Figure 10.1

The optimal advertising budget

Before considering the determination of the advertising level to satisfy objectives we should note that the advertising decision must be seen in the light of other aspects of company strategy, particularly pricing policy. We have seen that, in conditions of oligopoly, advertising competition may replace price competition because adverse reactions are less likely. More usually the relationship between advertising and price occurs when some aspects of advertising are concerned with publicising prices – i.e. advertising designed to draw attention to price differences. Later we shall see that recent developments in retail pricing have given increased importance to this area of advertising. This is considered more fully in Chap. 11.

For the profit maximiser, the optimal advertising expenditure occurs where the marginal revenue from the last advertisement is equal to its marginal cost, in a manner strictly analogous to the optimal output decision. In practice it is difficult to separate the marginal cost of advertising from the marginal cost of production. However, theoretically at least, it is possible to find average and marginal cost curves for advertising expenditure. We have seen that the cost per unit of advertising decreases as the quantity of advertising increases, because of quantity discounts and indivisibilities. However, we anticipate that at some point the cost per unit of advertising will increase, so that the average cost curve (per unit of advertising) has the familiar U-shape. Associated with this will be a marginal cost of advertising curve intersecting the average curve at its lowest point.

The relationship between advertising quantity and sales revenue is discussed above, where we derive an elongated S-shaped curve. From this curve the average and marginal revenue curves from advertising can be derived. The determination of the optimum quantity of advertising is then a simple matter of equating the marginal revenue and marginal cost from advertising.

From Fig. 10.2 the optimum quantity of advertising is A^*, and the maximum profit from advertising is equal to the area of the rectangle *abcd*. It is important to remember that in this model we have considered only the costs and revenues associated with advertising. In particular, we have assumed that output and there-production costs remain constant. Thus this model is only appropriate for situations where advertising has the effect of enabling the producer to sell a given *quantity* at a higher price.[5]

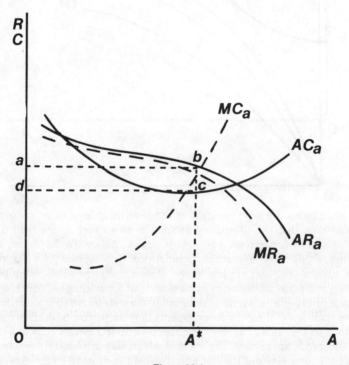

Figure 10.2

The more usual situation is where advertising shifts the demand curve so that more is sold at a higher price (i.e. the supply curve slopes upwards). Then any analysis of optimum advertising must take account of the cost of producing this higher output.

Suppose the effect of advertising is to increase both price and quantity sold. Then there will be a total revenue function corresponding to different levels of advertising. Because of diminishing returns to advertising, successive equal amounts of advertising will shift the total revenue function upwards by decreasing amounts. (Fig. 10.3) TR refers to the total revenue function without advertising, TR_{a_1}, to revenue with an amount of advertising a_1, etc. Assume that $a_2 = 2a_1$. Then increasing advertising from a_1 to a_2 increases total revenue but by less than advertising of a_1 increased total revenue.

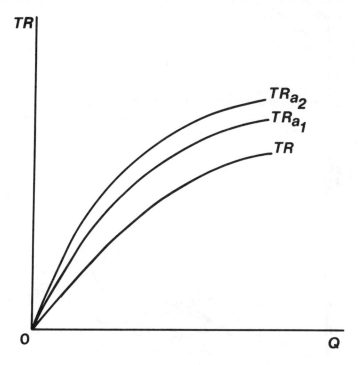

Figure 10.3

From a cost point of view there will be a total production cost curve independent of the amount of advertising. The shape of this curve is determined by factors outlined in Chap. 9. Advertising is then an addition to costs, with the effect of shifting the total cost function upwards by the amount of the advertising expenditure. Thus there is a family of total cost functions associated with different advertising expenditures. These are shown in Fig. 10.4.

The vertical distance between the total cost curve with advertising (TC) and the total cost curve with an amount of advertising, a_1, measures the amount of advertising a_1.

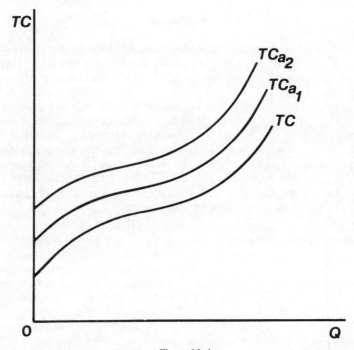

Figure 10.4

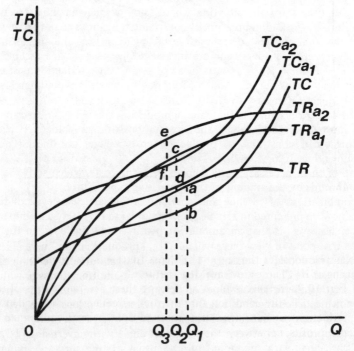

Figure 10.5

To find profit-maximising output for each level of advertising the total cost and total revenue curves are brought together in Fig. 10.5. For each advertising situation, profit maximisation occurs where the difference between total revenue and total cost is greatest (i.e. where the slopes of the total revenue and total cost curves are the same).

Thus without advertising, profit maximisation occurs at output level Q_1, with advertising level a_1 at output level Q_2, etc.

To determine the level of advertising to maximise profit all we need do is to compare the absolute magnitude of profit in different advertising situations. With no advertising profit is ab, with an amount of advertising a_1 profit is cd, etc. In the situation we have drawn, the level of profit initially increases with advertising ($cd > ab$) and then decreases. Thus to maximise profit an amount of advertising a_1 will be incurred, and the quantity Q_2 produced and sold.

Despite its apparent complexity the essence of this approach is that finding the level of advertising to maximise profit involves considering the *total* situation for different levels of advertising, and choosing that combination of advertising, sales and output which generate the greatest difference between total revenue and total cost.

Advertising and sales-revenue maximisation

The analysis of the optimum advertising budget has been extended by W. J. Baumol and others for the situation where sales-revenue maximisation is the objective, subject to a minimum profit constraint.[6] Again assume that advertising shifts the total revenue curve upwards, but by decreasing amounts as successive equal amounts of advertising are incurred. On the cost side assume that marginal production costs are constant so that the total production cost curve is a linear function of output. Added to production costs is a minimum level of profit (Π) which is necessary to satisfy shareholders. Although profit is normally considered to be a residual, in the Baumol model it is treated as a necessary cost the firm must generate to satisfy the expectations of shareholders. Hence by adding this profit constraint to production costs we get the linear function ($C + \Pi$) shown Fig. 10.6.

On top of these necessary costs come advertising costs, which shift the cost function upwards by the amount of the advertising expenditure.

The combinations of revenue and cost curves for particular levels of advertising can now be presented in a single diagram similar to Fig. 10.5. The important difference, however, is that an amount of profit is now included in the cost function.

For example, consider the revenue and cost functions associated with a level of advertising of A_1. These are drawn together in Fig. 10.7.

From Fig. 10.7, for this level of advertising there are two points of intersection which satisfy the condition that the total revenue generated will exactly pay for production costs and advertising costs, plus the necessary minimum level of acceptable profits, i.e. where

$$TR_{A_1} = C + \Pi + A_1 \text{ (output levels } Q' \text{ and } Q''\text{).}$$

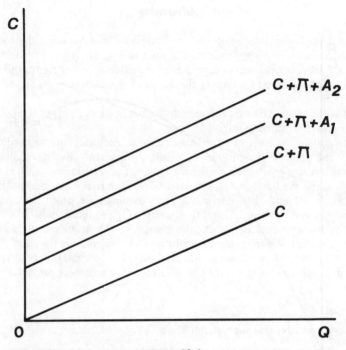

Figure 10.6

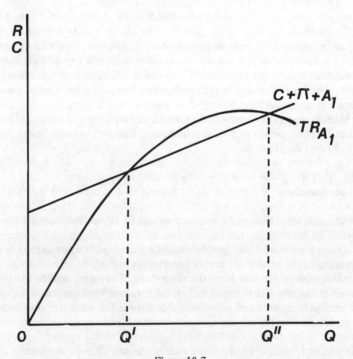

Figure 10.7

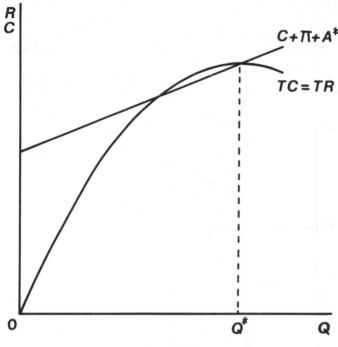

Figure 10.8

The same procedure can be repeated for different levels of advertising, generating a series of points where total revenue equals total costs (with the profit constraint included in costs). The locus of these points will trace a curve $TC = TR$, which will have the shape illustrated in Fig. 10.8 because of the way in which total revenue has been specified.[7]

The sales-revenue maximiser will select the advertising/output strategy which maximises total revenue - in this case output Q^* and advertising level A^*, at the top of the $TC = TR$ function.

Advertising and time

The above analysis misses one important aspect of advertising because it is *static* - the effect of advertising on sales is treated as immediate with no carry-over effect between different periods. In practice the effect of advertising is spread over a considerable period of time. For example, magazine advertisements may be read a considerable time after the issue date. The same applies to television advertising in the sense that brand images are retained in the minds of consumers and may influence purchases a considerable time after advertisement reception. This is especially true for age-specific consumption - for example, advertisements for alcoholic drink may mean that brand preferences are created in youth that are only realised when the consumer attains the age when he can legally partake of alcohol.

More generally, if we consider a single advertisement at one moment in time, its effect on demand may be spread over several periods. The rate at which the effect on demand changes over time will depend on both the nature of the product and the form of the advertisement. Fig. 10.9 illustrates three possibilities.

In case (*a*) the effect of the advertisement declines rapidly, in (*b*) the effect declines at a constant rate, and case (*c*) shows the effect first increasing and then declining.

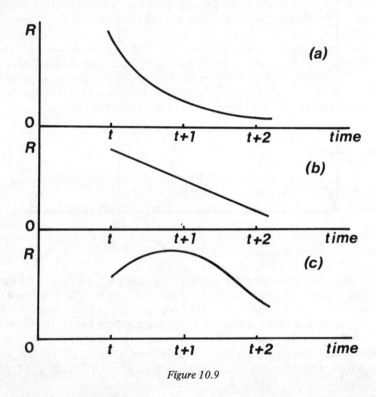

Figure 10.9

Normally an advertising campaign is conducted over several periods, so that advertising has a cumulative effect on consumers. Advertising may then be considered as any other of the firms assets, in that it has a cost and yields a return, however intangible the asset may be in terms of identification. Like any other asset the return deteriorates (i.e. the asset depreciates) without new injections of expenditure.

In this chapter we have concentrated on advertising as the firm's promotion activity. It is important to remember that there are other aspect of sales promotion that may be important; for example, sales force efforts, general publicity, etc. However, the general economic reasoning in these other decision areas is essentially the same as for advertising; cost and revenues must be considered and the decision made in the light of the firm's objectives.

It is important to remember that the effect of advertising is to increase sales revenue. Thus advertising will not be undertaken in situations where increases in sales revenue are not desired, or in situations of excess demand – where the only effect of advertising would be to make order backlogs or waiting lists longer. Certain luxury goods fall into this category, where the producer has no need to publicise the attributes of his product, or where the exclusiveness of the product forms a major part of its attraction, and may be diminished by advertising (for example, the Rolls-Royce motor-car).

However, for the more usual multi-product firm it is difficult to envisage a situation of satisfactory demand without some form of advertising. Even here the distribution of advertising between different products will be determined by the distribution of demand. Two extremes of policy can be defined. At the one end the firm may concentrate advertising expenditure on those goods that have not had a performance as satisfactory as other products. Alternatively, the best strategy may be to further expand demand for those products that have proved successful, reducing resource allocation to other products.

Further reading

P. Doyle, 'Economic Aspects of Advertising – A Survey', *Economic Journal*, vol. 78, no. 311 (Sep 1968). pp. 570–602.
Joel Dean, *Managerial Economics* (Englewood Cliffs, N.J.: Prentice-Hall, 1951) chap. 6.
P. Kotler, *Marketing Decision Making: A model-building approach* (New York: Holt, Rinehart & Winston, 1971).

Questions

1 The optimal advertising budget is where the marginal cost of the last advertisement equals its marginal revenue. How far is this statement relevant to the modern firm?

2 Examine the impact of an increase in production costs on the price, output and advertising decisions of a firm if:

   (i) the firm's objective is to maximise profit;
   (ii) the firm seeks to maximise sales revenue.

3 What factors determine the rate at which the effectiveness of an advertisement declines over time?

11
Pricing

The aim of this chapter is to consider certain practical aspects of pricing policy. Pricing policy has to be seen in the light of the objective(s) being pursued by the firm – it is a means to an end, not an end in itself.

Before proceeding to the topics on applied pricing policy it is useful to add some further observations relating to two of the market structures discussed previously[1] – monopoly and oligopoly.

Monopoly pricing

The application of the model presented in Chap. 6 requires knowledge of demand and cost conditions. Only if these are known can the monopolist arrive at the optimal combination of output and price. Obtaining this information is costly and time-consuming, and it seems reasonable to suppose that the monopolist always works with a level of information which is to some extent imperfect. The exact level of information obtained results from a trade-off between the cost of obtaining extra information and the benefits derived from the extra data.[2]

A deficiency of the model in Chap. 6 is that it applies to a single moment in time. In practice the monopolist will look not just to the present, but what effect his pricing policy will have on future events, particularly the possibility of potential competition. Generally the monopoly is likely to be transitory rather than permanent. In this situation the monopolist will take account not only of future demand patterns for the product range, but also the likely cost conditions of new entrants. In such circumstances the new entrant may have a cost advantage in that he can employ the latest technology in production. However, an offsetting factor may be higher marketing costs for new entrants if the present product is already well-established.

Where monopoly is of a transitory nature a number of factors affect the speed at which competitors enter the field:

(i) The ease of entry – this is affected by the existence of patents and licences, and the nature of the entrants' cost curves.

(ii) The degree of product differentiation – i.e. the ease of finding an acceptable substitute from the consumer's viewpoint.

(iii) The profit being made by the existing producer.

The economic theory of *limit pricing* has been developed to examine how prices may be set to deter entry.[3] The general conclusion drawn is that the limit price depends upon the relative cost conditions of existing and potential producers, the elasticity of demand and the extent of co-operation between existing producers.

The pricing of new products which are differentiated from those of rivals can involve a variety of possible combinations of price, advertising and output. Two combinations are of special interest: the Skimming Price Policy and the Penetration Price Policy.

The *Skimming Price Policy* involves setting a high initial price to recover fixed costs quickly, before competition erodes profits. However, as high profits are generated initially, competitors are likely to respond quickly unless there are substantial barriers to entry. The policy is normally operated under generally in-elastic demand conditions, and skims the market in layers, first, taking those with high incomes who can afford to pay a high price, and then gradually lower-ing the price over time to take in lower layers with smaller incomes. The policy is particularly applicable to goods which are only purchased one – e.g. books. Publishers often issue a hardback version in very limited numbers backed by substantial advertising. When these are sold out a paperback version is introduced in much larger numbers with lower price and lower advertising. In a world of uncertainty skimming prices may be more appropriate for risk-averters, because present revenue is more certain than future expected revenue. Skimming prices may ease cash-flow problems by recouping initial outlays quickly.

In contrast, the *Penetration Policy* sets initial prices at a low level, hoping to make an inroad into the product area through both product differentiation and a highly competitive price. The result is a lower profit margin, but on a larger volume and over a longer period. The policy is particularly useful if there are significant economies of scale to be gained from the production of a high level of output. These twin characteristics of significant scale economies and high price elasticity of demand characterise situations where penetration pricing is likely to be successful. The objective of the first entrant may be to entrench himself into a high market share by creating brand preference which may be easier and cheaper initially, before competitors are also engaged in advertising.

In essence the choice of pricing policy depends upon the elasticity of demand, the nature of cost conditions, the likelihood of future competition and the firm's rate of time preference between profits in different periods.

The Skimming and Penetration Price policies represent the extremes of alternative strategies that can be employed when a product of time-limited differentiation is launched. The optimal strategy for a particular new product is . likely to be somewhere in between.

Oligopoly pricing

Oligopoly is the form of market structure which characterises the modern economy, with a few firms being responsible for the majority of industry output. The product made may be identical (homogeneous oligopoly), or differentiated with a high cross-elasticity of demand (heterogeneous oligopoly). One important feature of oligopoly pricing is the strong aversion to price-cutting. This arises because of the expectation that rivals will match price cuts, leading to lower profits all round for firms in the industry. Therefore we expect price stability in oligopoly, since upward increases in price may not be matched (see Kinked Demand Model in Chap. 6, p. 86).

The basic problem for the firm in this market structure is how to assess what strategies the rival frims will undertake in any given set of circumstances. What can be said, however, is that a price rise by one firm is more likely to be matched if that firm is experiencing events which are typical of the industry. This may perhaps come from an upward pressure on costs, or from a shift in consumer demand towards the product. Conversely, the reaction of rivals to a price change becomes uncertain if rivals are affected differently by changed conditions, or if rivals differ in their estimate of the future. There are, however, means of reducing this uncertainty about price movements.

One possibility is to undertake more non-price competition – principally advertising or product improvement. By such means the product can be differentiated more from its rivals. In one case advertising creates a psychological differentiation from rival products, while product change makes the differentiation real rather than apparent.

Second, the existence of stocks and the possibility of order backlogs reduce the need for price changes. Any inequality between supply and demand can be accommodated by building up or running down stocks. This is discussed further in Chap. 14 (p. 228).

Finally, oligopolies often tend to become collusive in relation to pricing. By the formation of a cartel, or by price leadership by one of the firms, the uncertainty on pricing is removed. Cartels involve explicit price agreements which are often illegal or considered generally undesirable. In consequence price agreement tends to be implicit in practice, with price leadership commonly adopted. To qualify as the price leader the dominant firm will usually have a large market share together with a reputation for sound pricing practices. These practices will reflect not only what is desirable for the firm itself, but what is desirable for the industry to which it belongs. Price leadership generally only applies for upward price changes, since any firm may reduce price and others must follow to retain market shares. In heterogeneous oligopoly the leader must establish differentials between different products, a difficult task because of differences in design, quality, image, etc. Only when market shares are stable are accepted differentials achieved.

We now turn to discuss certain applied aspects of pricing policy – namely:

(1) Cost-plus pricing.
(2) Multi-product pricing.
(3) Price discrimination.
(4) Transfer pricing.
(5) Spare-part or component pricing.
(6) Retail pricing.
(7) Government regulations.

Cost-plus pricing

The procedure of cost-plus pricing has received increased attention following considerable empirical evidence of its favour in practice.[4] This determines price on the basis of the addition of three components: price = average fixed cost + average variable cost + a 'reasonable' profit margin. For the single-product case, the distinction between fixed and variable cost is unnecessary. In the multi-product case fixed costs must be distributed over the product range, so the distinction between fixed and variable costs has to be made.

The calculation of average fixed cost poses a number of problems. First, fixed costs have to be separated from variable costs, and, as this is purely a matter of time, subjective judgement is unavoidable. For example, an insurance premium may be estimated on last year's output level. As far as this year is concerned the insurance premium is fixed, but this year's output level will influence next year's premium. Depending on the time interval used, the insurance cost may be treated either as a fixed cost or as a variable cost with respect to output.

Second, the term 'average fixed cost' requires that an output must be specified (because the average fixed cost curve varies with output, particularly at lower output levels). But in order to know output we must presume the firm makes a decision on this. It may, for example, produce at the most efficient operating level (lowest average variable cost) – perhaps 80 per cent of maximum capacity. Having fixed output we can calculate average fixed cost. In theory, once output is determined, the pricing problem disappears, as price is determined from the position of the demand curve. In practice, however, there is room for pricing decisions, as the position of the demand curve is unknown.

The same problem of specifying output levels applies for the estimation of average variable cost. The notion of planned or optimal output may be again invoked, which can be used as a divisor for total variable cost.

Finally, there is the 'reasonable' profit margin to be added. This is purely a subjective judgement as to what is 'right' or 'just' rather than what is most profitable. There is a school of thought, however, that holds that the 'reasonable' profit margin in fact takes account of demand conditions, and the adoption of the cost-plus formula can lead to the same price as the profit-maximising approach. This can be seen as follows:

The profit maximiser will produce at the point where marginal revenue and marginal cost are equal. Price is then determined from the demand function for that output.

From Chap. 7 marginal revenue can be related to the elasticity of demand (E) because

$$MR = P \left(1 + \frac{1}{E}\cdot\right)$$

Therefore if P_1 is a profit-maximising price

$$P_1 \left(1 + \frac{1}{E}\right) = MC.$$

Rearranging

$$P_1 = \frac{MC}{1 + \dfrac{1}{E}} .$$

If production costs are linear over the relevant range, marginal cost is equal to average variable cost, and therefore the equation can be rewritten as

$$P_1 = \frac{AVC}{1 + \dfrac{1}{E}} ,$$

which can be rearranged by manipulation to be

$$P_1 = AVC - \frac{AVC}{E + 1} .$$

This implies[5] that the profit-maximising price is equal to average variable cost plus a margin, since E is less than -1 for a profit maximiser, so that $-AVC/E + 1$ is positive.

The size of the mark-up varies inversely with the elasticity of demand, so that price is higher the more *inelastic* demand.

There is considerable dispute about whether cost-plus pricing is compatible with standard economic theory. As we have seen above, it is possible that cost-plus pricing is identical with pricing which attains maximum profits, but this requires information which is likely to be unavailable in practice. This type of pricing procedure may be reconciled with economic theory if it can be shown that economic forces such as the extent of competition, attitudes to risk, etc., determine the size of the profit margin. However, to date there is little to suggest that margins are determined other than by rule of thumb.

If cost-plus pricing suffers from the deficiencies outlined above, why is the practice apparently so widely used? One answer is that the addition of a 'reasonable' profit margin is an objective of the firm – i.e. businessmen seek to get a fair profit rather than maximum profit. In oligopolistic situations cost-plus pricing may be safest, especially if other firms have similar cost structures and behave in the same way. The method is convenient and simple, especially for new products where normal profit margins have not yet been established. In inflationary times cost-plus pricing maintains real profits because prices rise in proportion to costs.

Thus while cost-plus pricing has its conceptual difficulties, its adoption in practice may reflect the impracticability of applying marginal analysis. In fact, the informational requirements of marginal analysis may be such that the cost of decision-making is greater under this approach than the increase in profit associated with it. Hence, the simpler method of cost-price pricing is preferred.

Multiple-product pricing

If we assume that the firm is a profit maximiser the addition of more than one
product causes no serious problems. The firm will in each case produce at the
point where $MC = MR$ and charge a price indicated by the demand function for
this optimal output. The only practical problem here is whether MC and MR can
easily be identified in each case. As far as the cost side is concerned it is necessary to be able to trace variable costs to particular products. In most cases this
poses few problems, e.g. the labour cost on a production line can be identified,
cost of materials separately assessed, capital equipment specific to that good
identified. In some cases, however, there may be more problems – some labour
may do work on more than one product, some machinery may be used to
produce parts for more than one product, etc. – then an apportionment of
labour and capital between different uses has to be undertaken. There may be
similar problems with fuel, e.g. electricity is a variable cost, but the measurement
of electricity may be at a single point in the factory. The variable cost of electricity to each product could be traced by separately metering each machine on
the product line. In most cases these difficulties can be overcome so that it is
possible to isolate variable costs to a particular product, although in some
instances subjective value judgements may have to be used.

On the demand side there are no special problems of estimation, so that
marginal revenue can be ascertained. The only exception to this is if the demand
for one product depends on demand for another product in the line, i.e. the case
of complementary or substitute goods. If these effects are strong it will be
difficult to derive the position of the marginal revenue curve, since it depends on
demand for other products. Taking the car industry as an example, the demand
for spare parts of a particular car is dependent partly on the past demand for the
final product. The two goods here are strong complements and higher demand
for cars will lead to greater demand for spare parts.

If these difficulties in estimating the separate marginal functions for cost and
revenue can be overcome for each product, then multiple products pose no
further problems for the firm's pricing policy. Optimal output and price will be
set for each product which will determine total revenue and total variable cost.
All that then has to be done is to deduct total fixed costs to arrive at profits,
which of course will be at a maximum.

We have noted above that firms may not wish to maximise profits and instead
pursue other objectives. We have seen that pricing often follows a different
pattern proceeding on a cost-plus basis. Additional problems are then posed by
moving from one to a number of products. Here the fixed costs have to be
'shared' between the several products, on the basis that no one product should
bear the full burden of fixed costs which are common to all products. We are
here considering costs such as rates, fire insurance on buildings, managerial
expenses, all of which can be regarded as common for each product, and can in
no sense be traced to particular products.

There is no obvious way in which this sharing should be done. In practice
purely arbitrary rules tend to be adopted, e.g. a product whose variable costs at
its 'planned' output are twice those of the 'planned' output of another product,

should bear twice the burden of fixed costs. It is noticeable that, in this allocation method, the demand characteristics of each product are of no relevance.[6]

Price discrimination

This is the practice of selling the same product at different prices to different
customers, or to the same customer at different times. The term 'price discrimination' is used without moral overtones, because price discrimination may be
socially desirable (for example, the practice of charging old-age pensioners
lower prices for haircutting).

Economic theory states that profit-maximising pricing requires equality of
marginal revenue and marginal cost. How then can it be profitable to charge
different prices for the same good? The answer is that the firm may not face a
single marginal revenue curve, but a variety of curves corresponding to different
markets. The firm facing different markets will maximise profit by operating in
each market so that marginal revenue in that market equals marginal cost. Generally this means that the firm will profit by setting the price lower in the more
elastic market.[7] Thus we can see that one requirement of profitable price
discrimination is that price elasticity of demand must be different in different
markets (otherwise there is no point in price discrimination). A second requirement is that markets must be separable, otherwise those buying at the lower
price can profitably resell to high-price buyers, although if segmentation is due
to consumer inertia or lack of price information, the degree of leakage between
markets will depend on the price difference.

There are a variety of possible methods of market segmentation. Price discrimination may be practised on the basis of geographical separation simply by
selling at different prices in different locations. Alternatively, different prices
may be charged on the basis of how the product is used; for example, the
practice of trade-discounts, according to whether the purchaser is a final consumer, or a provider of services to final consumers. Price discrimination may be
based on the timing of purchases; for example, the practice of differential rail
charges according to when the journey is made.

Apart from the function of profitably exploiting differences in price elasticity,
price discrimination may accomplish other objectives. Where demand fluctuates
in a systematic pattern, time price discrimination may reduce production costs
by reducing these fluctuations. A contribution to profit may be made by charging a low price in off-peak periods, as long as this price is greater than average
variable cost. Price discrimination may be a method of responding to market
differences in competition, i.e. by charging a lower price in the market with
strongest competition.

Another form of price discrimination is the quantity discount, whereby price
is inversely related to the quantity purchased. Quantity discounts are common
in both manufacturing and retail pricing. The basic rationale for the quantity
discount is the existence of economies of scale, whereby average cost is lower
the greater the quantity produced. If quantity discounts lead to greater sales
then they will influence the extent of economies of scale. In addition quantity
discounts may reduce stock and distribution costs by stimulating customers to

buy in bigger lots. Customer loyalty may be induced, especially if discounts are cumulative.

Transfer pricing

The growth of large multi-product firms has led to an increase in decentralisation as a form of business organisation, with many large corporations split into semi-autonomous divisions, each making its own price and output decisions in an attempt to eliminate the possibility of control-loss leading to diseconomies of scale. One problem this presents is the pricing of products transferred between divisions – how should products at one stage of production be priced to the division at the next stage of production, if both divisions are owned by the same firm? A related question is: should the firm charge the same price for the product to other divisions as it does to external purchasers or should it operate some kind of price discrimination?

The problem is the determination of transfer prices to maximise the overall profit of the company. One division may increase its profits by charging a higher transfer price to another division whose profits may then be reduced.

The general answer to the transfer pricing problem is that the transferred product should be priced at marginal cost, unless there is a perfectly competitive

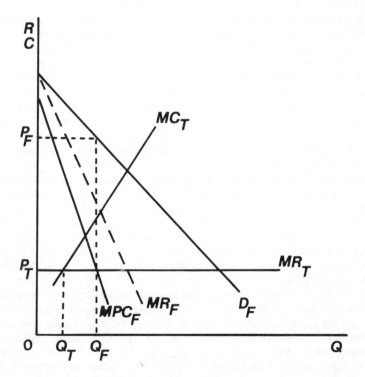

Figure 11.1

market for the transferred good, in which case it should be priced at the market rate. This case is sufficiently unusual to be of little practical interest, but the analysis of this situation demonstrates the principles of transfer pricing.

Division I produces the good T, which can be sold on a competitive external market for a price P_T, or transferred to Division II to be used in the production of good F for which there is an imperfect market. Division I faces a perfectly elastic demand curve (and therefore the average revenue of T is equal to marginal revenue of T) and an assumed upward-sloping marginal-cost curve MC_T. Division II, due to market imperfection, faces a downward-sloping demand (average-revenue) curve, and therefore a marginal revenue curve that lies below this. These are represented in Fig. 11.1.

We seek an appropriate price for the transferred good. There will be costs of producing F, irrespective of the price of the transferred good. Let the marginal cost of producing F, before the transfer price is paid, be MC_F. Then we can find the new curve MR_F-MC_F, which represents the marginal profit contribution of the final good, before transfer price is paid, denoted by MPC_F.

Assume one unit of the transferred good is required to produce one unit of the final good. The profit-maximising output of F will occur where the marginal revenue of F is equal to the marginal total cost of F, i.e. MC_F plus the transfer price. If the transfer price is P_T, optimal production of F is where $MR_F-MC_F = MPC_F = P_T$, i.e. where $MR_F = MC_F + P_T$. This is the output level Q_F, with a price of P_F.

Optimal production of T again requires $MC_T = MR_T$. Division I will therefore produce at Q_T, and sell at a price P_T. Both divisions will then be maximising profit, and total profit will be greater than at any other transfer price.

Note that with the situation as described, Division II will require more of good T than Division I produces. Because of the existence of a competitive market for T, this can be purchased externally at the same price P_T. If the optimal decision had resulted in Division I producing more of T than Division II required, the surplus would have been sold on the external market at the competitive price. Only if MC_T were to intersect MR_T at the point where MPC_F equals MR_T would neither division engage in external market operations.

If no external market for the transferred product exists, transfer prices should be based upon marginal cost. Here the demand schedule for the transferred good is difficult to define. Consider Fig. 11.2, with the revenue and profit contribution curves for F, and the marginal cost curve for T, as illustrated.

Optimal output of both T and F will occur at level Q^*. At Q^* the profit of Division II is maximised, as the marginal revenue from F is just equal to the marginal total cost of producing F $(MC_F + P_T)$.

This marginal-cost-pricing rule could be applied in two ways. The first is where Division II is given the marginal cost curve for T, from which it can deduce its marginal total cost by adding this to the marginal cost of producing F prior to purchasing T, and then proceed to maximise profits by equating this with marginal revenue as above. This is to treat MC_T as the supply curve for input T. The other method is to give Division I the profit contribution curve for F, which can then be treated as the demand curve for T.

These illustrations demonstrate the approach required for optimal transfer pricing, and can be applied in a variety of other situations (for example, when

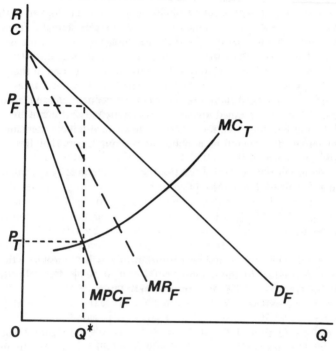

Figure 11.2

there is an imperfect market for the transferred good, where again the optimal
strategy is transfer pricing at marginal cost).

A further complication to transfer pricing occurs when divisions are situated
in different locations, with different tax structures. Then transfer pricing can be
used to minimise the tax liability, by redistributing profit so that it is actually
made in the location with least-profit tax.

Suppose a multinational corporation produced components in Country *A*,
which were then transported and assembled into the final good in Country *B*. If
the profit tax in Country *A* is high, the multinational can charge a low price for
components to the assembly division, so that Division *A* makes little or no
profit, while Division *B* makes high profit. If the profit tax in *B* is higher than
that in *A*, the transfer price is set high so that Division *A* makes most profits.

The practice of transfer pricing to minimise tax liability is now generally
illegal, but extremely difficult to monitor if there is no external market for the
transferred good, for then the respective legislatures can have little guidance to
what the transfer price would normally be.

Spare-part or component pricing

The essence of spare-part pricing is to recognise the complementarity of demand.
Whether spare parts are priced high or low will depend on the relative importance
of component sales compared to sales of the original good. For consumer

durables one of the factors determining demand is the cost of maintenance. Then setting the price of components low will increase demand for the durable good. On the other hand it may be that sales of the spare parts are more important and profitable than sales of the original good. The optimal strategy may then be to set the original goods price low, and therefore create a demand for the component. This is particularly well-illustrated by razor manufacturers, who tend to sell razors on perpetual 'special-offer' in order to expand the market for replacement blades which can then be sold at a high price. Although demand for the razors may be highly elastic, once the razor is purchased the consumer has little choice but to purchase the manufacturer's blades (probably the only blades compatible with the razor), and therefore blade demand is price inelastic. Profit maximisation will require the component price to be as high as possible without inducing the consumer to switch razors.

Retail pricing

The extent to which retailers will wish to handle a firm's goods will obviously depend on the profit available. The mechanism for achieving such profit is the trade discount system which we now discuss in more detail.

Profits for retailers come from being able to make a margin over the cost of buying goods, together with cost associated with selling them. The difference between the cost price (i.e. the price to the retailer) and his selling price, is termed the 'gross profit margin'. The margin after all selling costs are deducted is called the '*net* margin'. The normal method of quoting price to the retailer is for the manufacturer (or wholesaler) to state a recommended selling price for the good and then deduct the trade discount – in effect this *suggests* the gross profit margin. Whether this is the actual gross profit margin depends on policy over selling prices – if the manufacturer is able to control selling price then the trade discount is the gross profit margin to the retailer. However, the practice of setting prices in this way (usually termed 'resale price maintenance') has now largely vanished.[8] Instead, the retailer sets his own selling price and hence determines his own gross profit margin. We thus have a situation where the manufacturer (or wholesaler) cannot control the profit margin of the distributor, and because of this has greater difficulty in controlling the number and type of outlets for his goods. The price which is quoted by the manufacturer is merely a suggested or recommended price and has no legal status for enforcement.

How does this affect the retailing firm? We may adopt the traditional marginal analysis for the typical retail outlet. This is shown in Fig. 11.3.

The demand for the product is shown by the demand curve *AR*. Its associated marginal revenue curve is *MR*. On the cost side there are two elements to be considered: the cost of the good bought from the manufacturer and the associated selling costs (sales, clerical workers, rent, insurance, etc.). If we assume there are quantity discounts, i.e. that by purchasing more the retailer can buy at a lower cost, then the cost of an extra unit falls as the number of goods purchased rises. We may call this function the 'marginal buying cost curve' (*MBC*) and here it is presumed to fall linearly.

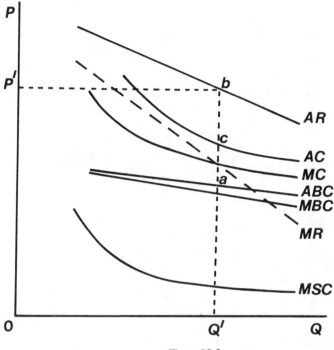

Figure 11.3

On the selling cost side we assume certain factors fixed in the short run (size of premises, fleet of delivery vehicles, etc.), but the number of sales staff is variable. It is likely that a certain amount of staff is necessary before the business can function at all, but that this level of staff can cope with a significant increase in retail trade before extra staff have to be called in. We would therefore expect the marginal selling cost curve (*MSC*) to fall significantly at low levels of output, and more gradually thereafter. There may come some point where the increase in staff combined with the given fixed factors tend to lead to decreasing returns, and hence to a rise in the *MSC* curve at high sales levels.

By adding *MSC* and *MBC* the marginal cost curve *MC* is derived. Profit is maximised where $MC = MR$, i.e. at sales of $0Q'$ and a price of $0P'$.

The *gross* trading margin at this level of sales will be determined by the difference between the average revenue and average buying cost (*ABC*), i.e. *ab* in Fig. 11.3. The *net* trading margin will be set by the difference between average revenue and average total cost (*AC*) at this output level – *bc* in the diagram.

We have made several simplifying assumptions in the above analysis – only one good traded, linear marginal buying cost curve, smooth selling cost curve. In practice the marginal buying cost curve is more likely to be as in Fig. 11.4, with *ranges* of output subject to the same discount, but then falling at critical points for a further output range. In this case the *MBC* is stepped.

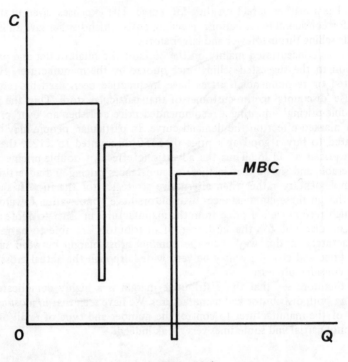

Figure 11.4

The curve dips at the critical points of change as the new marginal buying cost will apply to all of the previous output purchased, e.g. a retailer may be able to get a delivery of up to 20 items at a cost of £10 each, but on purchases of above 20 (and say under 40) the unit price drops to £9.00. Hence if we calculate the marginal buying cost for the 21st item.

Cost of 20 items
       20 × £10 = £200
Cost of 21 items
       21 × £9 = £189

In fact here the saving on all the 20 items previously purchased is such that the 21st item is 'free' – or more accurately has a *negative* buying cost of – £11. If we calculate the marginal buying cost of the 22nd item this will, of course, return to the £9 level as we are back on the 'flat' portion of the curve.

The terms of these discounts are of critical importance in determining the profitability of the outlet. In particular they have played a crucial role in explaining the movement towards retailing through large supermarkets and superstores rather than the traditional small shop. The terms of the discounts are highly favourable towards large orders.

On the selling cost side the change in method of distribution towards self-service has a marked effect on the *MSC* curve. The expenses saved in staff may make for considerable reductions in selling costs which further give an incentive towards selling through fewer and larger stores.

We have concentrated mainly on the costs of the retail outlet and paid little attention to the suggested selling price quoted by the manufacturer. However, suggested or recommended prices have in practice been used by retailers to advertise 'discounts' to the customer of that particular store. Thus the practice of 'double-pricing' – quoting a recommended price and then an 'own' price may have a marked effect on the demand curve. In particular, people may be more motivated to buy a good at a price of £150 discounted to £125, than if it's simply priced at £125. Thus the advertising effect of double-pricing may be considerable and shows that in these circumstances pricing and advertising may be complementary rather than alternative strategies for the firm. It should be noted that in these circumstances distributors have a motivation towards wanting a high recommended price from the manufacturer in order to quote a higher saving or discount for the customer. If distributors are able to bargain with manufacturers in this way then the nominal gross margin between suggested selling price and cost price may be very wide, although the actual gross margin will be considerably less.

We therefore see that the distributive margin is a highly complicated issue involving both distributor and manufacturer. We have seen that in most cases the ability of the manufacturer to control the number and type of retail outlets is often only partial and sometimes very weak indeed.

Government regulations

In the past few years it has become common for many governments to operate some kind of prices policy, as part of an anti-inflation strategy. This may take a variety of possible forms, but usually involves the setting of some limit on permissible price increases. The essential point from the managerial economist's view is that the firm's freedom of decision-making is reduced. The decision-maker must then set price at the optimum level within the legal or institutional constraints. For the firm launching a new product in a period of anti-inflation policy it becomes even more important to ensure that the original price is set correctly where demand equals supply, for if price is initially set too low, and therefore demand exceeds supply, it may be difficult or impossible to raise it sufficiently to avoid losing potential profit.

One strategy to avoid inflation controls is to relaunch the product in slightly different form, so that a new price can be charged. Generally, however, decision-makers recognise both the spirit and the letter of the law. This leads us to the whole question of social responsibility and the firm. Increasingly, firms set prices to earn less than maximum profit, or to stabilise employment, investment, etc. Unlike many economists this is a movement we would welcome, and recognise that in practice there are many factors to be taken into account in decision-making which may not be expressible in economic terms.

Further reading

E. F. Brigham and J. L. Pappas, *Managerial Economics* (New York: Dryden Press, 1972) chap. 11.

Joel Dean, *Managerial Economics* (Englewood Cliffs, N.J.: Prentice-Hall, 1951) chaps 7-9.

F. M. Scherer, *Industrial Pricing: Theory and Evidence* (Chicago: Rand McNally, 1970).

B. Taylor and G. Willis (eds), *Pricing Strategy* (London: Staples Press, 1969).

D. S. Watson (ed.), *Price Theory in Action*, 3rd ed. (Boston, Mass.: Houghton Mifflin, 1973).

Questions

1 'The development of a new product creates a monopoly that is likely to be transitory. In setting a price for the new product, it is essential to take account of the transitory nature of the monopoly the new product creates.' Discuss.

2 Given that cost-plus pricing is likely to result in less than maximum profit, how do we account for its widespread use in practice?

3 The economic theory of price is irrelevant to business decisions since the theory assumes that firms sell direct to consumers. Discuss.

4 What factors determine the discretion that firms have over the prices they charge for their products?

5 When the sale of a particular good creates a future monopoly market for components the optimum strategy is to charge a low price for the original good and a high price for components. Discuss.

12
Multi-Product Firms

Introduction

With one or two exceptions we have proceeded so far with the simplifying assumption that the firm is concerned with the production of a single good. This has greatly simplified the development of production, cost and demand functions. In practice the single-product firm is the exception, and we now consider the difficulties associated with the production of many goods by a single firm.

Prior to any formal analysis it may be helpful to illustrate the extent to which firms produce a variety of goods. A useful European example is that of the firm Unilever (Anglo-Dutch in origin), which produces goods including soap, margarine, toothpaste, meat products, ice-cream, frozen foods, perfumes, detergents, paper, transport, chemicals, etc. This product range is achieved through a whole series of subsidiary companies operating throughout the world. In fact the parent company of Unilever is rarely in the public view, and the consumer is generally only aware of the brand identities adopted by subsidiaries.

This example can be contrasted with another European company, Royal Dutch Shell (again Anglo-Dutch in origin), which is conventionally considered to produce a single good – oil. In practice, however, the Shell group consists of many subsidiary companies spread throughout the world, and although oil is a common feature, production of chemicals is also an important part of the operations of some subsidiaries. Even oil is more a product group than a single product. Thus Shell is also a multi-product firm.

The term 'multiple products' has so far been used in a rather loose sense. More rigorously, products are normally considered in terms of their physical attributes and this suffices for most purposes. However, difficulties can arise from reliance on physical characteristics alone. A firm may produce the same physical good for two separate markets; for example, a food manufacturer producing butter both for the retail market and for sale to other firms who use butter as an input. The manufacturer may have to organise production for the distinct markets on separate production lines. Then from the management point of view it may be more useful to think in terms of two separate products than in terms of a single product, despite the obvious physical identity of the two products.

Conversely, we can consider a firm producing a number of physically similar but not identical products; for example, saloon cars of different colours. In physical terms a yellow car is not the same as a blue one, yet to the manager yellow or blue cars may be considered the same product, since they are assembled from the same basic components and sold in the same market. The fact that both cars are produced in the same way and sold in the same market may be more important from a decision-making point of view than the difference in colour.

We can therefore infer that physical characteristics are not the sole factor of importance in product delineation. In general the way in which a product is defined is determined by the operational utility of the definition. Physical attributes will be important but some of these attributes are more significant than others. In addition other factors may be important: type of market, method of distribution, packaging, production method, etc., serve to differentiate physically similar products. Thus no hard-and-fast rules can be given as to how a product should be defined. Rather the best we can do is point to the sort of criteria that may be helpful. Again the judgement of the decision-maker is the best guide, defining a product according to the assistance this definition gives to decision-making.

The number of firms in the multi-product category has grown rapidly in recent decades. This has been the result of a number of factors, including the desire for growth, the associated merger movement, the drive towards multi-national rather than national organisation, increasing industrial concentration, etc. The addition of new products to the existing product line is generally termed the 'process of *diversification*', and will now be considered in more detail.

Diversification

The process of diversification is seen as a twofold expansion process: into new products *and* into new markets. Ansoff[1] provides the following diagrammatic representation (Fig. 12.1). There may be a variety of reasons for diversification: market saturation for existing products, excess cash flow, the profitability of

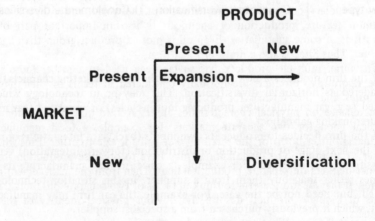

Figure 12.1

new products, etc. A useful starting-point for the analysis of diversification is in the examination of attitudes towards risk. Reliance on a single product brings with it the danger of a secular decline in demand over time. This is particularly so for products of limited life which may become obsolete through changing technology or the vagaries of consumer demand. In consequence, firms may seek new products for which demand is growing. What we are now considering is the balancing of risks. The risk of reduced future profits from the production of a single good is balanced against the risks associated with producing and marketing a new product. We shall see in the next chapter that the overall riskiness of the firm depends on the risk associated with the new product compared to the existing product, and the degree of independence between products. Suffice to say at this stage that in some circumstances the firm can reduce overall risk by taking on products more risky than existing products, if these are negatively correlated. However, for independent products, the new product must be less risky than existing products if overall risk is to be reduced. There are a number of ways in which the firm can diversify. Ansoff[2] again provides a convenient classification (Fig. 12.2).

NEW PRODUCT

Market	Related technology	Unrelated technology
Same type	Horizontal diversification	
Firm is its own customer	Vertical diversification	
Similar type	Concentric diversification	Concentric diversification
New type	Concentric diversification	Conglomerate diversification

Figure 12.2

If the firm produces a new good but uses the same marketing channels this is considered as horizontal diversification. This may be in technology which is related (e.g. car manufacturer producing motor-cycles) or unrelated (car manufacturer making car radios).

If the firm decides to produce its own inputs (backward integration) or move into the next stage of production or distribution (forward integration) vertical diversification is observed. For example, a car firm may manufacture its own engines rather than buy them from a supplier. In this situation technology is related, but need not be the case. For example, the car firm may manufacture paint, which it previously purchased from a specialist supplier.

Concentric diversification occurs when the firm introduces a new product into a similar market. This may be related in terms of technology (car firm making farm tractors) or unrelated (car firm producing accessories such as seat covers). Further concentric diversification is observed when new technically related products are sold in new markets. The term 'conglomerate diversification' is reserved for situations where the firm expands into a new market with a new product of unrelated technology. An example would be the car manufacturer making and selling drugs.

The above classification is helpful in the consideration of uncertainty. We can distinguish between that uncertainty which is due to future information being imperfect and that uncertainty due to a lack of information about the present. Consequently any diversification action is uncertain because the future is unknown, but different types of diversification differ in the extent to which present information is known. Then, for example, the introduction of a new product with related technology to a present market is, other things being equal, less uncertain than the introduction of a new technology product into a new market, simply because there is more information about expected returns.

The situation is further complicated by the lack of independence between new and existing products. This product dependence may arise because of production or demand interrelationships, or both. For example, the development of a product beyond the normal experience of the firm may have an adverse effect on consumer goodwill. If the Rolls-Royce motor company were to diversify (conglomerately) into the manufacture of ice-cream, the image of Rolls-Royce as a specialist motor manufacturer would be damaged. These production or demand dependencies must be taken into account in the decision to diversify. It is noteworthy that Unilever, which has diversified conglomerately, has circumvented the problem by retaining a low public profile and has preferred to give prominence to the subsidiary firms producing specialist goods.

A great deal of the recent diversification process has occurred because of mergers and take-overs between firms rather than a single firm adding to its product line. Growth by merger brings with it the inevitable consequence that *some* of the products taken over may not be seen as profitable.[3] Then after take-over such products are likely to be eliminated from the product line to achieve a balance between the different products of the merging firms. This process may present considerable difficulty in view of public, governmental and work-force opposition. Consequently the merging firms may have to 'carry' unprofitable products for a considerable time. It should be remembered, however, that the elimination of unprofitable products is as important to the success of a firm as the acquisition of new profitable products.

The production of multiple products

The production of many different goods within a single firm leads to special difficulties both because outputs need to be produced in optimal proportions and because inputs need to be distributed optimally between competing outputs.

We can now formalise the demand and production interrelationships suggested in the preceding section. In demand terms products may be substitutes or complements depending on how the price of one affects the demand for the other. Then the marginal revenue function for each good is not simply the derivative of price times quantity with respect to that good, but must take explicit account of the effect of demand for one on the demand for the other.

Suppose the firm produces two goods, X and Y. Then total revenue for the firm will be:

$$TR = P_x Q_x + P_y Q_y.$$

However, if the goods are demand-related, the demand for one depends not only on its price, but also the price of the other good, i.e.

$$Q_x = f(P_x, P_y)$$
$$Q_y = g(P_y, P_x).$$

The nature of the demand relationship is shown by the partial derivatives.

If $\partial Q_x / \partial P_y > 0$, then x and y are substitutes (and by implication $\partial Q_y / \partial P_x > 0$). If the goods are demand complements then these partial derivatives will be negative.

We can now find the marginal revenues associated with each good by differentiating the total revenue function, using the product rule (see p. 11).

Thus

$$MR_x = P_x \frac{\partial Q_x}{\partial Q_x} + Q_x \cdot \frac{\partial P_x}{\partial Q_x} + P_y \frac{\partial Q_y}{\partial Q_x} + Q_y \cdot \frac{\partial P_y}{\partial Q_x}.$$

Because of the way we have specified the demand function, $\partial Q_y / \partial Q_x = 0$ (although this may not be the case in terms of *production*).

Therefore we get

$$MR_x = P_x + Q_x \frac{\partial P_x}{\partial Q_x} + Q_y \cdot \frac{\partial P_y}{\partial Q_x},$$

and correspondingly,

$$MR_y = P_y + Q_y \cdot \frac{\partial P_y}{\partial Q_y} + Q_x \cdot \frac{\partial P_x}{\partial Q_y}.$$

The marginal revenue directly associated with each product is shown by the first two terms.[4] The third term refers to the change in the total revenue associated with one product when sales of the other product change, i.e. $Q_y \cdot \partial P_y / \partial Q_x$, gives the effect on the total revenue due to y when an extra unit of x is sold.

The sign of this cross-marginal revenue term depends on whether the goods are substitutes or complements in demand. If the goods are substitutes increased sales of one good leads to reduced sales of the other.

Production interrelationships occur when the goods are produced together. This may be in fixed proportions (for example, lamb and wool) or variable proportions (different breeds of sheep produce different proportions of meat and wool). If the goods are produced in fixed proportions it makes no economic sense to try and separate the products analytically. Consequently we have joint cost and demand functions, and maximise profit by simply equating joint marginal cost with joint marginal revenue.

Where products can be produced in variable proportions the problem is to determine optimal output combinations. If demand interrelationships exist as well then the most we could say is that an optimal solution involves considering the total revenue and total costs associated with each possible combination.

A related problem is to determine the optimal input combinations for different products to maximise overall profits. Where the total revenue and total cost functions can be completely specified this becomes an ordinary maximisation problem which can be solved by calculus. The addition of input or capacity constraints presents no particular problem if these can be expressed in equality form (for example, twenty units of labour *must* be employed) for then the classical optimisation techniques can be adjusted to take account of the constraints (by way of the method of Lagrangean multipliers). More commonly constraints take the form of inequalities (the amount of labour employed cannot *exceed* twenty units) and the classical constrained optimisation techniques are inadequate. For if there is more than one constraint we must allow for the possibility that not all constraints may be binding at the optimal position (the optimal solution may involve employing *less* than twenty units of labour). In this situation, if some simple assumptions are satisfied, we can use the techniques of *linear programming*.

Linear programming

The problem for the multi-product firm is to determine the optimal allocation of inputs between different outputs. To use the technique of linear programming we need to make certain assumptions about factor and product prices, and the nature of the production function. These assumptions rob the technique of *general theoretical* importance, but are often relevant in *practical* terms. In particular we assume:

(1) The profit contribution per unit of output is constant and known for each output.

(2) The firm faces a finite number of possible production techniques, and that technically efficient input combinations are fixed for each technique.

(3) Each technique has constant returns to scale, so that output is a linear function of inputs.

(4) The inputs to the firm are available in limited (known) amounts.

(5) The objective of the firm is to maximise profit.

These assumptions are often satisfied in modern productive situations (at least in the short run). If price is *taken* by the firm as fixed, and production is under conditions of constant average cost, then the profit contribution per unit of output is fixed, and therefore profit is a *linear function of output*. In practice once a technique is chosen it cannot be easily modified, and that given a particular technique output can only be increased by increasing inputs in the same proportion. Then output becomes a linear function of inputs. These inputs are usually available in fixed amounts, in the short run, so that capacity constraints are realistic. Finally, even if profit maximisation is not the sole objective of the firm it may be one objective, or the true objective of the firm may be a complement to profit so that the firm operates *as if* to maximise profit.

The decision problem for the firm can then be written in the following general form:

Maximise $Z = c_1 x_1 + c_2 x_2 + \ldots c_n x_n.$

subject to $a_{11} x_1 + a_{12} x_2 + \ldots + a_{1n} \leqslant b_1$

$\qquad\quad a_{21} x_1 + a_{22} x_2 + \ldots + a_{2n} x_n \leqslant b_2$

$\qquad\quad a_{m1} x_1 + a_{m2} x_2 + \ldots + a_{mn} x_n \leqslant b_m$

and $x_1, x_2 \ldots x_n \geqslant 0.$

The problem consists of a single linear *objective function* (Z) which is maximised subject to a finite number of linear *constraints*. In this formulation $x_1 \ldots x_n$ refers to the n outputs, each with a constant profit contribution £c_1 per unit of x_1. There are m capacity constraints represented by $b_1 \ldots b_m$. The a_{ij} coefficients show the input i requirements per unit of x_j in each technique. Finally, there is the non-negativity constraint that output of each final good cannot be less than zero.

Suppose that a firm produces two commodities, x and y, with a profit per unit of x of £4, and per unit of y of £6. The firm uses three inputs (A, B and C) and each unit of x produced requires 5 units of A and 8 units of B (input C is not used in the production of x). To produce a unit of y requires 10 units of A, 6 units of B and 10 units of C. The firm has at its disposal 50 units of A, 48 units of B and 40 units of C per time period. The constraints can then be written in tabular form:

	Product		Input available
Input	x	y	
A	5	10	50
B	8	6	48
C	0	10	40

Formulating in terms of the standard linear programming problem, the objective function Z is simply £4 times the output of x plus £6 times the output of y, i.e.

$Z = 4x + 6y.$

This is then maximised, subject to the three constraints (because there are three inputs). From the table we can see that 50 units of A are available, each unit of x requires 5 of A and each unit of y requires 10 of A. Then the constraint can be written as:

$$5x + 10y \leqslant 50.$$

Similarly, the constraints on B and C are written as $8x + 6y \leqslant 48$

and $0x + 10y \leqslant 40$

Finally, we have the condition that we cannot produce less than zero of either commodity, i.e.

$$x, y \geqslant 0.$$

If we combine the various components the problem becomes:

Maximise $Z = 4x + 6y$

subject to $5x + 10y \leqslant 50$

$\quad 8x + 6y \leqslant 48$

$\quad 0x + 10y \leqslant 40$

and $x, y \geqslant 0.$

Two alternative approaches are available to solve this problem: the *graphical method* and the *Simplex method*. The graphical method is simpler, but of limited application. The Simplex method is more difficult, but of general application. Both are discussed below.

The graphical method
This method is generally only used when there are two variables in the objective function, since the variables have to be plotted on a graph[5].

The first step is to define the vertical and horizontal axes as the outputs of x and y respectively. The constraints can then be incorporated in the following way: each constraint shows the maximum possible output combinations of x and y when the capacity of each input is fully used. If the input is fully used the constraint becomes an equality, for example taking the input A, at capacity,

$$5x + 10y = 50$$

when $x = 0, \quad y = 5$

and when $y = 0, \quad x = 10.$

Thus if all input A is used to produce y, 5 units can be produced, and when it is all used to produce x, 10 units can be produced. We can of course produce any linear combination of x and y between these points.

This procedure can be repeated for inputs B and C, i.e.

Second constraint $8x + 6y = 48$

when $x = 0, \quad y = 8$

$\quad y = 0, \quad x = 6$

Third constraint $0x + 10y = 40$

   when $x = 0,\ y = 4$

        $y = 0,\ x$ unconstrained.

These constraints can then be incorporated into the graph to identify the feasible solutions to the problem – i.e. solutions which satisfy all constraints. This is the innermost area bounded by the constraints and called the *feasible region* (the area 0*abcd* in Fig. 12.3 below).

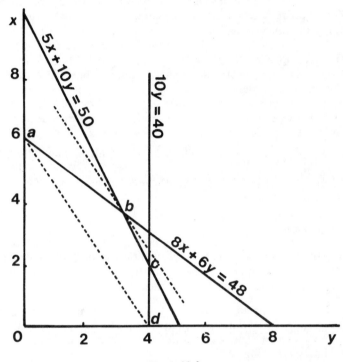

Figure 12.3

We now need to use the objective function to find the combination of x and y in the feasible region to maximise profit.

The objective function is

$$Z = 4x + 6y$$

which can be rewritten as:

   $4x = -6y + Z$, where Z is a constant.

This equation defines a straight line of negative slope. The value of Z will determine the exact position of this line. Increasing the value of Z will have the effect of moving this line parallel away from the origin.

We set the value of Z at a convenient figure so that the objective function can be located on the graph[6] (in this case set $Z = 24$).

Now if $x = 0$, $6y = 24$
                      $y = 4$
and if $y = 0$, $4x = 24$
                      $x = 6$.

The line $24 = 4x + 6y$ therefore shows combinations of x and y which yield £24 profit. The objective function can then be considered an *isoprofit* line.

The objective function can now be moved parallel to itself until the outermost point in the feasible region is achieved. This point is always at a corner of the feasible region (unless the objective function is parallel to one of the binding constraints). Thus by moving the objective function one can discover which corner point in the feasible region generates the most profit.

In Fig. 12.3 the objective function for $Z = 24$ is shown by the inner dotted line. This is moved outwards (increasing profit) until it just touches the outermost point of the feasible region. This shows the position which will achieve maximum profit *and* satisfy the constraints. The optimal solution is where x equals 3.6 units and y equals 3.2 units. These values can then be substituted into the objective function to find the corresponding level of profits.

$$Z = 4x + 6y$$
$$= 4(3.6) + 6(3.2)$$
$$= £33.6.$$

No other combination of x and y will yield a greater profit and satisfy the constraints.

The Simplex method[7]

The Simplex method is an algebraic technique for solving linear programming problems. It proceeds by starting from the origin and working around the corner points of the feasible region, testing for optimality at each corner, until the optimal solution is found.

The method will be demonstrated by solving the same problem described in the graphical method, i.e.

Maximise $Z = 4x + 6y$
subject $\begin{cases} 5x + 10y \leqslant 50 \\ 8x + 6y \leqslant 48 \\ 0x + 10y \leqslant 40 \end{cases}$
to
and $x, y \geqslant 0$.

Note that the constraints can be simplified by dividing throughout by the highest common denominator, e.g.

$$5x + 10y \leqslant 50$$

implies $x + 2y \leqslant 10$.

These two constraints are then equivalent (any combination which satisfied the first formulation must also satisfy the second and vice versa). Consequently the problem can be simplified to:

Maximise $Z = 4x + 6y$

subject to
$$x + 2y \leqslant 10$$
$$4x + 3y \leqslant 24$$
$$0x + y \leqslant 4$$
$$x, y \geqslant 0.$$

As with the graphical method, the Simplex approach requires that the constraint inequalities be transformed into equalities. This is achieved by the introduction of three *slack variables* (S_1, S_2 and S_3).

Thus $x + 2y \leqslant 10$

becomes $x + 2y + S_1 = 10$

or $S_1 = 10 - x - 2y$.

When the constraint is binding, $S_1 = 0$. If this input is not fully used up, then $S_1 > 0$. Similarly for the other two constraints:

$$S_2 = 24 - 4x - 3y$$
$$S_3 = 4 - 0x - y.$$

The Simplex method requires that we start at the origin to find the *basic feasible solution*. Thus we set both x and y equal to zero, and immediately achieve a corner point in the feasible region. This is obviously not optimal, as when there is no production there is no profit. Nevertheless, the origin serves as a starting-point, and we can set out the resulting equations as follows:

$$Z = 0 + 4x + 6y$$
$$S_1 = 10 - x - 2y$$
$$S_2 = 24 - 4x - 3y$$
$$S_3 = 4 - 0x - y.$$

For convenience these can be copied into a matrix which becomes the first solution.

FIRST SOLUTION
(zero variables)

			x	y	*Ratio*
	Z	0	4	6	
	S_1	10	-1	-2	5
(non-zero	S_2	24	-4	-3	8
variables)	S_3	4	0	$\boxed{-1}$	4

The variables set to zero appear at the column head – in this case x and y are both zero. The non-zero variables are shown in the row heads of the constraints – i.e. the slack variables take on the values of 10, 24 and 4 because there is no production.

We now move away from the basic feasible solution towards another corner of the feasible region. To do this we exchange a slack variable (previously non-zero) for an output variable (previously zero). Thus we increase output of one of the goods until the innermost constraint is reached.

This process of exchanging variables is done about a *pivot* which is one of the elements of the solution. The location of the pivot proceeds as follows:

Pivot column
Select the column with the largest positive coefficient in the objective function. In the example, both x and y are positive but y is chosen because it is the largest. Thus y becomes non-zero because it has the greatest profit contribution per unit.

Pivot row
Select the row with the lowest *absolute* ratio of the first column (constraints) to the corresponding elements in the pivot column. This identifies which constraint is binding first. In the example the absolute values of these ratios are shown in the final column, as 5, 8 and 4 respectively. This tells us that if we produce only y, the maximum output is 4 units (point d in Fig. 12.3, p. 187).

The pivot is then located as the element -1 and is conventionally emphasised by drawing a circle around that element. Thus the first operation is to introduce the output y up to the point where input C is fully utilised, and the slack variable (S_3) becomes zero.

To find the elements in the second solution we perform operations on the pivot. These operations take the form of four rules which simplify a series of otherwise tedious algebraic manipulations. These are:

1. *New element in place of pivot* – the reciprocal of the pivot element.
2. *Other elements in pivot row* – change the sign of the element and divide by the pivot.
3. *Other elements in pivot column* – divide the element by the pivot.
4. *All other elements* – new element = previous element − (product of corner elements)/pivot.

The fourth operation usually causes most difficulty. The term 'corner element' in the equation refers to an imaginary box drawn from the element being replaced back to the pivot. Two other elements are determined by the box, and these are referred to as 'corner elements'. Thus to replace the zero in the top left-hand corner of first solution we draw a box from this zero back to the pivot -1 (dotted line)

0	4	6
10	−1	−2
24	−4	−3
4	0	⊖−1

The new element becomes (rule 4):

$$0 - \frac{6 \cdot 4}{-1} = 24.$$

Thus for the second solution we implement the rules as follows:

Element in place of pivot $1/-1 = -1$
Pivot row $-4/-1 = 4; -0/-1 = 0$
Pivot column $6/-1 = 6; -2/-1 = 2; -3/-1 = 3$

Other elements $0 - \dfrac{6 \cdot 4}{-4} = 24; \quad 4 - \dfrac{6 \cdot 0}{-1} = 4$

$$10 - \frac{(-2) \cdot 4}{-1} = 2; \quad -1 - \frac{(-2) \cdot 0}{-1} = -1$$

$$24 - \frac{(-3) \cdot 4}{-1} = 12; \quad -4 - \frac{(-3) \cdot 0}{-1}$$

Now we have all elements of the second solution. All we need to remember is that y becomes non-zero and S_3 becomes zero.

SECOND SOLUTION

		x	S_3	*Ratio*
Z	24	4	−6	
S_1	2	−1	2	2
S_2	12	−4	3	3
y	4	0	Ⓐ−1	∞

We can now interpret this second solution. Reading down the first column we see that profit Z is £24. The slack S_1 is 2 units (meaning there are two units of input A unused), slack S_2 is 12 units (of input B unused) and 4 units of y are produced. Reading across the column heads we note that both x and S_3 are zero (no x is produced and all input C is used up).

The coefficients in the first row also have an interpretation. The coefficient under x is positive and indicates that introducing x into production will increase profit. Thus the coefficients in the top row provide a *test of optimality*. If there is a positive coefficient in this row (apart from the first element, which is total profit), then the solution is non-optimal, and profit can be improved by making the corresponding variable non-zero. The coefficient under S_3 has an interpretation we shall discuss later.

Having discovered that the second solution is non-optimal we proceed as before to derive the new pivot element and then implement the pivoting rules (moving to the next corner in the feasible region).

In the table x has a positive coefficient and this is then introduced in place of one of the non-zero variables, i.e. x provides the pivot column.

The pivot row is identified by the lowest absolute ratio of the first column to the pivot column. The lowest ratio is 2, and so we pivot around the element -1. Thus we introduce x up to the point where the first slack variable, S_1, is used up - i.e. we exchange x and S_1.

Using the pivotal rules as before we can now find a third solution; at the third corner of the feasible region.

New element in place of pivot $1/-1 = -1$

Pivot row $-2/-1 = 2; -2/-1 = 2$

Pivot column $4/-1 = -4; -4/-1 = 4, 0/-1 = 0$

Other elements $24 - \dfrac{4 \cdot 2}{-1} = 32; \quad -6 - \dfrac{4 \cdot 2}{-1} = 2$

$$12 - \frac{(-4)(2)}{-1} = 4; 3 - \frac{(2)(-4)}{(-1)} = -5$$

$$4 - \frac{2 \cdot 0}{-1} = 4; \quad -1 - \frac{0 \cdot 2}{-1} = -1.$$

Hence we get the third solution, exchanging x for S_1

THIRD SOLUTION

	S_1	S_3		*Ratio*
Z	32	-4	2	
x	2	-1	2	$\frac{1}{2}$
S_2	4	4	(-5)	$\frac{4}{5}$
y	4	0	-1	4

In this situation, $x = 2$ and $y = 4$, resulting in a total profit of £32. Reading along the top row we note that the optimum is not yet reached, since the co-efficient under S_3 is positive. Thus we can increase profit by reintroducing S_3 into the non-zero variables. S_3 defines the pivotal column. To determine the pivotal row, again consider the ratio of the first-column coefficient to the corresponding element in the pivotal column. This ratio has an absolute minimum for the S_2 row, so the pivot is the element -5. Thus to increase profit we exchange S_3 for S_2. The pivotal operations are performed again about the pivot -5, to move to the next corner of the feasible solution (from c to b In Fig. 12.3, p. 187).

New element in place of pivot $1/-5 = -\frac{1}{5}$

Pivot row $-4/-5 = \frac{4}{5}; -4/-5 = \frac{4}{5}$

Pivot column $2/-5 = -\frac{2}{5}; 2/-5 = -\frac{2}{5}; -1/-5 = \frac{1}{5}$

Other elements $32 - \dfrac{2 \cdot 4}{-5} = 33\frac{3}{5}; \quad -4 - \dfrac{2 \cdot 4}{-5} = -\frac{12}{5}$

$$2 - \frac{2 \cdot 4}{-5} = 3\tfrac{3}{5}, \quad -1 - \frac{2 \cdot 4}{-5} = \tfrac{3}{5}$$

$$4 - \frac{4 \cdot -1}{-5} = 3\tfrac{1}{5}; \quad 0 - \frac{4 \cdot -1}{-5} = -\tfrac{4}{5}$$

FOURTH SOLUTION

		S_1	S_2
Z	33.6	$-\frac{12}{5}$	$-\frac{2}{5}$
x	3.6	$\frac{3}{5}$	$-\frac{2}{5}$
S_3	$\frac{4}{5}$	$\frac{4}{5}$	$-\frac{1}{5}$
y	3.2	$-\frac{4}{5}$	$\frac{1}{5}$

Reading along the first row we note that both coefficients are negative, indicating that an optimal solution has been found. The slack variables S_1 and S_2 are both zero, indicating that inputs A and B are fully utilised.

The optimum solution is to produce 3.6 units of x and 3.2 units of y, yielding a profit of £33.6, the same solution as generated by the graphical method. In this case we also know that at the optimum $S_3 = \frac{4}{5}$ showing that 0.8 unit of input C are not being used. The coefficients under S_1 and S_2 will be interpreted later.

The Simplex method is more powerful than the graphical method since it can handle any number of variables. However, it is considerably more tedious to calculate, but since each *iteration* (process of moving from one solution to the next) follows the same procedure, computer programs have been developed to handle the routine arithmetic involved in achieving the optimal solution.

Minimisation problems
Linear programming is an optimisation procedure that can solve both maximisation and minimisation problems. Minimisation problems can be expressed in the following general form:

Minimise $\quad A = c_1 x_1 + c_2 x_2 + \ldots + c_n x_n$

subject to $\quad a_{11} x_1 + a_{12} x_2 + \ldots + a_{1n} x_n \geqslant b_1$

$$a_{21} x_1 + a_{22} x_2 + \ldots + a_{2n} x_n \geqslant b_2$$

$$\vdots$$

$$a_{m1} x_1 + a_{m2} x_2 + \ldots + a_{mn} x_n \geqslant b_m$$

and $\quad x_1, x_2 \ldots x_n \geqslant 0.$

Here the objective function A is a linear function of x_i and is to be minimised, subject to the m constraints. The only changes in the format compared to the maximisation problem are:

1. A change in the objective function from maximisation to minimisation.
2. A reversal of the inequality signs from less than or equal to ($\leqslant$) to greater

than or equal to ($\geqslant$).

Minimisation problems in two variables can be solved graphically. This will be illustrated by the 'Blending Problem'. Suppose the multi-product firm produces two goods and wishes to produce a blended third product, consisting of the first two goods combined, so that the third product has certain defined characteristics. The the problem is to determine the optimal combination of the first two goods which satisfied the necessary characteristics at minimum cost.

Suppose the firm produces two animal feeds y_1 and y_2 at a constant average cost of £6 and £9 per unit respectively. Each unit of y_1 contains 2 units of starch and 6 units of protein, while each unit of y_2 contains 4 units of starch and 3 units of protein. The firm wishes to produce a third animal feed, y_3, by blending y_1 and y_2, so that each unit of y_3 contains *at least* 3 units of starch and 4 units of protein. Then the problem is to determine which combination of y_1 and y_2 will satisfy these requirements at minimum cost.

The problem can be set out in the standard form as:

Minimise $\quad A = 6y_1 + 9y_2$
subject to $\quad 2y_1 + 4y_2 \geqslant 3 \qquad \left[\begin{matrix} \text{starch} \\ \text{protein} \end{matrix} \right\} \text{requirements} \Bigg]$
$\qquad\qquad 6y_1 + 3y_2 \geqslant 4$
and $\qquad y_1, y_2 \geqslant 0.$

We proceed as before, setting the constraints in *implicit* form, i.e.

$$2y_1 + 4y_2 = 3$$
when $\quad y_1 = 0, y_2 = \frac{3}{4}$
$\qquad\quad y_2 = 0, y_1 = \frac{3}{2}$

and $\quad 6y_1 + 3y_2 = 4$
when $\quad y_1 = 0_1 \qquad y_2 = \frac{4}{3}$
$\qquad\quad y_2 = 0_1 \qquad y_1 = \frac{2}{3}.$

This procedure finds the intercepts of each constraint with the y_1- and y_2-axis and the constraints can then be plotted (Fig. 12.4).

The feasible region is now the area to the right of the outermost constraints, i.e. from *klm* outwards. The area inside this, including the origin is not feasible since the constraints are unsatisfied.

We now introduce the objective function

$$A = 6y_1 + 9y_2,$$

which can be located by choosing a convenient value for A (in this case where $A = 9$).

Then $\quad 9 = 6y_1 + 9y_2$
when $\quad y_1 = 0_1 \qquad y_2 = 1$
and when $\quad y_2 = 0, \quad y_1 = 1\frac{1}{2}$

This is represented on Fig. 12.4 by the outer dotted line. To find the minimum cost point in the feasible region this line is shifted parallel to itself until it just

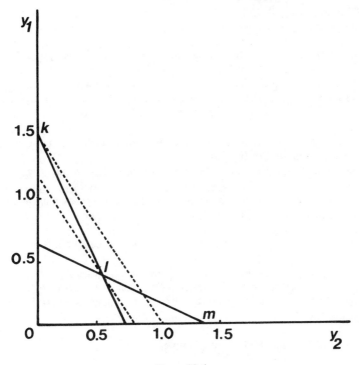

Figure 12.4

touches the feasible region at point *l* in the diagram. This is then the combination of y_1 and y_2 that satisfied the constraints at minimum cost, i.e. where $y_1 = \frac{7}{18}$ and $y_2 = \frac{5}{9}$. Then the two products should be blended in the ratio,[8] $\frac{7}{18} : \frac{5}{9}$ or 7:10.

The total cost of the new product per unit will be:

$$A = (6 \times \tfrac{7}{8}) + (9 \times \tfrac{5}{9}) = £7\tfrac{1}{3}.$$

The graphical method can solve minimsation problems without much difficulty if there are only two variables in the objective function. If there are more than two variables the Simplex method can be used, but the minimisation problem cannot be solved as it stands. Instead, the minimisation problem needs to be transformed into a maximisation problem and then solved in the normal way. To achieve this transformation we need the concept of *duality*.

Duality

To every linear programming problem there is a corresponding *dual* problem with the property that the optimal value of the dual is equal to the optimal value of the original (*primal*) problem. The dual of a maximisation problem is a minimisation problem, and vice versa.

The dual of a primal problem in standard form is found by implementing the following rules:

(1) Change the problem from maximisation to minimisation (or vice versa).

(2) Introduce new variables into the dual objective function so that the number of new variables equals the number of constraints in the primal problem.

(3) The coefficients of the new variables in the dual objective function are formed from the magnitude of the constraints of the primal (read from top to bottom).

(4) The number of constraints in the dual is equal to the number of variables in the objective function of the primal.

(5) The variables in the new constraints are formed from the variables in the new objective function.

(6) The coefficients of the variables in the dual constraints are formed from the coefficients of the variables in the primal constraints (read from top to bottom).

(7) The inequalities are reversed (from less than or equal to, to greater than or equal to; or vice versa).

(8) The constraints of the dual (read from top to bottom) are formed from the coefficients of the primal objective function (read from left to right).

(9) Add the non-negativity conditions for the new variables in the dual objective function.

These rules can be illustrated by an example:

Primal

Maximise $Z = p_1 q_1 + p_2 q_2$
subject to $a_{11} q_1 + a_{12} q_2 \leqslant c_1$
$\qquad\qquad a_{21} q_1 + a_{22} q_2 \leqslant c_2$
$\qquad\qquad a_{31} q_1 + a_{32} q_2 \leqslant c_3$
and $\quad q_1, q_2 \geqslant 0$.

Dual

Minimise $A = c_1 v_1 + c_2 v_2 + c_3 v_3$
subject to $a_{11} v_1 + a_{21} v_2 + a_{31} v_3 \geqslant p_1$
$\qquad\qquad a_{12} v_1 + a_{22} v_2 + a_{32} v_3 \geqslant p_2$
and $\quad v_1, v_2, v_3 \geqslant 0$

Notice that in the primal there are two variables and three constraints and in the dual there are three variables and two constraints.

At the optimum, minimum A = maximum Z, so that by solving the dual we also solve the primal. Note also that the dual of the dual is the primal so that the duality process is symmetrical.

Minimisation problems can now be solved by finding the dual maximisation problem and solving it.

Suppose we have the primal problem:

Maximise $\quad Z = 3x_1 + 2x_2$
subject to $\quad 2x_1 + x_2 \leqslant 5$
$\qquad\qquad x_1 + x_2 \leqslant 3$
and $\qquad x_1, x_2 \geqslant 0$.

This has an optimal solution shown in Fig. 12.5 with $x_1 = 2$, $x_2 = 1$ and $Z = (3 \times 2) + (2 \times 1) = 8$.

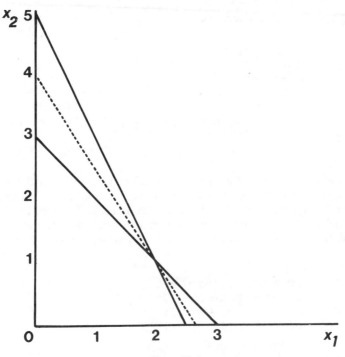

Figure 12.5

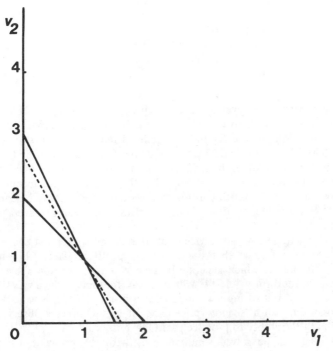

Figure 12.6

The corresponding dual problem is:

Minimise $\quad A = 5v_1 + 3v_2$
subject to $\quad 2v_1 + v_2 \geqslant 3$
$\qquad\qquad v_1 + v_2 \geqslant 2$
and $\qquad v_1, v_2 \geqslant 0.$

The optimal solution to this is shown in Fig. 12.6 and occurs when $v_1 = 1$, $v_2 = 1$, so that $A = 5(1) + 3(1) = 8$.
Then maximum $Z = $ minimum $A = 8$.

Because of the property of equivalent solution complex minimisation problems can be optimised by finding the dual maximisation problem and solving by the Simplex method. Moreover the Simplex method can be extended to solve both the primal and the dual without the need for additional computation.
Consider the original problem solved by the Simplex method.

Primal
Maximise $\quad Z = 4x + 6y$
subject to $\quad x + 2y \leqslant 10$
$\qquad\qquad 4x + 3y \leqslant 24$
$\qquad\qquad 0x + y \leqslant 4$
and $\qquad x, y \geqslant 0.$
This has the following dual

Dual
Minimise $\quad 10v_1 + 24v_2 + 4v_3$
subject to $\quad v_1 + 4v_2 + 0v_3 \geqslant 4$
$\qquad\qquad 2v_1 + 3v_2 + v_3 \geqslant 6$
and $\qquad v_1, v_2, v_3 \geqslant 0.$

The primal problem is given an economic interpretation on page 185 above. The variables x and y refer to the quantities of the two goods produced, while the primal constraints show the input availabilities and requirements to produce the two goods. The coefficients in the objective function represent the per unit profit contribution of each good. The primal problem is to maximise profit subject to the input constraints. Note that the problem takes account of input prices by assuming the profit contribution per unit of x and y to be constant. We saw that this was the situation if output prices were fixed and average cost was constant.

The dual problem assigns a valuation to each input over and above the input price accounted for, so that the maximum profit is effectively 'shared out' between the inputs which generate it. Thus v_i is the premium above the input price, which the firm would be willing to pay for input i, since v_i is the amount which an extra unit of input i would add to profit. Then this valuation is what the economists call a 'shadow price' since it is not directly observable, but a reflection of the ability to produce profitable output.

The dual can be solved simultaneously with the primal by adding slack variables (L_i) to the dual constraints so that these become:

$$v_1 + 4v_2 + 0v_3 - L_1 = 4$$
$$2v_1 + 3v_2 + v_3 - L_2 = 6$$

in our example. The slack variables are negative since these have to be deducted to make the greater than or equal to constraint into a strict equality.

Then we simply add extra labels to the Simplex solutions. These are added to the right-hand side to represent the v_i variables and to the bottom to represent to new (L_i) slack variables. Note that the new slack variables are of negative sign.

The procedure can be demonstrated by example, reproducing tableaux from the Simplex section with the new variables added.

FIRST SOLUTION
(zero variables)

		x	y	
	Z	0	4	6	
(non-zero	S_1	10	−1	−2	v_1
variables)	S_2	24	−4	−3	v_2
	S_3	4	0	⊝−1	v_3

(zero variables)

$$A \qquad -L_1 \qquad -L_2$$
(non-zero variables)

The normal Simplex rules then apply to the combined solution. We pivot around the −1 element in the bottom row. This not only exchanges y for S_3 but also exchanges $-L_2$ for v_3 in the dual.

SECOND SOLUTION

	x	S_3	
Z	24	4	−6	
S_1	2	⊝−1	2	v_1
S_2	12	−4	3	v_2
y	4	0	−1	L_2

$$-L_1 \qquad -v_3$$

We then pivot around the −1 element in the second row, exchanging x for S_1 and $-L_1$ for v_1. This generates the third solution.

THIRD SOLUTION

	S_1	S_3	
Z	32	−4	2	
x	2	−1	2	L_1
S_2	4	4	⊝−5	v_2
y	4	0	−1	L_2

$$-v_1 \qquad -v_3$$

The negative coefficient under S_1 indicates that the optimum has not yet been found so we pivot once more around the element -5 to achieve the fourth solution, which is optimal, exchanging S_3 for S_2, and v_2 for $-v_3$.

FOURTH SOLUTION

		S_1	S_2	
Z	33.6	$-\frac{12}{5}$	$-\frac{2}{5}$	
x	3.6	$\frac{3}{5}$	$-\frac{2}{5}$	L_1
S_3	0.8	$\frac{4}{5}$	$-\frac{1}{5}$	v_3
y	3.2	$-\frac{4}{5}$	$\frac{1}{5}$	L_2
		$-v_1$	$-v_2$	

The coefficients $-\frac{12}{5}$ and $-\frac{2}{5}$ can now be interpreted as the dual solutions for $-v_1$ and $-v_2$ respectively. Thus $v_1 = \frac{12}{5}$, $v_2 = \frac{2}{5}$ and $v_3 = 0$, since it is among the zero variables. Therefore positive shadow prices are assigned to the inputs (A and B) which are fully used, whereas a zero shadow price is assigned to the third input (c) which is not fully utilised at the optimum position. These shadow prices, over and above the input prices accounted for, show the amount by which profit would be increased if there was a single extra unit of that input available.[9] These shadow prices are valuations in the sense that it would be profitable for the firm to pay up to £12/5 extra for an extra unit of input A, since this extra unit would lead to an increase in profit of £12/5.

If this extra unit of A was made available profit would be increased by re-allocating inputs between the two outputs to produce a different combination of x and y. Adding extra input A to either production process would not increase output on its own, since inputs are used in fixed proportions. Rather the extra output would occur from the *reallocation* of inputs between outputs.

Consider again the maximisation problem:

Maximise　$Z = 3x_1 + 2x_2$

subject to　　$2x_1 + x_2 \leqslant 5$

$x_1 + x_2 \leqslant 3$

$x_1, x_2 \geqslant 0$.

This is solved in Fig. 12.5 above, with $x_1 = 2$ and $x_2 = 1$. The dual minimisation problem was found and solved in Fig. 12.6. From this we found that $v_1 = 1$, $v_2 = 1$. These figures can now be interpreted as the shadow prices of the two constrained inputs. If an extra unit of either input was made available, maximum profit increases by 1 unit.

Suppose an extra unit of the second input was made available. Then the second constraint becomes $x_1 + x_2 \leqslant 4$.

This is shown in Fig. 12.7 (reproducing Fig. 12.5) by the shift in the constraints.

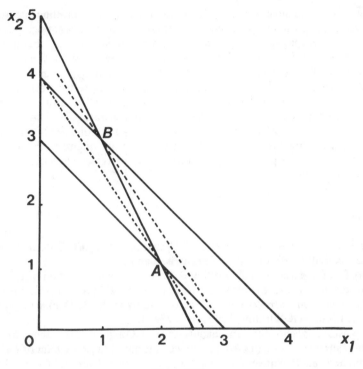

Figure 12.7

We are then able to move the objective function outwards until it just touches the new feasible region at B. This shows the new optimal output combination $x_1 = 1, x_2 = 3$, generating at new profit of $(3 \times 1) + (2 \times 3) = £9$. When we compare this to the previous optimum we see that profit has increased £1, which is the shadow price of input 2.

The important point is that a new output combination becomes optimal. Output of x_1 is reduced, releasing more of *both* inputs which can be used to produce x_2.

The techniques of linear programming have wider application than in the analysis of multi-product firms. Various examples of the sort of problems in which the linear programming approach can be utilised are:

(1) To determine the optimal advertising mix, minimising the cost of various media usage, subject to various audience requirements.
(2) To allocate rationed capital funds between various investment projects to maximise return.
(3) To determine the optimal distribution network, given a number of producing locations and required destinations, subject to the productive capacity and goods requirement of the various locations.
(4) To determine the optimal stock mix, given the various costs and magnitudes of stocked goods, subject to budget constraints and warehouse capacity.

However, to be of practical value the linearity assumptions must be a reasonable approximation to actual business conditions. Other programming techniques have been developed for constrained optimisation under different circumstances. *Integer programming* can solve problems of a similar kind, when the variables in the objective function are discrete rather than continuous; for example, when people are allocated different tasks according to their relative efficiencies to minimise overall time taken to perform these tasks. Obviously a non-integer number of people cannot be allocated to a particular task. *Non-linear programming* deals with situations where the linearity assumptions are unrealistic; for example, when price is a quadratic function of output quantity. For these and other variants of the programming approach the interested reader is referred to specialist texts on operations research.

Further reading

W. J. Baumol, *Economic Theory and Operations Analysis*, 3rd ed. (London: Prentice-Hall International, 1972) chaps. 5 and 6.

R. Dorfman, 'Mathematical or "Linear" Programming: A Non-Mathematical Exposition', *American Economic Review* (Dec 1953) pp. 797–825, reprinted in *Readings in Microeconomics*, ed. W. Breit and H. M. Hockman (London: Holt, Rinehart & Winston, 1969) pp. 173–94.

J. F. Weston, 'The Nature and Significance of Conglomerate Firms', *St. Johns Law Review*, vol. 40 (1970) pp. 66–80, reprinted in *Economics of Industrial Structure*, ed. B. Yamey (Harmondsworth, Penguin Books, 1973) pp. 305–21.

For the definitive study on applications and extensions of the programming approach the interested reader is referred to R. Dorfman, P. A. Samuelson and R. Solow, *Linear Programming and Economic Analysis* (New York: McGraw-Hill, 1958).

Questions

1 'Since the future is unknown, any expansion activity is a gamble.' Comment on this statement, considering how attitudes towards risk determine the direction of expansion activity into new products and/or new markets.

2 'The delineation of products is simple. If the cross-elasticity of demand is unity, the products are the same. If not, they are different.' Discuss.

3 Using the Simplex method solve the following problem:

$$\text{maximise} \quad Z = 2x_1 - 3x_2 + x_3$$
$$\text{subject to} \quad 3x_1 + 6x_2 + x_3 \leqslant 6$$
$$4x_1 + 2x_2 + 4x_3 \leqslant 4$$
$$x_1 + x_2 + x_3 \leqslant 3$$
$$\text{and} \quad x_1, x_2, x_3 \geqslant 0.$$

4 Suppose a firm produces two goods, x_1 and x_2. Each requires three inputs: machine time, labour time and a single raw material. The amount of each input required to produce a unit of each output, together with the amount of inputs available, are given in the following table:

		Product		Input available
		x_1	x_2	
	Machine time	3	3	18
Input	Labour time	1	2	8
	Raw material	2	1	10

Given that the profit contribution per unit of x_1 and x_2 is £6 and £9 respectively, find the output combination that maximises profit, using the Simplex method.
What assumptions are implicit in your answer?

5 A manufacturer produces two products, A and B, using 3 inputs X, Y and Z. To produce one unit of commodity A requires 8 units of X, 5 units of Y and 4 units of Z; to produce one unit of B requires 3 units of X, 4 units of Y and 7 units of Z. The total supply of inputs available in any production period are 24 units of X, 20 units of Y and 28 units of Z. If profit per unit of output obtained on A is £200 and profit per unit of B is £300, what are the levels of output of the two commodities which will maximise profits?

6 Form and solve the dual of the following production problem:

maximise $Z = 2X + 3Y$
subject to $10X + 10Y \leqslant 600$
            $9X + 15Y \leqslant 600$
and $X, Y \geqslant 0,$

where Z is total profit from two products X and Y; production is subject to two input constraints.

Designate the valuations of these two inputs as V_1 and V_2, and solve accordingly. Prove that the solution to the dual is identical to that of the original problem. Interpret the significance of V_1 and V_2.

13
Investment

Introduction

The role of management is to determine the optimal combinations of decision variables to achieve the firm's objective(s). A temporal distinction can be made between utilising the firm's *existing* resources in an optimal manner and determining the *optimal level* of such resources. So far we have concentrated on the first set of decisions, although we have in several chapters referred to factors which span a longer time period (e.g. in relation to cost and demand estimation). It is to an explicit examination of the second set of decisions – the choice of an optimal level of resources at the firm's disposal – that we now turn.

It is again important to note that the investment decision, like pricing, is a means of obtaining the firm's objective(s) rather than an end in itself. The level and type of projects accepted may therefore be different, assuming profit maximisation as a goal, to (for example) projects accepted under Williamson's assumption of maximisation of managerial utility.[1] A common feature in most investment decisions, however, is the desire for profit, although one may argue about whether the firm will necessarily wish to invest in the *most* profitable project. The analysis of the investment decision in this chapter will therefore place particular importance on the profit criteria for decision-making in this area. It is also important to realise that pricing and investment decisions should be considered as *related* rather then separate decisions. The flow of returns to a particular project will partly depend on physical values (e.g. tons of steel produced), but also on the pricing policy in relation to the product (in this case, steel). Thus pricing and investment are both means of attaining an objective, and are particularly related to one another.

Investment can be defined as the acquisition of durable productive facilities, undertaken in the expectation of a future gain. Investment will normally consist of physical capital such as buildings, plant, machinery, equipment, vehicles, etc., but will also include non-physical items such as staff training, which may be regarded as investment in human capital. The value of investment is the potential profit that it allows in the future. Because investment is durable its promised services stretch over many time periods. Consequently there are two problems to be overcome in successful investment appraisal. The first is the need to make *intertemporal* comparisons of money sums. The return generated by an investment is not a single sum but a flow over a time period. We shall see that the correct procedure is *discounting*, which enables comparisons of different sums at different points in time by expressing all future sums in terms of their *present value.* The second problem arises because the future is uncertain. In order to determine the returns to an investment, future costs and revenues must be estimated, with all the attendant problems described in Chaps 7 and 9 (pp. 100, 145). The investment decision is extremely important, with the future performance of the firm largely dependent upon it, and therefore on the accuracy of estimated returns. In many circumstances the best that can be achieved is stochastic estimates, deriving the probability distribution of expected returns. Then the techniques of decision theory (outlined in Chap. 3, p. 35) can be used for decision-making, adjusted by the need to make intertemporal comparisons of money sums.

Types of investment decisions

Investment decisions may be subdivided into three types. The simplest is the decision to invest or not; the accept/reject decision. The criteria used will be to accept all decisions which are profitable.

The second type of investment decision is the ranking of investment projects. This enables a choice to be made by placing investment projects in order of attractiveness, particularly useful when for some reason investment funds are limited. The choice is then made to maximise returns for the given outlay.

The final type of investment decision is the choice between mutually exclusive projects. Some kind of ordering is then necessary independent of the availability of funds. For example, suppose the firm must choose between different methods of producing the same good, requiring different plant and equipment. Then the projects are mutually exclusive because the choice of one precludes the choice of the other.

Finally, we can make a further distinction between investment decisions, into the acquisition of new productive capacity for goods within the experience of the firm, which may be for expansion or replacement, and the decision to invest in new product areas (diversification)[2]. Theoretically all of these decisions can be appraised in the same manner. In practice the distinction between them is in terms of the degree of uncertainty about future returns. The replacement decision is likely to be least uncertain and may often be handled in a routine manner. At the other extreme in the uncertainty range is the diversification decision, involving entry into markets beyond the present experience of the firm. Not only future revenues and costs, but also the reaction of existing producers, will be uncertain.

Traditional appraisal methods

We shall proceed by examining three particular investment appraisal methods which have historically been used extensively and may therefore be called traditional. We shall especially consider the deficiencies of these methods, and then examine the more modern methods of discounting.

Consider two investment projects, *A* and *B*, with the following time profiles of net returns. Both cost initially £100 and return profit streams for four years.[3]

Net profit (£)

	YEAR	0	1	2	3	4
PROJECT	A	−100	50	50	20	10
	B	−100	30	30	40	40

Assume the investment becomes worthless after five years. The problem is to determine which project to choose. The three traditional methods will be considered in the light of this example.

1. THE PAYBACK METHOD

This involves choosing that project which repays the initial investment in the shortest time.

According to this method, project *A* is preferable, as the initial outlay is recovered within two years, while *B* has a *payback period* of three years. The main advantage of this method is its simplicity. Also it builds in *risk-aversion* by valuing early returns highly. However, returns beyond the payback period are ignored, and therefore profitable opportunities may be forgone.

Under-investment is likely because if, for example, the payback period is five years, the firm will not accept projects with an average rate of return of less than 20 per cent in these first five years, even if the cost of capital to the firm is much lower. In addition, if there is positive correlation between risk and expected return, this method may mean adopting only very risky projects, since few low-risk projects give such high return.

2. THE PEAK-PROFIT METHOD

This involves expressing the level of profits in the best year as a percentage return on the sum invested. Therefore project *A* has a peak profit of 50 per cent, while *B* has a peak profit of 40 per cent. *A* is then preferable to *B*.

The peak-profit method assumes that peak profit is a reliable guide to the average profitability of the project, an assumption that can never be universally valid. Some projects reach a peak early; others take a considerable time to reach maximum returns. A project with a low but early profit peak may be more profitable than one with a later but higher peak, because early profits may be reinvested. Therefore maximising peak profit may not lead to overall profit maximisation.

3. THE AVERAGE-PROFIT METHOD

The average-profit level of the project is expressed as a rate of return on the initial investment, and projects ranked accordingly. This method therefore takes account of returns over the project's entire life.

Project *A* has an average profit return of 32.5 per cent and *B* of 35 per cent. Project *B* would therefore be chosen. Notice, however, that the average-profit method may mean a project with greater aggregate returns is given a reduced ranking. Suppose, for example, that project *B* now gave an extra return of £10 in year 5. In any sense of the word the project is more profitable than before, extra revenues being provided. But the average profit of the project is reduced simply because total profits are now spread over a longer period. The average profit of *B* now becomes 30 per cent. The average-profit method is inadequate for comparing projects of different duration.

Suppose, further, that one had a choice of two mutually exclusive projects, one lasting five years with an average return of 10 per cent and one lasting ten years with an average return of 9 per cent. The choice between them requires more information, in particular about investment opportunities available in five years' time. The average-profit method does not allow for profits to be reinvested and therefore attaches more weight to early returns.

Discounting

The last point brings us directly to the need to take explicit account of the timing of returns. This problem was referred to in Chap. 5 (p. 62), where we noted that the solution involved attaching weights to temporally distinct sums. We shall proceed to examine how these weights may be determined.

The basic problem is that £1 today is worth more than the same £1 in a year's time, regardless of inflation because the £1 today can be invested to grow to a larger sum in the future. All the traditional methods fail to take explicit account of this, which can be achieved by *discounting*.

Discounting involves reducing the value of future returns to make them directly comparable to present sums. Suppose that we could invest any money today in the capital market for a return of 10 per cent. Then £1 today would be worth £1.10 p. in one year's time. Conversely we can say that £1.10 p. in a year's time is worth £1 now at a rate of interest of 10 per cent. Therefore £1 in a year's time is worth 91 p. (1.00/1.10) now because 91 p. now could be invested to get £1 in a year's time. Consider £1.21 p. in two years' time. To find its present value if we can invest at 10 per cent, we divide it by $1 + 0.1$ twice, i.e.

$$PV_{1.21} = \frac{1.21}{(1.1)^2} = \text{£}1.$$

This is the logic of discounting, and can be applied in all cases to make intertemporal comparison of money sums. All we do is multiply the future sum by a discount factor (*df*) which depends on the time period involved and the rate at which sums can be invested. In the case of £1.21 in two years' time, as money could be invested at 10 per cent, the discount factor was $1/(1.1)^2 = 0.826$.

To avoid the tedium of calculating a new discount factor for every situation, a table of discount factors is produced as an appendix to this chapter, showing the relevant multiple for common time periods and rates of discount. Then, for example, to find the above discount factor we would examine the row for two years and the column for 10 per cent.

The discounted present value method of investment appraisal involves two useful concepts, those of gross and net present value (GPV and NPV). The gross present value of a flow of sums $A_1 \ldots A_i \ldots A_n$, where A_i is return in year i is:

$$GPV = \frac{A_1}{1+r} + \frac{A_2}{(1+r)^2} + \ldots \frac{A_i}{(1+r)^i} + \ldots \frac{A_n}{(1+r)^n}$$

$$= \sum_{i=1}^{n} \frac{A_i}{(1+r)^i} \text{ , where } r \text{ is the appropriate rate of discount.}$$

Once all future profits have been discounted to their present value this can be compared with the initial outlay to discover if the project is profitable, i.e. to find the net present value, where

$$NPV = GPV - C_0, \; C_0 = \text{initial investment outlay.}$$

If the rate of discount used is the rate of interest a positive net present value shows that the firm can achieve greater profit by investing in the project than by investing in the capital market.

A variant of discounting involves calculating the internal rate of return (IRR) on a project. Instead of discounting at a fixed rate, that rate of discount is found which sets the net present value of the project to zero. We find d such that

$$\sum_{i=1}^{n} \frac{A_i}{(1+d)^i} - C_0 = 0.$$

Thus we can see that when the net present value of a project is zero the internal rate of return is equal to the rate of discount. Projects are accepted if the internal rate of return is greater than the *opportunity cost* of capital, or alternatively ranked according to the magnitude of the internal rate of return. If, for example, the firm must borrow money to undertake an investment, paying a rate of interest of r, any project will be undertaken if the internal rate of return is greater than r.

With either discounting method, no allowance should be made for depreciation because both methods allow for the replacement of capital. In terms of meaning, the net present value of a project is the value of the surplus the firm makes by investing in the project above what it could make by investment at the discount rate. The internal rate of return is the return on capital after allowing for recoupment of the initial outlay. Both methods assume that returns can be reinvested at the discount rate (for example, by investing in financial assets).

The discounting procedure takes no account of uncertainty because the forecast returns are assumed to be achieved. The maximisation of net present value can be extended to maximising expected present value simply by replacing the single estimate of returns by a probability distribution of returns for each year.

Inflation confuses the situation by making present returns more valuable than future returns, *independent* of the reinvestment opportunities of the firm. In investment appraisal it is therefore essential that inflation does not distort the picture. Two solutions can be envisaged.

One method is to anticipate the rate of inflation through the project life, and if this is done the cash-flow estimates reflect the price level assumed to be holding in each year. Assuming the capital market to be perfect the nominal rate of interest is appropriate as the discount rate to be used in this case

The other possibility is to disregard future inflation rates, and work solely in terms of the price level at the present. Time cash flows are based at the price level in time period '0' – the present. In this case the appropriate discount rate is the present *real* rate – i.e. the nominal rate *less* the current level of inflation.

This latter method is obviously more attractive since it avoids having to forecast inflation rates. We need only concern ourselves with forecasting the flows of returns in terms of the present price level. We should, however, remember that in estimating the rate of discount most interest rates are in nominal form and we shall specifically have to deduct the current inflation rate to arrive at the real return. We now turn to discuss the discount rate in more detail.

The discount rate

The choice of an appropriate rate of discount is critical for both discounting methods. It is needed to find present value and as a yardstick against which the internal rate of return can be compared.

We have stated that a project is profitable if the internal rate of return is greater than the opportunity cost of capital. The opportunity cost of capital depends on the circumstances the firm is in. If the firm must borrow to finance investments the *borrowing* rate will be the appropriate rate of discount. Alternatively the firm may find itself with surplus funds, in which case the opportunity cost of capital will be the rate at which the firm could *lend* the funds. If a project is to be financed partly from surplus funds and partly by borrowing, the discount rate reflects the weighted average of the two components. For example, if three-quarters comes from internal funds which had an opportunity cost of r_1 per cent, while the residual quarter is borrowed at r_2 per cent, the appropriate discount rate is

$$(\tfrac{3}{4} \times r_1) + (\tfrac{1}{4} \times r_2)$$

or more generally

$$W_1 r_1 + W_2 r_2,$$

where W_1 and W_2 respectively represent the proportion of internal and borrowed funds.

If we plot the internal rate of return against the level of investment we anticipate a downward-sloping curve – the return on the marginal project decreases. This curve is known as the marginal efficiency of capital (*MEC*).

Assume that the firm must borrow to undertake physical investment and that

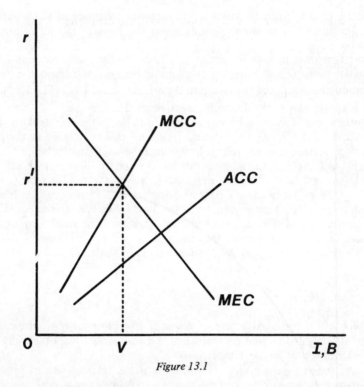

Figure 13.1

the cost of funds increases with the level of borrowing. Then the cost curves for capital (*ACC, MCC*) will be upward-sloping. If these curves are combined we find the optimal level of investment (*I*) or borrowing (*B*) and the optimal discount rate (*r*) (Fig. 13.1).

At *V* the marginal cost of borrowing the last £1 is equal to the internal rate of return on the marginal project. At levels of investment below *V* the last £1 of borrowed money returns more than it costs, while the converse holds for levels of investment above *V*. Then the optimal amount of investment (borrowing) is *V*, and the optimal rate of discount is *r'*.

Therefore we discount at *r'*, and accept all projects with a positive net present value. This is equivalent to accepting all projects with an internal rate of return greater than *r'*.

With a perfect capital market the cost of borrowing would be invariant with respect to the amount borrowed, and the marginal cost of borrowing would equal the average cost of borrowing. The rate of discount would then be the rate of interest and all projects would be undertaken with an internal rate of return greater than this rate of interest.

Comparing net discounted present value and internal rate of return

Consider a firm with an amount of profits. These can either be distributed to shareholders or invested. If the firm decides to invest all or some of these this can be accomplished in two ways: the purchase of *financial* or *productive* assets.

If the firm invests in financial assets it will receive a return equal to the rate of interest. Investment in productive assets yields the internal rate of return on these assets.

Assume two time periods for simplicity. Then the firm will face productive opportunities curve (P) showing the relationship between the amount invested (I_1) in productive assets and the return in the second period (R_2) (Fig. 13.2).

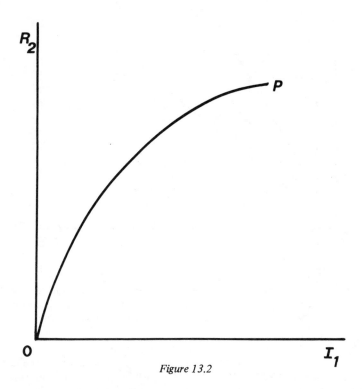

Figure 13.2

The slope of P shows the internal rate of return on the marginal project, while the slope of a line from the origin to the curve shows the average rate of return. The shape of the curve shows that as investment increases the total return increases, but at a decreasing rate.

Assume a perfect capital market, so that the borrowing rate equals the lending rate i. Then the return on financial investment is constant and can be represented by a straight line (F) from the origin with a slope equal to $1 + i$. Figs. 13.2 and 13.3 can be combined to determine the optimal distribution of investment between physical and financial assets.

If the firm invests I_a it will get the same return (R_a) whether it invests in productive or financial assets. At I_a the average rate of return on productive assets is equal to the rate of interest. Beyond I_a the return is greater from financial than from productive assets.

Suppose the firm has the amount I_a to invest. We shall show that the return is higher if the firm invests in both physical and financial assets than exclusively

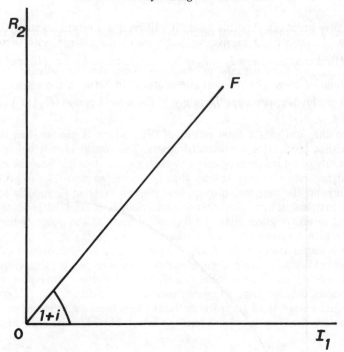

Figure 13.3

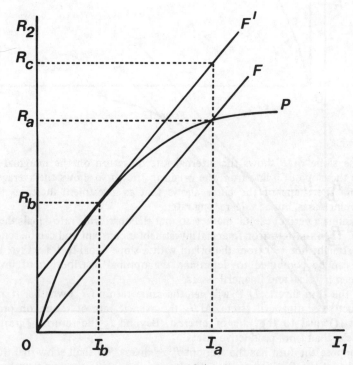

Figure 13.4

in either. To maximise overall return the firm invests I_b in productive assets, for which it receives a return of OR_b.

The firm can then invest $I_a - I_b$ in financial assets and get a return of $R_c - R_b$ on this, since

$$(I_a - I_b)(1 + i) = R_c - R_b.$$

Then the firm gets a total return of OR_c, which is greater than the return from either productive or financial assets. The reason is that beyond I_b the average rate of return on productive assets is greater than for financial assets, but the marginal rate of return is less. Thus I_b is invested physically to get the highest return on the marginal project, and the rest invested financially to get the highest marginal return after this. If more than I_b is invested productively the marginal return is lower than the rate of interest. At the point I_b the internal rate of return is equal to the rate of interest.

The financial assets curves F and F' can be considered as present value lines. The present value criteria is to invest to maximise net present value, i.e. to achieve the highest present value line which occurs at I_b. Therefore, given our assumptions, the two discounting methods are equivalent.

The next stage is to compare methods when these assumptions are relaxed. Suppose our firm has no surplus funds to invest, but still faces productive invest-

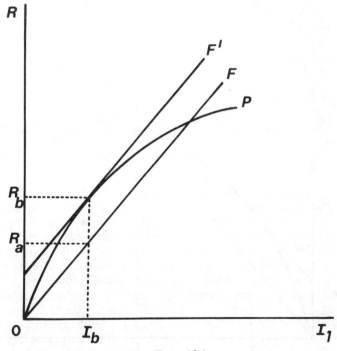

Figure 13.5

ment opportunities. The only way for the firm to exploit these opportunities is to borrow money and pay the rate of interest (Fig. 13.5).

The optimal position for the firm is to invest where the financial opportunities curve is again tangential to the productive opportunities curve (I_b). Here the firm receives R_b on its physical investment and pays R_a on the money borrowed, enjoying a surplus of $R_b - R_a$, which is the maximum possible. The internal rate of return on the marginal project is again equal to the rate of interest (and the net present value of the marginal project is zero). Hence the analysis works equally well whether the firm is a borrower or a lender.

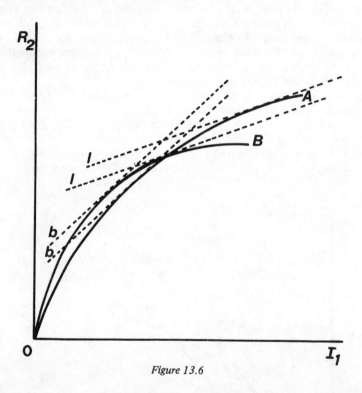

Figure 13.6

However, suppose the capital market is imperfect so that the borrowing rate (b) does not equal the lending rate (l). The rate of interest the firm should use for discounting depends upon whether the firm is a net lender or borrower. Unfortunately whether the firm is a borrower or lender depends upon the funds at its disposal and the amount it wishes to invest, which in turn depends on the rate which it uses to discount. Thus to arrive at an optimal decision we need to know whether the firm is a borrower or lender, which in turn depends on the optimal decision. For example, suppose there are two mutually exclusive investment projects A and B, both with decreasing internal rate of return, but at different rates. Then if the lending rate is used (l) A will be chosen, whereas if the (higher) borrowing rate is used B will be chosen. If the borrowing rate is used A is preferable to B, while using the lending rate B is preferable to A.

Multi-period analysis

As long as investment decisions are independent the future can be considered as a series of two-period combinations. The net-present-value method works through any time period by generalising across any two periods. However, the internal-rate-of-return (*IRR*) method will not generalise, because the nature of the *IRR* changes in multiple-period analysis.

For any normal project the net discounted present value (*NDPV*) is a decreasing function of the discount rate. Thus *NDPV* can be plotted against the rate of discount to get a downward-sloping curve. The point of intersection of this curve with the horizontal axis shows the internal rate of return, because here the *NDPV* of the project is zero. Suppose we must choose between two projects A and B, with the following curves (Fig. 13.7):

The internal rate of return on project A is r_1 and for project B equals r_2. Thus using the *IRR* method, project A would be chosen ($r_1 > r_2$). With the *NDPV* method the choice depends upon the appropriate discount rate (d). If $d > t$ A will be chosen, and if $d < t$, B has the highest present value.

When a project involves more than two time periods there may be more than one internal rate of return which sets the present value to zero. Consider a three-period project, with an initial cost of C_0, and returns A_1 and A_2 in the next two time periods respectively.

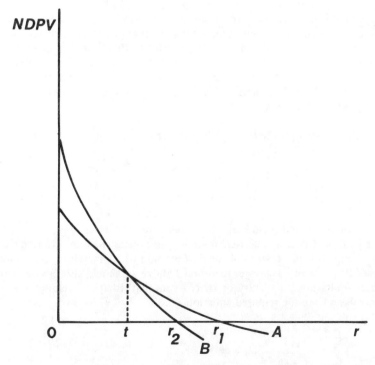

Figure 13.7

Then the internal rate of return is r, so that:

$$\frac{A_1}{1+r} + \frac{A_2}{(1+r)^2} - C_0 = 0,$$

i.e.

$$-C_0(1+r)^2 + A_1(1+r) + A_2 = 0.$$

This is, then, a quadratic equation in r and therefore there may be two values of r which set this equation equal to zero. In general, a n-period problem may have as many as $n-1$ solutions for r. The problem is then to decide which internal rate of return is appropriate for decision-making.

However, the problem is reduced by the mathematical *change-of-sign rule*. This tells us that there will be as many positive solutions as there are changes in the sign of the cash flow. Therefore if all flows after the initial investment are positive there is only one solution for r. Unfortunately this is to confine investment appraisal to a specific type of problem. Generally there may be several changes of sign in an investment project (for example, if the project requires expenditure in the future).

The essence of the problem is that there are a whole set of rates of return for a particular project, with different rates in different periods. The *IRR* method reduces these into one or more average figures.

Suppose the net cash flow for a particular project over three periods is -1, 1, 1. Then there are a number of possible combinations of rates of return over the two time intervals (i_1 and i_2) which result in this flow. For example, the gross return in the second period could be 1.75 of which 0.75 is reinvested to get 1 in the third period. In this case $i_1 = 75$ per cent, $i_2 = 33$ per cent. Various second-period proceeds generate the given cash flow at the rates of return specified in the table below:

Second-period proceeds	Reinvestment	i_1	i_2
2	1	100	0
1.75	0.75	75	33
1.618	0.618	61.8	61.8
1.5	0.5	50	100

Each of these second-period proceeds generates the given cash flow at the specified rates of return. The *IRR* method compresses these into the average of 61.8 per cent. It is this feature of the *IRR* method which may lead to paradoxes.

Apart from the disadvantages mentioned above we should also draw attention to the computational difficulty of *IRR*. As no mathematical technique is available to solve r from the required equation

$$\sum_{i=1}^{i=n} \frac{A_i}{(1+r)^i} - C_0 = 0$$

(given A_i, C_0 and n) the only alternative is to adopt an iterative procedure. This involves a trial-and-error method of using different values of r which come nearer and nearer to zero. This difficulty has, however, been greatly diminished by the use of computer programs for this purpose.

Consequently we can conclude that the *NDPV* method is superior with the proviso that the appropriate rate of discount for the firms financial position must be used.

Uncertainty and investment decisions

As we have seen, discounting proceeds on the assumption the future net returns are known. This is obviously unrealistic and we shall now consider methods of taking account of the uncertainty of future costs and returns.

Table 13.1

Net returns

PROJECT A	year 1	year 2	P_2	year 3	P_3	year 4	P_4
	−1000	500	$\frac{1}{2}$	600	$\frac{1}{2}$	400	$\frac{1}{2}$
		200	$\frac{1}{4}$	400	$\frac{1}{4}$	600	$\frac{1}{4}$
		600	$\frac{1}{4}$	200	$\frac{1}{4}$	100	$\frac{1}{4}$
		$EA_2 = 450$		$EA_3 = 450$		$EA_4 = 375$	
PROJECT B	year 1	year 2	P_2	year 3	P_3	year 4	P_4
	−1000	400	$\frac{1}{2}$	500	$\frac{1}{2}$	400	$\frac{1}{2}$
		440	$\frac{1}{4}$	400	$\frac{1}{4}$	480	$\frac{1}{4}$
		360	$\frac{1}{4}$	360	$\frac{1}{4}$	360	$\frac{1}{4}$
		$EB_2 = 400$		$EB_3 = 440$		$EB_4 = 410$	

There are basically two methods of accounting for uncertainty. The first is the *risk premium* approach, whereby the discount rate is increased in proportion to the uncertainty of the project. Consequently high-risk projects will need to have a higher present value or internal rate of return to be acceptable. The twin problems are how is uncertainty to be estimated and how is the discount factor to be adjusted. Usually the premium added to the discount factor represents a subjective assessment of risk and must in some sense be arbitrary. For the risk-averse investor the risk premium will be an increasing function of the riskiness of the project.

A second approach is possible when the probability distribution of future returns is known or can be estimated with a degree of confidence. Investment projects can then be ranked according to their *expected net present values* (*ENPV*). Consider two projects, A and B, each costing £1000 initially, with the probability distribution of returns as shown in Table 13.1. Assume the appropriate rate of discount is 10 per cent.

Therefore there is a $\frac{1}{2}$ probability that project A will return £500 in year 2, a probability of $\frac{1}{4}$ this return will be £200, and the same probability of this will be £600. The expected return for project A in year 2 (EA_2) is therefore:

$$EA_2 = 500 \times \tfrac{1}{2} + 200 \times \tfrac{1}{4} + 600 \times \tfrac{1}{4}$$

$$= £450.$$

In the same way we can find expected returns for project A in year 3 and year 4, and expected returns for project B in all years.

All we now need to do is multiply each expected return by the appropriate discount factor, to find the expected gross present value ($EGPV$) of each project.

From the table of discount factors, $df_1 = 0.909$, $df_2 = 0.826$ and $df_3 = 0.794$. Therefore the expected gross present value of project A is:

$$EGPV_A = 450 \times 0.909 + 450 \times 0.826 + 375 \times 0.794$$

$$= 1078.5.$$

Similarly $EGPV_B = 1052.58.$

Given that the initial investment cost for each project is £1000, the expected net present value of project A is £78.5 and for project B is £52.58. Therefore project A would be chosen.

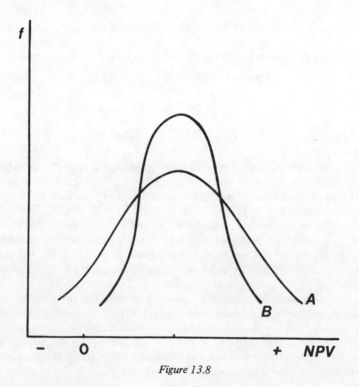

Figure 13.8

However, as we have seen in Chap. 3, the expected-value criteria does not take account of attitudes to risk, even in the more sophisticated present-value form.[4]

If attitudes to risk are important the single calculation of expected net present value is insufficient, as it provides only a measure of central tendency and ignores dispersion. Full information on the net present value for *each* combination of possible outcomes is now necessary, so that a picture of net present value in the form of a frequency (*f*) distribution can be drawn up. For example, in Fig. 13.8 projects *A* and *B* have the same expected net present value, but *A* has higher dispersion. The choice between *A* and *B* will then depend on attitudes to risk on the basis of this information.

If the expected *NPVs and* dispersions are different the position is more complicated still. If *A* has both a higher expected net present value, and greater dispersion, than *B*, we have the situation illustrated in Fig. 13.9.

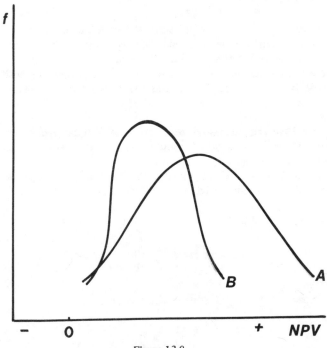

Figure 13.9

Risk-averse decision-makers will be willing to accept some reduction in expected net present value if this reduces the dispersion of possible outcomes. For example, the returns on project *B* are less dispersed than those for *A*. A risk-averse firm may therefore prefer project *B* even though its expected present value is lower.

One analytical technique for decision-making under uncertainty is to compare risky outcomes to their *certainty equivalent*. We anticipate a risk-averse decision-maker to be indifferent between a project with a given expected return and variance and a project with lower expected return but zero variance. Theoretically the set of indifference curves can be found illustrating the trade-off between expected value and variance (see Chap. 3, p. 32). The obvious difficulty is locating the exact position of these indifference curves. If this can be accomplished, the analysis can proceed using expected utility as the decision criteria.

The covariance approach

The firm does not consider projects in isolation, but faces a series of projects which define the *risk structure* of the firm. The risk structure of the firm depends upon two factors: the degree of correlation between projects, and differences in the degree of risk associated with each project.

In determining the risk stucture of the firm there are two important results we must consider.[5] We are now concerned with how new projects will affect the overall riskiness of the firm.

1. If the riskiness of the new project is the same as the riskiness of existing projects, the lower the degree of correlation between projects, the more the new project reduces the overall risk structure of the firm.

2. Where the new project is more risky than existing projects, positively correlated projects will increase overall risks, while negatively correlated projects will reduce risk.

Therefore we have the interesting result that the firm can reduce its degree of overall risk by taking on high-risk projects, as long as these are negatively correlated with existing projects.

Suppose the firm has existing assets whose present value depends on future economic conditions, summarised in the following table:

Existing assets	Boom £	Slump £
Net present value	400	−200
probability	$\frac{1}{2}$	$\frac{1}{2}$

Then the expected net present value of these assets is

$$400 \times \tfrac{1}{2} + -200 \times \tfrac{1}{2} = £100.$$

The firm is considering investing in new plant to produce a good whose demand varies inversely with economic conditions (i.e. has high negative income elasticity).

The present value of the new project can be summarised:

New project	Boom	Slump
Net present value	−220	200

The expected net present value of the new assets is £−10, and therefore, considered in isolation, the project would not be undertaken.

However, there is negative correlation between the projects (when one perform badly the other performs well).

When combined, the projects give a net present value of £180 in periods of boom and £0 in a slump. Therefore the variability of returns is reduced by the addition of the new project, even though by itself it has a negative expected present value. By undertaking the new project the possibility of losses is eliminated.

Capital rationing

Problems for discounting arise when firms are limited in their ability to utilise funds; for example, by administrative problems, government-imposed constraints, etc. The problem is then not whether to invest or not, but to choose projects that obtain maximum benefit from limited funds.

It is unusual for alternative investment projects to have similar durations or require initial outlays. If project lives differ, the optimum decision will require consideration of reinvestment possibilities. For example, if project A has shorter duration than project B it may be possible to reinvest funds released from A more profitably than funds tied up in project B.

If projects differ in the initial outlay required, and investment funds are limited, one solution is to seek to maximise not present value, but present value per £ invested, up to the limit of available funds. Thus projects are ranked according to present value per £ of investment and undertaken until the sum of investment outlays equals the funds constraint.[6]

Taxation

The discounting procedure can take account of the effect of taxation by discounting tax payments and allowances correctly, at the time of payment or relief.

Generally tax laws give assistance to investment projects by allowing relief during the early part of the life of the asset. If the firm is allowed to write-off the asset quickly for tax purposes, the rate of return on the project will be higher than if depreciation allowances are given over the life of the asset. Early tax allowances are more advantageous because early returns are weighted heaviest by discounting.

Appendix Table of discount factors (df) for durations up to twenty years and discount rates up to 20 per cent

Discount rate
Per cent

Year	1	2	3	4	5	6	7	8	9	10	12	14	16	18	20
1	0.990	0.980	0.971	0.962	0.952	0.943	0.935	0.926	0.917	0.909	0.893	0.877	0.862	0.847	0.833
2	0.980	0.961	0.943	0.925	0.907	0.890	0.873	0.857	0.842	0.826	0.797	0.769	0.743	0.718	0.694
3	0.971	0.942	0.915	0.889	0.864	0.840	0.816	0.794	0.772	0.751	0.712	0.675	0.641	0.609	0.579
4	0.961	0.924	0.889	0.855	0.823	0.792	0.763	0.735	0.708	0.683	0.636	0.592	0.552	0.516	0.482
5	0.951	0.906	0.863	0.822	0.784	0.747	0.713	0.681	0.650	0.621	0.567	0.519	0.476	0.437	0.402
6	0.942	0.888	0.838	0.790	0.746	0.705	0.666	0.630	0.596	0.564	0.507	0.456	0.410	0.370	0.335
7	0.933	0.871	0.813	0.760	0.711	0.665	0.623	0.583	0.547	0.513	0.452	0.400	0.354	0.314	0.279
8	0.923	0.853	0.789	0.731	0.677	0.627	0.582	0.540	0.502	0.467	0.404	0.351	0.305	0.266	0.233
9	0.914	0.837	0.766	0.703	0.645	0.592	0.544	0.500	0.460	0.424	0.361	0.308	0.263	0.226	0.194
10	0.905	0.820	0.744	0.676	0.614	0.558	0.508	0.463	0.422	0.386	0.322	0.270	0.227	0.191	0.162
11	0.896	0.804	0.722	0.650	0.585	0.527	0.475	0.429	0.388	0.350	0.287	0.237	0.195	0.162	0.135
12	0.887	0.788	0.701	0.625	0.557	0.497	0.444	0.397	0.356	0.319	0.257	0.208	0.168	0.137	0.112
13	0.879	0.773	0.681	0.601	0.530	0.469	0.415	0.368	0.326	0.290	0.229	0.182	0.145	0.116	0.093
14	0.870	0.758	0.661	0.577	0.505	0.442	0.388	0.340	0.299	0.263	0.205	0.160	0.125	0.099	0.078
15	0.861	0.743	0.642	0.555	0.481	0.417	0.362	0.315	0.275	0.239	0.183	0.140	0.108	0.084	0.065
16	0.853	0.728	0.623	0.534	0.458	0.394	0.339	0.292	0.252	0.218	0.163	0.123	0.093	0.071	0.054
17	0.844	0.714	0.605	0.513	0.436	0.371	0.317	0.270	0.231	0.198	0.146	0.108	0.080	0.060	0.045
18	0.836	0.700	0.587	0.494	0.416	0.350	0.296	0.250	0.212	0.180	0.130	0.095	0.069	0.051	0.038
19	0.828	0.686	0.570	0.475	0.396	0.331	0.276	0.232	0.194	0.164	0.116	0.083	0.060	0.043	0.031
20	0.820	0.673	0.554	0.456	0.377	0.312	0.258	0.215	0.178	0.149	0.104	0.073	0.051	0.037	0.026

Further reading

C. J. Hawkins and D. W. Pearce, *Capital Investment Appraisal* (London: Macmillan, 1972).

J. Hirshleifer, 'On the Theory of Optimal Investment Decision', *Journal of Political Economy*, vol. lxvi, no. 4 (Aug 1958) pp. 329–52, reprinted in S. H. Archer and C. A. D'Ambrosio (eds), *The Theory of Business Finance: A Book of Readings* (New York: Macmillan Co., 2nd ed. 1976).

A. J. Merrett and A. Sykes, *The Finance and Analysis of Capital Projects* (London: Longman, 2nd ed. 1973).

J. Simon, *Applied Managerial Economics* (Englewood Cliffs, N.J.: Prentice-Hall, 1975) part 5.

Questions

1 A firm must choose between investment projects A and B, with the following timed returns:

Return £	Year 0	1	2	3
A	−100	45	45	34
B	−100	50	50	10

Advise the firm, using the following alternative appraisal methods:

(i) payback;
(ii) average rate of return;
(iii) discounting.

Which method do you consider most appropriate?

2 Examine the impact of an increase in interest rates on the investment activity of a profit-maximising firm.

3 Comment on the difficulties raised for discounting by the existence of an imperfect capital market or multi-period returns.

4 'The uncertainty surrounding future costs and revenues interacts with the difficulties of determining the discount rate to make discounting an investment appraisal method of significance only to academic economists.' Discuss this view, comparing the difficulties of discounting with the problems encountered with other appraisal methods.

5 A firm has a choice between two mutually exclusive investment projects, A and B, with the following initial outlays and timed returns:

Project	Initial outlay	Year 1	2	3	4	5
A	800	−100	200	250	400	500
B	1000	300	400	300	200	−100

Assume the firm's opportunity cost of capital is 12 per cent.

(i) Find the discounted net present value of each project.
(ii) Find the internal rate of return on each project.
(iii) Which, if any, of the projects should the firm undertake?
(iv) What assumptions must be made to answer question (iii)?
(v) What would be the effect of choosing either project on the overall risk structure of the firm, given that the firm's existing projects are more risky than, and negatively correlated with, the new project?
(vi) If the returns specified are in terms of constant prices in year 0, and the rate of inflation is 6 per cent, how is your answer to question (iii) affected?

14
Inventories

Introduction

The term 'inventories' refers to stocks held by the firm. These may be of raw materials, intermediate goods or final goods. Usually inventories are treated either as a residual which arises when output does not equal sales or as a minor aspect of the production process. However, we shall see that the decision to hold inventories may be of prime importance to the firm and in certain situations the level of inventories may be the firm's best source of information and strategic variable.

There are considerable costs involved in holding inventories, primarily the opportunity cost of capital tied up in specific forms. Stocks with a high value represent a non-interest-bearing and generally illiquid asset. The opportunity cost of this asset could be productive opportunities, or at the very least the interest forgone on financial assets. In addition to this capital cost there may be cost of storage, not only space but handling, protection both physical and environmental, etc. Generally the cost per unit of holding inventories is assumed constant.

Given that inventories are expensive, why then are they held? The simplest reason for holding stocks is speculation. If the value of the stock is an increasing function of time, it is obviously profitable to hold stock if the increase in value is greater then the holding cost. This is especially true in times of inflation. The decision to hold stocks for speculative purposes will depend on the expectation of price increases. Let the value of stocks held at time t be $P_t I_t$. Assume that the cost of holding stock is i per unit. Then a *nominal* profit on holding stock due to an increase in price to time $t + 1$ will occur if:

$$P_{t+1} \cdot I_t - P_t \cdot I_t > i \cdot I_t$$
$$(P_{t+1} - P_t)I_t > i \cdot I_t$$

i.e. if $\quad P_{t+1} - P_t > i.$

However, it is somewhat unrealistic to assume that stock price will increase and holding cost remains constant. More generally, holding cost per unit will increase from i_t to $i_t + 1$. Then the nominal profit made will equal[1]

$$(P_{t+1} - P_t) - \frac{(i_{t+1} + i_t)}{2} \ I_t.$$

If holding costs have included the opportunity cost of capital tied up in stocks this nominal profit will equal real profit as alternative investment possibilities will have been accounted for. If i only represents actual expenditure the nominal profit made will need to be compared to alternative investment possibilities to discover if an actual economic profit is made. In practice the calculation can only be performed in terms of expected price and holding cost and therefore the return from the speculation in inventories is uncertain.

A more common motive for holding stocks is to enable a constant rate of output. This may involve holding stocks of raw materials or unfinished goods to ensure production is not interrupted by shortages, or it may involve adjusting stock levels when output is not equal to sales to keep output at an optimum level from a production cost point of view. The first decision depends on the probability distribution of future shortages. For example, if the component supply industry is frequently disrupted by industrial relations problems, it may be necessary to hold large stocks of components to enable the final good industry to produce continuously. Generally these *precautionary* holdings per unit of output decrease as output expands and therefore represents an economy of scale. The second decision to hold stocks of final goods to ensure constant output rates is more interesting and depends on both the shape of the firm's average cost curve, and the market structure within which the firm operates.

If the average cost curve is constant over the relevant range there is obviously no production cost advantage from an unchanged output rate. We anticipate, at least in the short run, that the firm's average cost curve will be U-shaped. Then keeping the output rate constant at the bottom of the average cost curve, when demand is temporarily deficient, will be beneficial if the saving in production cost is more than the cost of holding stock. The saving in production cost will depend on the slope of the average cost curve.[2] Note that this assumes that demand will increase in the future, not only to take up the output produced, but also to remove the accumulated surplus of output.

This decision is also related to market structures. In perfect competition demand is certain in the sense that all output can be sold at the given price. Then there is no point in holding stocks of finished goods either in the expectation of future price increases or to maintain an optimal output rate, because at the optimum output rate all can be sold.

Only in imperfect competition is demand uncertain. We know that more will be sold at a lower price, but not how many more. The problem is not just one of estimating the slope of the demand curve (or the elasticity of demand), because it is a fact of experience that sales vary over time even at a constant price. The true demand curve for the product is not a straight line but a series of probable sales at a given price. Then, for example, the demand curve in Fig. 14.1 shows only *expected* sales at various prices.

At the price P_1 expected sales are Q_1. Actual sales may be anywhere in the range Q_a to Q_b with the probability of a particular sales level highest in the neighbourhood of Q_1.

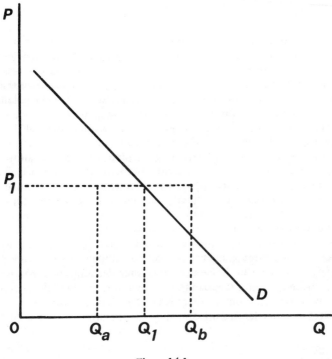

Figure 14.1

The ordinary straight-line demand curve

$$D = a - bP$$

can now be replaced by the more realistc stochastic demand curve

$$D = a - bP + \epsilon,$$

where ϵ is a random variable and $E(\epsilon) = 0$.

Given that demand is a random variable, stocks must be held if profitable sales opportunities are not to be forgone.[3] The optimum level of inventory will depend on the variability of sales and the relationship between revenue and cost. Generally the greater the price-marginal cost difference the more inventories will be held, because the greater the possible allowance for inventory cost.

Often the difficulties of demand estimation may be such that the level of inventory provides the greatest source of demand information to the firm. Increases in inventories of final goods provide evidence that demand is less than output and conversely; by keeping a careful check on stocks of final goods and the stream of orders, the *location* of the demand curve can be identified.

Inventory and oligopoly

Oligopoly is characterised by a tendency for price stability. In oligopolistic situations the reactions of competitors are critical in demand determination. Stocks of finished goods provide the adjustment mechanism necessary when demand does not equal supply. According to Scherer, 'The uncertainties rendering demand curve estimation difficult even under favourable conditions interact with the problems of predicting oligopolistic rival reactions in a manner which undermines the operational utility of the orthodox profit maximisation calculus.[4]

The point is that when demand does not equal output, rather than undertake price changes which may be destabilising, oligopolists prefer to allow short-run adjustments to be made in the level of stocks. However, when stocks fall quickly the possibility of forgone sales opportunities increase pressure for price increases. Similarly when stocks increase quickly the costs of holding stocks mean that pressure for a price decrease increases.

We hypothesise the existence of critical stock levels. Within these limits the inequality of demand and supply is allowed to affect only the level of stocks. When stocks reach the upper limit the cost of holding stock is higher than the cost of a price decrease and price falls, increasing demand and therefore reducing stocks. Conversely, when stocks fall to the minimum limit the cost associated with the possibility of forgone sales is greater than the costs associated with a price increase.[5] Consider Fig. 14.2:

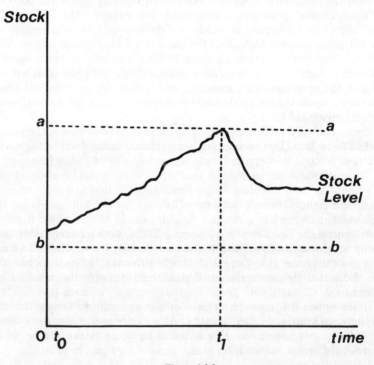

Figure 14.2

From t_0 demand is less than output so that stocks increase. When the stock level rises to the upper limit, a, price falls so that demand increases and stocks fall. This inequality of demand and supply affects the stock level only until a critical level is reached, whereupon price changes. The size of the upper limit will depend upon the cost of holding stock and the decision-maker's perception of the likely effect of a price decrease (other things being equal, the more unfavourable the likely rivals' reactions the higher will be the critical level).

We should note that the nature of the product is also important. Non-durable goods will be less susceptible to inventory holding because of the likely cost of perishability and obsolescence. Thus the above behaviour pattern is anticipated in oligopolistic industries with a homogeneous durable good; for example, oil.[6]

Inventory models

Suppose the firm faces an annual demand of S units per year at a uniform rate, and further suppose that S is known with certainty. Then the strategic implication of inventories discussed above can be ignored, and the problem for the firm is to determine the optimum level of inventories to meet the *known* demand.

Assume that the firm can obtain replacement items instantly from an outside supplier but there are ordering costs involved which depend only on the number of orders and do not vary with the quantity ordered on each occasion.

Then the problem is to balance the cost of ordering against the cost of holding stock, so that total cost is minimised. For example, the firm could order small quantities frequently, in which case the average level of inventory will be low but order costs are high, since the *number* of orders placed is high. Alternatively the firm could infrequently order in large amounts, in which case holding costs will be high as average inventory levels are high, but order costs will be low. We seek the optimum order quantity, which is where the marginal change in order costs equals the marginal change in holding costs, i.e. where total inventory costs are minimised.

Since orders are fulfilled immediately there is no need to place an order until stocks fall to zero. This assumption is unrealistic, for in practice there will be a *lead time* interval between order-placing and receipt of order. However, if this lead time is known the problem is unaltered. Since demand is assumed uniform all we need to do is calculate demand over the lead time and order when stocks fall to this point. Then at the time of delivery, stocks will have fallen to zero (Fig. 14.3).

At time t' the stock level is q, where q is the order quantity. This falls uniformly to zero at time t_2. Assume the lead time is $t_2 - t_1$. Then all we need to do is place the order at t_1 and the stock will arrive at t_2 when stock has fallen to zero. Note that the average level of stock held is simply the order quantity q divided by 2.

To determine the optimum order quantity we need to examine the relationship between costs and order quantity. As we have seen, order costs will fall as the order quantity increases. If q is the order quantity the number of orders placed in the period will be S/q.

Assume the order cost is £a per order. Then total order costs (C_o) will be aS/q.

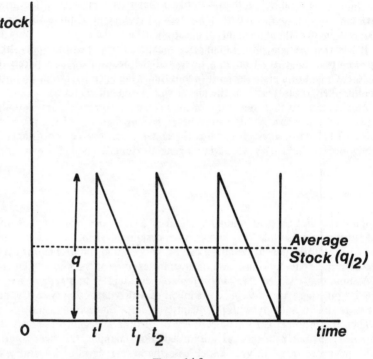

Figure 14.3

Graphically the relationship between total order costs and order quantity then describes a rectangular hyperbola. An increase in order quantity of one unit will *decrease* order costs by an amount given by the derivative of order costs (the marginal order cost) with respect to order quantity.

i.e. if $\qquad C_o = \dfrac{aS}{q}$

marginal order costs $= \dfrac{\mathrm{d}C_0}{\mathrm{d}q} = -\dfrac{aS}{q^2}$.

Thus, given our assumptions, order costs decrease at a decreasing rate as order quantity increases.

Assume that the cost of holding stock is a constant proportion (b) of the value of that stock. We have seen that the average level of stock will be $q/2$. Then if the purchase price of stock is £c per unit, then the average value of stock will be £$cq/2$. Then the holding cost (C_h) will be $bcq/2$. Therefore holding costs increase in proportion to the magnitude of the order quantity. Marginal holding costs are positive and equal to $bc/2$.

Now we have seen that as the order quantity increases, order costs fall and holding costs increase. The point of minimum cost will be where the increase in holding cost just equals the decrease in order costs. This position defines the optimum order quantity q^*. If more than q^* is ordered, holding costs rise more than order costs fall, and total cost increases.

If less than q^* is ordered, increasing quantity ordered will reduce order costs by more than holding costs are increased, and therefore total costs fall as q increases. Graphically the relationship between total cost and order quantity can be plotted (Fig. 14.4).

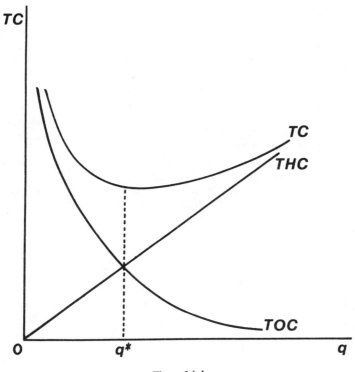

Figure 14.4

It is a peculiarity of this particular model that the optimum order quantity occurs at the point where total order costs equals total holding costs. The *determining* feature of this equilibrium is that here marginal order cost is equal and opposite to marginal holding cost.[7] Thus to determine q^* we merely equate marginal order costs $(-aS)/q^2$ with the negative of marginal holding cost $(bc)/2$ and solve for q.

i.e. if $\qquad \dfrac{bc}{2} = \dfrac{aS}{q^2}$

then $\qquad q^* = \sqrt{\dfrac{2aS}{bc}}$ defines the optimum order quantity

The optimal average inventory level is then $q*/2$, and the optimum number of orders per period is simply $S/q* = n$. The interval between orders is then just the total time period divided by n. Note that optimum reorder quantity increases with demand, but at a slower rate. Thus, if demand doubled, optimum order quantity would increase by a factor of $\sqrt{2}(= 1.414)$. As we would expect, optimum reorder quantity increases as order cost (a) increases since less orders will be made, and decreases with holding costs.

Algebraic formulation

It will be useful to demonstrate an alternative method of finding the optimum order quantity $q*$. To do this all we need is the total cost function, which is then minimised.

Total cost will consist of the sum of three components. The first is simply the stock purchase cost, and is equal to total demand (S) times stock price per unit c. Total order costs are simply $(Sa)/q$, and total holding costs $(cbq)/2$.

Let T equal total cost. Then $T = Sc + (Sa)/q + (cbq)/2$.

The first cost component is the stock purchase cost and is independent of the order quantity. The second and third components (order costs plus handling costs) form the *acquisition* cost of the stock.

We seek q to minimise T. We find the derivative of T with respect to q, set equal to zero and solve. This identifies a turning-point which we ensure is a minimum by considering the second derivative.

$$\frac{dT}{dq} = -\frac{Sa}{q^2} + \frac{cb}{2}.$$

If this equals zero

$$q^2 cb = + 2Sa$$

$$q* = \sqrt{\frac{2Sa}{cb}},$$

which is the same result as we achieved using the marginal approach.[8]

This result can now be substituted into the equation for total cost T to find the minimum total cost.

$$T* = Sc + \frac{Sa}{\sqrt{2Sa/cb}} + \frac{cb}{2}\sqrt{2Sa/cb}$$

$$T* = Sc + \sqrt{2Sacb}.$$

Thus minimum total cost is the sum of stock purchase cost and the second term which is referred to as the minimum acquisition cost (*MAC*).

We can now consider the effect on cost of ordering a quantity different from this optimal amount. Suppose for some reason a quantity K times this optimal reorder quantity is ordered. Then the cost of this (T') will be

$$T' = Sc + \frac{cb}{2} Kq^* + \frac{Sa}{Kq^*}.$$

Substituting

$$q^* = \sqrt{\frac{2Sa}{cb}}$$

$$T' = Sc + \frac{cb}{2} \sqrt{\frac{2Sa}{cb}} \cdot K + \frac{1}{K} \cdot \frac{Sa}{\sqrt{2Sa/cb}}$$

$$= Sc + K \left[\sqrt{\frac{Sacb}{2}} \right] + \frac{1}{K} \left[\sqrt{\frac{Sacb}{2}} \right]$$

$$T' = Sc + \left(K + \frac{1}{K} \right) \sqrt{\frac{Sacb}{2}}.$$

Note that if $K = 1$, so that the optimal quantity is ordered, $T' = Sc + \sqrt{2Sacb}$, which is the same result as before.

Now we can see how the acquisition cost varies with K. In particular, the acquisition cost when $K = \frac{1}{2}$ is the same as when $K = 2$ (Fig. 14.5).

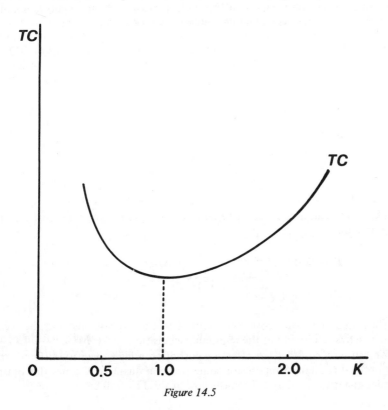

Figure 14.5

If an amount Kq^* is ordered, we can find the *increase* in costs compared to when q^* is ordered, simply by subtracting T^* from T'

$$= \left(K + \frac{1}{k} - 2 \right) \sqrt{\frac{Scab}{2}}$$

$$= \frac{(K-1)^2}{2k} \sqrt{2Scab}.$$

Therefore, if K times q^* is ordered, the associated increase in costs is $(K-1)^2/2$ times minimum acquisition cost. This is particularly useful when discounts are offered for ordering in large quantities, for then the increase in costs can be compared to the benefit of the discount to see if it is worthwhile taking advantage of the discount.

An example

So far we have considered optimal inventory policy in abstract algebraic terms, but this can also be illustrated by a numerical example. Suppose our firm faces an annual demand of 270,000 units per year. The stock cost-price is £12 per thousand units, with a cost of ordering of £2 and a cost of holding stock of 15 per cent of average stock value per annum. We seek the optimum order quantity and the minimum acquisition cost. Suppose, further, that the manufacturer is prepared to offer a discount of d per cent for stock bought in lots of 100,000. How high must d be for the discount to make ordering in these lots worth while? Using the above notation, $S = 270$ (thousands), $a = 2$, $b = 0.15$ and $c = 12$ (per thousand).

We saw that

$$q^* = \sqrt{\frac{2aS}{bc}}$$

$$= \sqrt{\frac{2(270)(2)}{0.15(12)}}.$$

Therefore the optimum order quantity = 25 (thousand) units.

The minimum acquisition cost is given by the formula:

$$MAC = \sqrt{2Sacb}$$

$$= \sqrt{2(270)(2)(0.15)(12)}$$

$$= £44.09.$$

No other order quantity will give a lower acquisition cost. Note that the annual number of orders will be $270/25 \simeq 11$ and the average inventory level will be 12,500.

The discount is offered for purchase in lots of 100,000 which is *four* times the optimum reorder quantity. We saw that the increase in acquisition costs when a multiple of K times the optimum order quantity was ordered was

$$\frac{(K-1)^2}{2K}\sqrt{2Sacb}.$$

If $K = 4$, acquisition costs will increase by $9/8$ times MAC,

i.e. by $\quad 44.09 \, (9/8) = £49.60.$

This is equal to an increase in the *purchase* cost of stock of

$$\frac{49.60}{12\,(270)} = 1\tfrac{1}{2} \text{ per cent.}$$

Therefore if the discount is greater than $1\tfrac{1}{2}$ per cent of stock price the reduction in cost associated with the discount will be greater than the increase in cost due to ordering more than the optimum level.

We have achieved specific answers to the questions of optimum order quantities and the average inventory levels by making particular assumptions about demand and cost conditions. In particular the assumption of uniform and known demand is most unrealistic and robs inventories of any strategic importance. An approach to inventory control when the probability distribution of future sales is known is outlined in Chap. 3 (p. 24) as an example of decison-making under uncertainty. The most we can say is that if demand is uncertain an optimum inventory policy must take account of the likelihood of running out of stock and therefore forgoing potential sales (or production), and the opportunity cost of these events. If the cost of 'stock-out' is high the optimum policy for the firm is likely to be to hold some kind of 'buffer stock' in reserve. Similar problems arise when the lead time between order placement and fulfilment is uncertain.

The particular cost functions we have assumed are probably considerably simpler than their real-life counterparts. In particular both order costs and holding costs may be increasing functions of the quantity ordered. For example, suppose that holding costs vary with the cube of the average level of inventory. At low inventory levels holding costs are low but these increase rapidly as higher stock levels are reached.

For example, suppose

$$C_h = cd(q/2)^3, \text{ where } d \text{ is a constant.}$$

If ordering costs remain the same total cost becomes

$$T = Sc + \frac{Sa}{q} + \frac{cdq^3}{8}.$$

Minimising as before:

$$\frac{dT}{dq} = -\frac{Sa}{q^2} + \frac{3cdq^2}{8} = 0$$

$$q^* = \sqrt[4]{\frac{8Sa}{3cd}}.$$

Thus the analysis is capable of handling various cost functions,[9] as long as these can be pre-specified, if only at the expense of greater complexity.

A further problem we have partially handled is that of the stock purchase price varying with the quantity purchased. This can be accommodated by letting price be a function of quantity ordered in some specific way.

However, in practice the specific form of this function may be stochastic or even unknown.

Despite these difficulties we believe that inventory control is a fundamental requirement of successful business behaviour. In fact, many forms of business enterprise, such as the retailer or wholesaler, may be considered as inventory systems themselves, with their prime activity being the purchase of goods in large quantities, which are then resold in smaller lots.

Further reading

M. H. Agee, R. E. Taylor and P. E. Torgersen, *Quantitative Analysis for Management Decisions* (Englewood Cliffs, N.J.: Prentice-Hall, 1976) chaps 10–11.

F. M. Scherer, *Industrial Pricing: Theory and Evidence* (Chicago: Rand McNally, 1970) chap. 1.

Questions

1 Examine the impact of market structure on the stock-holding decisions of the firm.

2 A company uses raw materials at a rate of 30 tons per year. The purchase cost is £30 per ton, order cost £10 per order, and stock-holding cost 20 per cent per annum.

  (i) Find the economic order quantity and minimum acquisition cost.

  (ii) The firm is offered a discount of 2 per cent of the purchase cost if it orders in lots of 15 tons. Is it worth accepting the discount?

  (iii) As a result of external factors the purchase price of the raw material increases to £40 per ton. However, at the same time new technology reduces the stock-holding cost. If the optimum number of orders stays the same as in question (i), what must the new holding cost fall to?

3 'The most economical point as regards total inventory costs is at the point where ordering costs are the same in amount as carrying costs'. (LEVIN and KIRKPATRICK.)

'As a matter of fact it is accidental that ordering costs equal holding costs at the minimum total cost'. (AGEE *et al.*)

Discuss the assumptions implicit in these two statements, indicating which opinion you regard as correct. How important is inventory policy for the modern oligopolistic firm?

15
Conclusion

By this stage we hope that the reader has been convinced of the intrinsic value of Managerial Economics as an object of study. At the same time we have tried to link the academic content to practical issues – not in the sense of preparing the reader so that he is now able to confidently pronounce on business problems, but in the sense he is aware of the sort of concepts and method of thinking that should lead to better decisions.

As with any text there are a number of topics that have been omitted to keep its length within reasonable bounds. Perhaps the most obvious omission is explicit discussion of decision-making in public utilities. A rigorous and comprehensive treatment of this would have probably doubled the length of the book. However there is much that is retained which is relevant. For whatever the objectives of the enterprise these will be better accomplished by using resources efficiently. For example, planning for the provision of public services involves estimating future demand and cost conditions in order to achieve maximum provision from limited resources.

The penalty to be paid in attempting to be comprehensive is that scant justice is given to other subjects which may be important. Although Managerial Economics has a firm base in economic theory, other disciplines are relevant to the study of business decisions. There could be much to be gained from undertaking study of mathematics, operational research and the whole host of approaches loosely termed 'management science'.

However for many students this book can be treated as self-contained. For them it is perhaps optimal that they seek to combine their knowledge of theoretical principles with practical experience. But a word of caution is necessary. The best economist in the world is of little value to the firm if he fails to communicate effectively and sympathetically with those responsible for business decisions. The ability to do this is an essential element of the 'art' of management.

Notes and References

1. In a famous example, Carnegie used to estimate future demand for steel by counting the number of chimneys issuing smoke in Pittsburgh.

CHAPTER 2

1. This reads: 'Total revenue is a function of output.' The letter f is conventionally used, but any other letter would suffice.
2. Averages themselves may be difficult to find, even if totals are known, if output is of more than one kind.
3. Strictly speaking, where $\Delta x = 1$ unit.
4. Mathematically

$$\frac{dy}{dx} = \mathop{\Delta x \to 0}^{\text{limit}} \frac{\Delta y}{\Delta x}.$$

5. The proof of all these rules of differentiation is given in Alpha C. Chiang, *Fundamental Methods of Mathematical Economics*, 2nd ed. (Tokyo: McGraw-Hill, Kogakusha, 1974) chap. 7.
6. Similarly if $y = u - v$
$$\frac{dy}{dx} = \frac{du}{dx} - \frac{dv}{dx}.$$

7. Implicit in the concept of a derivative is the assumption that x is continuous, i.e. we can produce $0.5, 0.1, 0.001$, etc., units of x.
8. As total revenue equals price times output, this is equivalent to the demand function $P = 6 - x$. Then total revenue $= Px = (6 - x)x = 6x - x^2$.
9. Mathematically, $x = -2$ gives the minimum of this function, as $(d^2 \Pi)/dx^2$ is positive at this point.
10. The symbol ∂ is used rather than d to refer to the partial, rather than the total, derivative.
11. The modern technique of linear programming, however, can deal with inequality constraints. See Chap. 12.
12. This is a maximum as $d^2 \Pi/dy^2 = -8$.

CHAPTER 3

1. J. Wiseman, 'Costs and Decisions'. Paper presented at Association of University Teachers of Economics Conference at York, 1978, (forthcoming).

2. To concentrate attention on essential aspects of decision-making, a number of simplifying assumptions have been made throughout this example, e.g. only three possible levels of sales are considered.

3. This precludes the possibility of stocking bread for more than one day, which we have removed by assumption.

4. With more durable goods the cost of holding stock must be considered. This is another type of decision problem (see Chap. 14).

5. This utility function corresponds to diminishing marginal utility of money. The marginal utility of money = $\Delta U/\Delta M$, which is the slope of the utility function.

6. An indifference curve shows combinations of characteristics that yield the same total utility.

See R. G. Lipsey, *An Introduction to Positive Economics*, 3rd ed. (London: Weidenfeld & Nicolson, 1972) pp. 173–80.

7. This is a decision-theory convention. The economist would regard losses as having negative utility, but this can create problems for the approach adopted here.

8. This section is quite complicated and may be omitted without loss of continuity.

CHAPTER 4

1. Capital gains on sale of assets by a firm give rise to profits which are in a rather different category from those profits arising from the normal activities of the firm in producing goods and services.

2. Throughout this chapter we are concerned only with the accountant in his role of correctly recording monetary items. We are not concerned with how accountants may interpret these amounts in practice. However, there is evidence that such interpretations are made on the basis of historic cost.

3. *Inflation Accounting*: Report of the Inflation Accounting Committee; Chairman, F. E. P. Sandilands (London: H.M.S.O., 1975).

CHAPTER 5

1. We should note that some economists, notably Professor Milton Friedman, would deny the importance of realistic assumptions in formulating theories. In essence he says that a theory is only to be judged by its predictive power, and it is sufficient for the firm to act 'as if' it were maximising profits. Whether it actually wants to maximise profits is irrelevant and hence not worthy of employing economists' time (see M. Friedman, *Essays in Positive Economics* (Chicago: University of Chicago Press, 1935) pp. 3–43.

2. The values to be attached to these weights, as well as the whole concept of present value, are discussed in Chapter 13.

3. A. A. Berle and G. C. Means, *The Modern Corporation and Private Property*, rev. ed. (New York: Harcourt, Brace & World, 1967).

4. J. K. Galbraith, *The Affluent Society*, 2nd ed. (Harmondsworth: Penguin Books, 1970); J. K. Galbraith, *The New Industrial State*, 2nd ed. (Harmondsworth: Penguin Books, 1975).

5. In many cases the main shareholders, directors and managers would be the same individuals. In other cases they would be closely associated.

6. W. J. Baumol, *Business Behaviour, Value and Growth* (New York: Macmillan Co., 1959; rev. ed. New York: Harcourt, Brace & World, 1967).

7. This is at the point of unit elasticity on the demand curve – see Chap. 7 (p. 98) – total revenue of OT' is generated.

8. O. E. Williamson, 'A Model of Rational Managerial Behavior', in *A Behavioral Theory of the Firm*, ed. R. M. Cyert and J. G. March (Englewood Cliffs, N.J.: Prentice-Hall, 1963).

9. It is formulated in mathematical form and the interested reader is referred to Williamson, op. cit., for greater detail.

10. R. L. Marris, 'A Model of the Managerial Enterprise', *Quarterly Journal of Economics*, vol. 77 (1963) 185–209.

11. See Marris, op. cit., for further details.

12. H. A. Simon, 'A Behavioural Model of Rational Choice', *Quarterly Journal of Economics* (Feb 1955) pp. 99–118.

13. R. M. Cyert and J. G. March, *A Behavioral Theory of the Firm* (Englewood Cliffs, N.J.: Prentice-Hall, 1963).

14. This has links with Williamson's concept of 'managerial slack', discussed previously.

CHAPTER 6

1. Under certain conditions the firm may be able to influence the external environment by planning, advertising and political activity (see Chap. 10, p. 153).

2. We should also note the possibility of physically identical goods being perceived as *different products* by the public. For example, a certain physical good may be manufactured under brand label X for the general market, and manufactured under license to a retailer who will sell it under an own brand of Y. It may well be the case that consumers do *not* see Y as a close substitute for X, especially if they are not competitively displayed in the store.

3. A further complication is that the price charged to the retailer is often arrived at *indirectly* by a discount from the retail price to the consumer. Hence the demand curve itself is related to final retail prices in a complex way. This is discussed in more detail in Chap. 11 (p. 174).

4. There may be further complications in regard to tax – e.g. delay or relief on corporation tax on specific investment expenditure – e.g. setting up new plant and equipment in areas of high unemployment where the Government gives tax incentives.

5. Ownership by a firm of a given area often does not carry the legal right of ownership of minerals under the area, or any right of extraction.

6. See A. Koutsoyiannis, *Modern Microeconomics*, 2nd ed. (London: Macmillan, 1979), chap. 6: 'Monopoly', pp. 177–9.

7. This is comprised of the aggregate of firms' marginal cost curves.

8. See Chap. 4, p. 49, for discussion on this point.

9. SAC_2 is the short-run average cost curve associated with the optimal plant size.

10. A similar difficulty in respect of monopoly was discussed earlier in this chapter (p. 77).

CHAPTER 6 – APPENDIX

1. This is a two-person zero-sum game, since the gains for one are equal the losses for the other. Both cannot gain or both lose.
2. The problem can also be solved by linear programming (see Chap. 12, p. 184).
3. The modulus symbols $|x|$ refer to the *absolute* value of x. Therefore if $x > 0$, $|x| = x$, and if $x < 0$, $|x| = -1$ times x.
4. The decision theory of Chap. 3 (p. 24) can now be seen as a game against nature, with events interpreted as the moves of nature. However, in this situation the maximin criteria may be inadequate, as it is inappropriate to assume that nature would react in the worst possible way.

CHAPTER 7

1. See, for example, W. Duncan Reekie, *Managerial Economics* (Oxford: Alan, 1978) p. 117.
2. It should be obvious that an unconstrained sales-revenue maximiser would operate where $Ep = 1$.
3. This problem is not specific to price elasticity, but applies to all elasticity measures.
4. This problem is discussed more explicitly in the section on multi-product pricing (see Chap. 11, p. 169).
5. Alternatively the 'raw' data can be adjusted to take account of seasonal or cyclical variations.
6. For example, see Julian Simon, *Applied Managerial Economics* (Englewood Cliffs, N.J.: Prentice-Hall, 1975) pp. 304–7.
7. The method of least squares is adequate in providing a straight line of best fit through the observations. However, there are circumstances where the linear approach is inadequate and polynomial functions (for example, quadratic or cubic) must be estimated. The procedure is then more difficult and is more fully described in Alpha C. Chiang, *Fundamental Methods of Mathematical Economics*, 2nd ed. (Tokyo: McGraw-Hill Kogakusha, 1974).
8. Thus $\bar{D} = (\Sigma D)/n$ and $\bar{P} = (\Sigma P)/n$.
9. We would now have four equations to solve simultaneously for the four parameters α, β_1, β_2 and β_3. For a more detailed explanation of multiple regression, see K. A. Yeomans, *Statistics for the Social Sciences*, vol. 2 (Harmondsworth: Penguin Books, 1973) pp. 191–234.
10. The conditions for identification are discussed in more detail in Baumol, *Economic Theory and Operations Analysis*, 3rd ed. (London: Prentice-Hall International, 1972) appendix to Chap. 10.
11. See, for example, M. Dutta, *Econometrics* (Cincinnati: Southwestern Publishing Co., 1975) chap. 4, on the problems of serial correlation and heteroscedasticity.
12. There are other supplementary tests of the goodness of fit of a regression equation. These can be found in any intermediate statistical text.
13. The least-squares method of estimates is too complicated to be used for the logistic function. The 'three-points method' is normally used to estimate values of a, k and b (see, for example, Yeomans, op. cit., chap. 5). The functional forms outlined above are by no means exhaustive.

14. One of the problems of market experiments is that unless the experiment is performed for long enough only the first two stages may be reported, resulting in misleading sales projections.

15. For a more comprehensive discussion of estimate appraisal see H. Theil, *Applied Economic Forecasting* (Chicago: Rand McNally, 1966).

CHAPTER 8

1. The isoquant is convex since a concave isoquant would represent *technically* inefficient production methods, i.e. production technique involving more of *all* inputs for a given output level compared to an alternative technique.

2. For example, take output Q_1 and techniques T_1 and T_2.

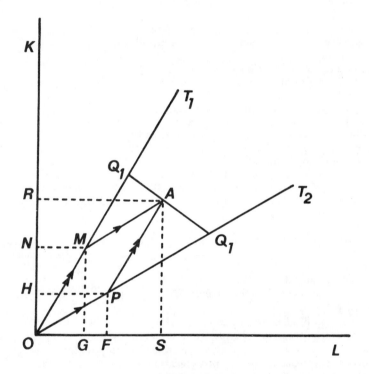

Figure 8.9(a)

A point A (involving $0R$ of capital, and $0S$ of Labour) is possible via factoring $0A$ into its constituent vectors $0M$ and $0P$ using the Parallelogram Law of vector addition. Thus $0N$ of K and $0G$ of L on T_1, plus $0H$ of K and $0F$ of L on T_2 will give the required output Q_1 with total input use $0R$ of K and $0S$ of L.

3. Except in the rare case of the relative cost of K and L being equal to the slope of a portion of the isoquant – in which case there are multiple solutions on the 'flat' portion, rather than a unique corner solution.

4. Except in the rare case where the cost of labour and capital is equal to the

slope of the isoquant, and hence all combinations (i.e. any technique) are optimal.

5. This is a multiplicative production function analogous to the exponential function described in Chap. 7 (p. 108).

6. These probabilities are calculated using the binomial distribution introduced in Chap. 3. Denote by p the probability of each man not being absent ($p = 0.9$). Then $q = 1 - p = 0.1$ We wish to find the probability of at least 10 men being available if 11 are employed. Then $x = 10$, $n = 11$.

$$P(x \geqslant 10) = P(x = 10) + P(x = 11)$$
$$= {}^{11}C_{10}(0.9)^{10}(0.1)^1 + {}^{11}C_{11}(0.9)^{11}(0.1)^0$$
$$\approx 0.7.$$

CHAPTER 9

1. From Chap. 2 (p. 10) the slope of the total cost function is equal to marginal cost. Thus if marginal cost is determined, the slope of the cost function is also determined.

2. For a fuller explanation see Chap. 8, p. 124.

3. In fact, for the mathematically initiated, average fixed cost describes a rectangular hyperbola.

4. This provides us with the justification for 'standby tickets' at greatly reduced prices. Suppose the aircraft has a capacity for 200 passengers and 170 seats filled at time of take-off. Then as long as the standby ticket price is more than £8.00, selling standby tickets will increase total profit (as long as demand for standard tickets is not affected).

5. A. A. Alchian, 'Costs and Outputs', in *The Allocation of Economic Resources*, ed. M. Abramovitz (California: Stanford University Press, 1959), reprinted in *Price Theory*, ed. H. Townsend (Harmondsworth: Penguin Books, 1973) pp. 228–49.

6. Ibid. p. 233.

7. Note that because costs are incurred at different time intervals they are here expressed in *present value* terms (see Chap. 13 (p. 207) for a discussion of present value).

8. Alchian, op. cit., p. 242.

9. The differences between economists' and accountants' cost concepts are discussed in Chap. 4.

10. Joel Dean, *Managerial Economics* (Englewood Cliffs, N.J.: Prentice-Hall, 1951) p. 260. Others, notably J. Wiseman, have forcefully argued that opportunity cost is a subjective concept, and therefore impossible to record. 'Costs and Decisions'. Paper presented at Association of University Teachers of Economics Conference at York, 1978 (forthcoming).

11. J. Johnston, *Statistical Cost Curves* (New York: McGraw-Hill, 1960).

12. C. A. Smith, 'Empirical Evidence on Economies of Scale', in *The Theory of the Firm*, ed. G. C. Archibald (Harmondsworth: Penguin Books, 1971) p.28.

CHAPTER 10

1. D. Dunbar, *Advertising: Facts and Figures*. Paper No. 8 of series 'The Case for Advertising' (London: J. Walter Thompson, 1976).

2. Factory cost, administration, royalties, etc.

3. National Board for Prices and Incomes, Report No. 113, Cmnd 4066 (London: H.M.S.O., 1966).

4. See Table 10.1 for a comparison of the importance of advertising for different products.

5. This is equivalent to assuming that the supply curve for the good is perfectly inelastic, so that when advertising shifts the demand curve, the same quantity is sold at a higher price.

6. The general Baumol sales-revenue maximisation model is introduced in Chap. 5, p. 66).

7. I.e. total revenue is a positive but decreasing function of advertising.

CHAPTER 11

1. Note that the pricing decision only occurs in markets which are *imperfectly competitive*. Under perfect competition price is *given*, and the only element to be decided by the firm is the quantity to be produced.

2. This data problem also applies to other market structures: oligopoly, monopolistic competition, etc.

3. For an excellent concise discussion see F. M. Scherer, *Industrial Pricing: Theory and Evidence* (Chicago: Rand McNally, 1970) chap. 4.

4. Probably the most influential of these was the study by R. L. Hall, and C. J. Hitch, 'Price Theory and Business Behaviour', *Oxford Economic Papers* (1939) pp. 12–45, reprinted in *Oxford Studies on the Price Mechanism*, ed. P. W. S. Andrews and T. Wilson (Oxford: Oxford University Press, 1951) pp. 107–38.

5. This result is dependent on the assumption of linear costs. If production is on the downward part of a U-shaped average-cost curve, then MC is less than AVC, and the equation will result in a price higher than that which maximises profit.

6. This contrasts with the profit-maximising approach where fixed costs are paid out of the revenue from each product depending on the cost *and* revenue functions for the product. However, there is no process of 'sharing' the fixed costs. They are determined residually in the process of arriving at the optimal price and output combinations for each product.

7. The calculus of price discrimination is demonstrated in E. F. Brigham and J. L. Pappas, *Managerial Economics* (New York: Dryden Press, 1972) pp. 297–302.

8. Except for a few exempt goods, e.g. in the United Kingdom, books and certain pharmaceutical goods.

CHAPTER 12

1. I. H. Ansoff, *Corporate Strategy: An Analytic Approach to Business Policy for Growth and Expansion* (Harmondsworth: Penguin Books, 1968) p. 113.

2. Ibid. p. 116.

3. I.e. firm A taking over firm B considers its acquisition as desirable as a whole, but does not see *each* product taken over as desirable in the light of demand and cost conditions, and its own rival products.

4. If competition is imperfect the second term is negative (price falls as output expands) and $MR < P$.

5. The method can also be used for three variables, by drawing in three dimensions, but the necessary geometry becomes complex.

6. In practice this means choosing as Z a common multiple of coefficients in the objective function, so that the objective function is located conveniently on the graph.

7. There are several (equivalent) procedures termed the Simplex method. The one adopted here we find most useful.

8. Note that if units of y_1 and y_2 are measured in kilograms, each unit of y_3 will weigh $\frac{7}{18} + \frac{5}{9} = \frac{17}{18}$ kilograms. Thus each $\frac{17}{18}$ kilograms of y_3 will contain 3 units of starch and 4 units of protein.

9. Note that these shadow prices refer to the problem after the constraints have been simplified by dividing through by the common denominator. Thus the shadow price of A above refers to the effect on profit of changing the first constraint from $x + 2y \leqslant 10$ to $x + 2y \leqslant 11$ and this refers to 5 units of A in the original problem (see p. 188).

CHAPTER 13

1. See Chap. 5, p. 68, above.

2. See Chap. 12, p. 180, for discussion of diversification.

3. It is conventional to use '0' to denote the present, so that year 1 is one year into the future, etc.

4. One solution is to combine the expected-value and risk-premium approaches. If, for example, project A is considered more risky the discount rate could be raised to 12 per cent, and the new expected net present value calculated.

5. H. M. Markowitz, 'Portfolio Selection', *Journal of Finance*, vol. vii, no. 1 (Mar 1952) 77–91, reprinted in *The Theory of Business Finance: A Book of Readings*, ed. S. H. Archer and C. A. D'Ambrosio (New York: Macmillan Co., 2nd ed. 1976) pp. 150–63.

6. It is unusual for the sum of required outlays to exactly equal the funds constraint. The constraint can be written in inequality form (where sum of required funds is less than or equal to the constraint), and the problem solved by linear programming, with the maximisation of present value as the objective function.

CHAPTER 14

1. This is assuming holding costs increase at a constant rate from i_t to i_{t+1} over the period. Then the average cost per unit of stock held is $(i_t + i_{t+1})/2$.

2. This point is similar to that made about plant size and flexibility: see p. 139.

3. The loss of sales through lack of stock depends on the *reactions of customers* which in turn depends on the type of good (is demand postponable?), the availability of alternative supplies and the strength of customer loyalty.

4. F. M. Scherer, *Industrial Pricing: Theory and Evidence* (Chicago: Rand McNally, 1970) p. 21.

5. This assumes a steep U-shaped average cost curve, so that there are strong incentives for keeping output constant.

6. Scherer, *Industrial Pricing*, provides general empirical evidence for this pattern of behaviour. The example provided – copper, machinery and fabricated metals – all satisfy the conditions outlined above.

7. This coincidental feature of this model (that total order costs equals total holding costs at the optimum) is due to the particular geometrical properties of the rectangular hyperbola. Note that at $q*$ the tangent to total holding cost curve is equal and opposite to the tangent to total ordering costs.

8. This is a minimum as $(\mathrm{d}^2 T)/(\mathrm{d}q^2) = (2Sa)/(q^3) > 0$.

9. This is a minimum as

$$\frac{\mathrm{d}^2 T}{\mathrm{d}q^2} = \frac{6cdq}{8} + \frac{2Sa}{q^3} > 0.$$

In this example optimum order quantity does *not* occur when total holding cost equals total ordering cost.

Answers to Numerical Questions

CHAPTER 2

1 (i) $MPL = 5 - 2L + K$. $MPK = L + 4 - 6K$.
   (ii) $MPL = 10 + 2L + 9L^2 + 2K - 2LK$.
   $MPK = 2L - L^2 + 8K - 6K^2$.

2 (i) $Q = \alpha/2\beta$, (ii) $Q = \sqrt{a/c}$ (iii) $Q = (\alpha - b)/2(\beta + c)$.

3 $x_1 = 8$. $x_2 = 14$. $Z = 128$.

CHAPTER 3

1 (i) Produce 1000 books (expected profit = £1000).
   (ii) Produce 2000 books (expected opportunity loss = £0).

2 (i) No overhaul (expected cost = £340).
   (ii) Overhaul (expected cost = £400).

CHAPTER 6

4 (i) A plays III, B plays II, value of game = 2.
   (ii) A plays II and III in the proportions $\frac{1}{4}$, $\frac{3}{4}$, while B plays I and II in the proportions $\frac{1}{4}$, $\frac{3}{4}$. The value of the game = $-\frac{1}{2}$.

CHAPTER 7

5 $D = 80 - 5P$.

   (i) $TR = 16Q - (Q^2)/5$. $AR = (80 - Q)/5$. $MR = 16 - (2Q)/5$.
   (iii) $D = 50$. $Ep = -0.6$ (iv) $Ea = -0.78$. (v) $P = 8$.

CHAPTER 8

3 $MPL = 5 - 2K + 2K^2$. $MPK = 4LK - 2L - 10K$.

  (i) Returns to labour constant.
     Returns to capital depend on the size of L.
     If $L > 2\frac{1}{2}$ then increasing returns to capital
     If $L < 2\frac{1}{2}$, diminishing returns to capital.
 (ii) Returns to scale vary with the magnitude of L and K.

CHAPTER 12

3 $Z = 2$. $x_1 = 1$. $x_2 = 0$, $x_3 = 0$.

4 Profit $= 42$. $x_1 = 4$, $x_2 = 2$.

5 $Z = 1242$ $A = 1.47$ $B = 3.16$

6 $V_1 = 0.05$, $V_2 = 0.17$. $Z = 130$. $X = 50$, $Y = 10$.

CHAPTER 13

5 (i) $PV_A = -14$. $PV_B = -129.2$.
  (ii) $IRR_A = 11.5$. $IRR_B = 4.8$.

CHAPTER 14

2 (i) E.O.Q. $= 10$ tons.   M.A.C. $= £60$.
  (ii) Yes. Stock costs increase £5, purchase costs fall £18.
 (iii) If the number of orders stays the same as in (i), E.O.Q. must remain at 10
     tons. Then holding costs must fall to 15 per cent.

Index